"I've used the *Ultimate Guide to Google AdWords* since the first edition. Transforming a client's unprofitable AdWords account into a cash cow—churning out $30 to $35k profits every month. Just scratching the surface of the book's contents.

"This is the best book on AdWords, period. Plus, it's a dang good book on internet marketing. Not only can you use it to tap Google's huge traffic stream, you'll also convert the thundering hordes of traffic into buyers and profits in your pocket. Do what I do—don't just buy and use it yourself, buy copies for your friends!"

—Roy Furr, Editor, Breakthrough Marketing Secrets, Direct Marketing Consultant

"I'm often asked by peers in my niche how I manage to rank so well in search engines and not go broke using Google AdWords. There are a couple of reasons—I've been subscribing to Perry Marshall's newsletters since 2003; I've read every one of his books; I listen in on all the conference calls he organizes; and finally, I IMPLEMENT his strategies and tactics."

"The *Ultimate Guide to Google AdWords* lists for $24.95. Only a fool would continue to run Google AdWords campaigns and NOT invest in, study, and implement the ideas in it. And no, you'll not find an affiliate link to Amazon here. Just get the book!"

—Jer Ayles-Ayler, AdWords User, Trihouse Enterprises, Inc.

"I bought this book to learn how to get better results from AdWords for my clients. The advice given is easy to follow, and following up on the results of your campaign is exciting. I've already seen a huge increase in clickthrough rates for the different customers and campaigns I run. I get far better results for less money.

"I would recommend reading *Ultimate Guide to Google AdWords* to anyone interested in starting AdWords marketing, or tuning their current campaigns for better results. On the other hand, I'd like to keep what's in here a secret."

—Henrik Hedberg, AdWords User

"Naming this the Ultimate Guide is not a fluke. I have been tweaking the hell out of the ads I'm using to lead searchers into my funnel. Over the past few weeks, I've managed to get one of my ads up to just over 7% CTR from a previous 1 to 2%!"

—Bill Perry, AdWords User

"I thought I knew it all. I set up an AdWords account and a couple of days later I came back to check if I was rich yet. Unfortunately, the only thing that happened was Google enjoyed free access to my bank account. Luckily the traffic was not that high so it was just a couple hundred dollars. And I made no money.

"Frustrated, I went online and did some research. Every forum, article, and blog seemed to be talking about Perry Marshall, so I decided to get *Ultimate Guide to Google AdWords*. 30 minutes into reading my mind was blown away.

"Next, my Quality Score went up from an average of two and three to a six and nine for various keywords. At the same time, my cost-per-click went down from over $4 to about $0.50.

"The rest is history. Seriously, if you don't know the stuff in this book don't even think of AdWords. This is THE guide."

—Jean Paul Essiam, AdWords User

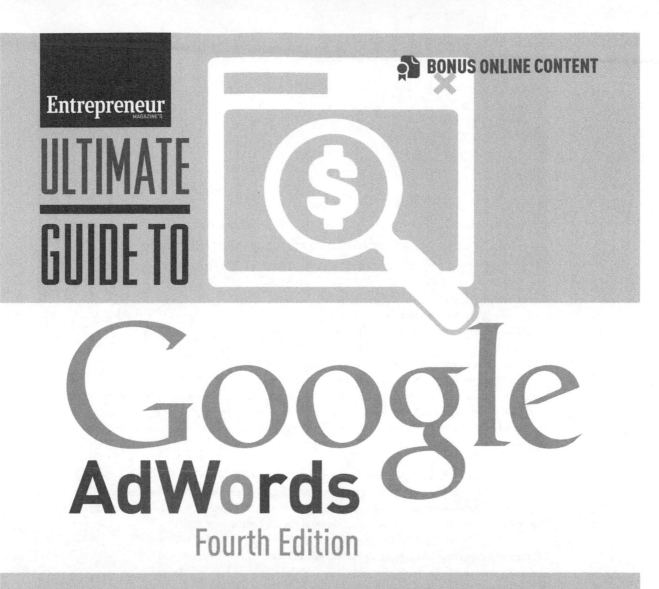

BONUS ONLINE CONTENT

Entrepreneur MAGAZINE'S

ULTIMATE

GUIDE TO

Google
AdWords
Fourth Edition

- Access 1 billion people in 10 minutes
- **Double your website traffic overnight**
- Build a profitable ad campaign today—from scratch

PERRY MARSHALL MIKE RHODES BRYAN TODD

Entrepreneur
PRESS®

Entrepreneur Press, Publisher
Cover Design: Andrew Welyczko
Production and Composition: Eliot House Productions

This publication is designed to provide accurate and authoritative information in regard to the
subject matter covered. It is sold with the understanding that the publisher is not engaged in
rendering legal, accounting or other professional services. If legal advice or other expert assistance is
required, the services of a competent professional person should be sought.

Library of Congress Cataloging-in-Publication Data
Marshall, Perry S.
 [Entrepreneur magazine's ultimate guide to Google AdWords]
 Ultimate guide to Google AdWords: how to access 1 billion people in 10 minutes / Perry
Marshall, Mike Rhodes, Bryan Todd.
 pages cm. — (Ultimate series)
 Rev. ed. of: Entrepreneur magazine's ultimate guide to Google AdWords : how to access 100
million people in 10 minutes / Perry Marshall and Bryan Todd. 3rd ed.
 ISBN-10: 1-59918-542-3 (paperback)
 ISBN-13: 978-1-59918-542-2 (paperback)
 1. Google AdWords 2. Internet advertising. 3. Web search engines. I. Todd, Bryan. II. Title.
HF6146.I58M36 2014
 659.14'4—dc23 2014020040

Printed in the United States of America

18 17 16 10 9 8 7 6

Contents

Wait! Before You Read This Book . . .

If you're brand new to Google AdWords and you're just getting started, you MUST read this short section first.

And:

If you've got years of AdWords experience under your belt or you already own an earlier edition of the *Ultimate Guide*, at the end of this introduction I'll give you shortcuts and page numbers for the advanced new material in the book.

The first thing you need to do is get your online bonus material at www.perry-marshall.com/supplement. There you'll also find a collection of supplemental

material that I consider vital to this book and you'll get in line for a series of updates you'll need as Google's system changes.

OK, now that you've done that, let me tell you *how* to go about learning AdWords. Please listen carefully, pay attention.

IF YOU'RE A RANK BEGINNER . . .

There's an old saying "You can't learn to ride a bicycle at a seminar," and it definitely applies to AdWords. AdWords and really everything you ever do in direct marketing is hands-on. It's not theory. It's real world. It's the school of hard knocks.

About the school-of-hard-knocks part: When AdWords was brand new, there were lots of inexpensive clicks and you could find your way by making lots of cheap mistakes.

Those days are over. Today that strategy will get you slaughtered.

When you open a Google AdWords account, go ahead and enter your keywords, write some ads, and set some bid prices. It's OK if you don't really know what you're doing; you'll learn. The first few chapters of this book will show you exactly how to do it. But here's the most important thing of all:

Set a low daily budget, say $5 or $10 per day, to make absolutely sure that your first experience with AdWords is a GOOD one, not a painful one. Because:

The worst thing you can do in your new career as a Google advertiser is accidentally run up $2,500 of clicks that you have no idea how you're going to pay for. Most advertisers have to go through some trial-and-error before things really come together. There are many assumptions Google will make about how to set up your account that are wrong, and if you blindly follow its menus, you'll make some costly mistakes.

The best thing you can do is enjoy the process of watching those clicks come in and seeing your handiwork produce results.

Then, if you're hands-on from the word go, everything you read in this book will make ten times more sense.

So yes, go ahead and get started. Create your AdWords account, roll up your sleeves, and jump in. As you go from one chapter to the next, make changes to your account. You'll literally be able to see the performance difference in a few hours.

Before you've even spent $10 on Google clicks, please make sure you're using this book as your guide. If you don't, you'll make a slew of common mistakes and blow a lot of cash that you could have used to grow your business.

Also, make sure you access the special reports and see the audios and videos in the Book Bonus member's area. They're at www.perrymarshall.com/supplement.

IF YOU'RE A VETERAN PAY-PER-CLICK MARKETER . . .

This is the 4th edition of the *Ultimate Guide to Google AdWords*. We've added a bunch of new chapters and segments that reflect the sharpest and most current Google strategies. They include five "Chisel Your Way In" strategies that make ultra-competitive markets much easier to win. Here are some of our favorites:

■ *Chisel Your Way in with YouTube.* Plain vanilla AdWords is thick with competition. YouTube is the world's second largest search engine and is far less competitive than Google Search *and* Google Display Network. You can buy clicks for far less money and there's a *lot* of clicks—and a lot of quality traffic—to be had. See Chapter 19, page 179

■ *Chisel Your Way in with Advanced Display Network Strategies.* Bypass costly mistakes and test ideas in the marketplace, for a fraction of what big fat-cat corporations spend on their market research. See Chapters 17 (page 157) and 18 (page 169).

■ *Chisel Your Way in by Crafting a Superior USP and Offer.* Awesome AdWords strategy + Flaccid USP = Bankruptcy. In Chapter 14 (page 123) you'll learn all about how to make not just your ads and your offers but your entire business stand out from your competitors, and how to translate that into better Google ad copy that gets clicks. I cannot emphasize how important this is.

■ *Chisel Your Way in with Bionic Google Ads.* I've devised a clever method that beats any control ad, any time, anywhere. This special chapter gives you the two best blades out of 16. If your competitors don't know this technique, they won't know what hit 'em. See Chapter 10, page 89.

■ *Chisel Your Way in by Fighting Battles You Can Win.* Some markets will drain all of your resources and aren't even worth fighting over; some you can never win at all. Chapters 7 and 8 (page 67 and 73, respectively) are all about the BIG picture. Find your sweet spot and dominate. This material is cutting edge—yet it will stay with you the rest of your life.

If you're brand new, just starting out, our five Chisel Your Way In strategies are how you get a toe-hold in a fierce, unforgiving market.

If you're a seasoned veteran, if you've read the previous editions of this book, or if you're already a pay-per-click ninja, I bet you've never seen these before.

ADVANCED MATERIAL FOR GO-GETTER GOOGLE ADVERTISERS

I've added new, advanced material at www.perrymarshall.com/supplement/ for aggressive marketers, including extended reports and videos for all five Chisel Your Way In

strategies I just named: YouTube advertising, advanced Display Network techniques, building killer USPs, Swiss Army Knife Formula for "Bionic Google Ads," and savvy market selection.

Once you've registered for the bonus material, you'll also receive the regular updates we send out about Google's ever-changing system.

One last thing: I mince no words. Google is THE benchmark for advertisers and information providers worldwide. In fact, from the standpoint of ordinary people getting things done every single day in the world, Google is the most trusted brand on the web. If you're up to Google's standards, you're world class.

I'm not saying it's easy. It is not. **Don't bring a knife to a gunfight.** But I do promise—it IS rewarding. Make no mistake.

Follow the guidelines in this book and you'll be a world-class promoter in your market, your niche, and your chosen profession. I wish you the very, very best of success.

—Perry Marshall
Chicago, Illinois

Chisel Your Way In
Frank Talk about the Google AdWords of Today

Two or five or ten years from now, the story of you and all the other players in your market will be just like the story of Google vs. Excite, HotBot, InfoSeek, AltaVista, Yahoo!, and MSN. A bunch of losers; a couple who turned out sort of OK; and one massive success story.

I want YOU to be the success story. The Alpha Dog.

If you want to get to the meaty stuff fast, don't skip this. This is not the typical book intro where someone yammers on about the last three editions and gushes about all the wonderful souls who were helped along the way.

I'm going to outline a few vital strategies that determine whether YOU succeed or fail in online marketing and Google AdWords. I'll conclude with some frank discussion on what it takes to make AdWords work today. Stick with me a minute for a brief internet history lesson.

Remember the dotcom bubble? Remember when half the world thought Jeff Bezos of Amazon was a genius and the other half deemed him a bloody fool? Do you remember the late '90s when it was obvious to everybody (OK, almost everybody) that the internet was a Very Big Deal and it was here to stay and the stakes were very, very big?

The internet is not merely another communication medium. As my friend Tom Hoobyar said, it is a fundamental shift for humanity that's as important as the discovery of fire.

The reason the dotcom bubble happened was, investors and entrepreneurs alike knew that winning this game would be a very, very big deal.

I remember sometime around 1999–2000, Yahoo! Auctions was trying to make a go of it. I was selling stuff on eBay, so I tried Yahoo! Auctions, too. They were advertising all over the place and their fees were lower.

I quickly found out Yahoo Auctions didn't have as many buyers. My stuff didn't fetch as high a price on Yahoo as it got on eBay. I didn't want sell an item for $17 on Yahoo if it would fetch $20 on eBay.

As a seller, I wanted to go where the buyers are. Buyers want to go where the sellers are. The synergy between buyers and sellers is called the *Network Effect*. The Network Effect says the value of a network is equal to the number of members squared. So if in 1999 Yahoo had one million users and eBay had two million, eBay wasn't twice as powerful; eBay was four times as powerful. Nothing Yahoo might do could overcome eBay's 4X power advantage.

As you know, eBay went on to become the #1 auction site. A respectable #2 doesn't even exist today. And unless eBay makes some major, catastrophic mistake, no one will ever be able to displace them—no matter how much money they spend. Someone could spend $100 billion trying to revive Yahoo! Auctions and it would never work.

The Network Effect is twice as big a deal on the internet as in the brick-and-mortar world. Why? Because the internet is almost frictionless. The frictionless quality of the internet paradoxically introduces a new kind of friction: *the nearly effortless dominance of the #1 player over all others;* the other players are at their mercy. If someone tried to revive Yahoo! Auctions, eBay would always be only one click away. So Yahoo! Auctions doesn't stand a chance.

This has *everything* to do with you, and your quest to dominate your market. I will get to that in just a minute. First, a quick story.

In 2002 I went to my first internet marketing conference, Ken McCarthy's System Seminar. There, I heard Jon Keel speak on pay per click (PPC). Jon was my first true inspiration as an online marketer. He devoted most of his presentation to Overture, which was the dominant PPC service at the time. It was a total revelation when he explained the dynamics of PPC and showed us the Overture Keyword tool, an early forerunner of Google's Keyword Planner tool.

Jon spent a few minutes talking about Google AdWords, which he hadn't played with much yet. I went home and opened my first AdWords account. Within a few days I knew I'd discovered the most amazing direct-response marketing tool in the history of man. A beautiful magic carpet ride began, and the rest, as they say, is history.

By this time eBay was already the king of online auctions. I understood that once they had this position, it would be so hard for anyone to ever steal it away from them. So while Jon was talking, I raised my hand and asked:

"Jon, is it possible for a pay-per-click engine to become a search monopoly sort of like eBay has a monopoly on auctions?"

Jon didn't know. I had a hunch it was true. But I didn't know why.

This was April 2002. At this time, Google was just yet another player in the dogfight between MSN, Yahoo, AltaVista, HotBot, Excite, Infoseek, and a dozen others. At that point there was no clear winner. They were all just beginning to move away from the "free" model. Search engine optimization (SEO) was still easy to game.

I personally liked Google much more than the rest, but I was a minority. Many people still didn't even know what Google was. Nobody at the time dreamed that Google was poised to become the 800-pound gorilla of the internet.

In those early days of AdWords, I wondered:

In this frictionless world, where every search engine is only one click away from any other, only one browser setting away from being the default, how is any one search engine going to dominate?

In hindsight that was a dumb question. Here's the right question:

If one _____ (search engine, auction site, map, e-commerce store, butcher, baker, candlestick maker) is clearly just a little bit better than everyone else, what is going to keep EVERYBODY from clicking over to them and buying from them instead?

And when that fabled tipping point happens, and they get thousands or millions or billions more dollars in their coffers, what is going to keep them from re-investing the profits and getting better and better until they are absolutely unbeatable—like eBay?

What Google did next after that conference in 2002 was the thing I couldn't quite foresee.

A year later, AdWords hit critical mass. It reached that spot where everyone was seeing their competitors' ads on Google and wanted to know how they got there. Google became a gravitational force where affiliate marketers figured out every word in the whole English language (and most other languages) was up for sale. The world got sucked in.

Where Overture was clunky and poorly thought out, AdWords was elegant and magnificently executed. Sure, AdWords had its flaws, but it was fundamentally *right*. It was a marketer's dream. During the next five years, Google exploded with breathtaking force. Google fast outpaced Overture as a PPC platform, raking in billions of dollars and going public.

Google, which was a *little bit* better than all the other search engines, started getting a *lot* better.

Google Maps became almost dreamlike in its sophistication. Soon you could take a virtual tour of anywhere with Street View. Google bought YouTube, which became the world's #2 search engine, the default place where everyone uploads videos of their kids' ballet recital.

AdWords started adding features, eventually getting to where almost every form of targeting you can imagine became possible, no matter how granular. Local businesses started tuning into Google Maps. Consultants and agencies started selling "I'll get you listed on Google."

Add Gmail and Google News and smaller services like Google Scholar (a search engine for academic books and papers) and Google becomes entrenched, as unbeatable as eBay. The other search engines were and are vastly inferior. You'd have to spend a trillion dollars to unseat Google, and you would *still* probably fail.

This "winner take all" phenomenon is what the dotcom excitement was really all about. Sure, there was a lot of dumb stuff, talking socks and whatnot. People do dumb stuff when trillions of dollars are on the line. But they knew the rewards would be big. The present dominance of Google, Amazon, Apple, and Facebook proves that out.

OK, so what does this have to do with you?

The winner-take-all phenomenon is just as true at *your* level and in *your* market as it was for Google and eBay. Right this very minute. Especially if you run a pure online business. Or any business with national or international borders.

In my book *80/20 Sales and Marketing*, I describe how it's a law of nature that 80 percent of the money comes from 20 percent of the customers, 80 percent of the sales come from 20 percent of the products, 80 percent of the cars drive on 20 percent of the roads. 80/20 applies to almost everything you do in business.

But here's what I don't really explain in that book:

On the internet, most things aren't 80/20. They're 90/10!

The web, the "great equalizer," the leveler of all playing fields, is even more unequal. 90 percent of the customers use 10 percent of the search engines. 90 percent of your

traffic comes from 10 percent of your ad campaigns. 10 percent of the advertisers get 90 percent of the traffic.

Winners win BIG on the internet.

Losers lose BIG on the internet because it's so frictionless.

Winners rise to the top faster.

Online marketing is a blood sport. You are playing for keeps. If you think Google AdWords is just going to be this little thing that you do, some task you delegate to your part-time assistant . . . if you're going to stick your toe in the water and dabble in it . . . if you think you're just going to spend an hour or two, buy some clicks and get rich

Then ditch this book right now and go find some other delusion to indulge in.

Because it's NOT going to work that way.

You're either going to do this right, and dominate, and go home with the spoils, or you're going to go home with your tail between your legs. You'll be like the long-extinct Yahoo! Auctions and the whole thing will be a painful lesson and tax write-off.

This is not some interesting miscellaneous activity that's going to make you a little extra money. This is big.

If you want it to be.

Know this going in. If you're not serious, don't even start.

If you're in business at all, this is the game you are playing. It is a 90/10 game and you're either among the broke wannabe 90 or the opulent 10. There isn't much of an in-between space. If you're not one of the top three, you're toast. And this is not just true on Google. It's true everywhere on the internet.

Some may tell you otherwise... but they are lying. There's no lack of flimflam men on the web. So if you want to make a middling living doing mediocre work and getting paid mediocre money, go get a job as a barmaid or security guard. Go babysit a kiosk at the mall where you're guaranteed that you can accost a few dozen people every hour as they walk by.

But if you're going to play on the internet, you need to pick a game you can win. And then you need to play for keeps.

It is FAR easier to be #1—and stay there—than it is to be #4 or #5 or #10, and fight over the scraps with all the other losers. As the "#1 AdWords guy" for the last ten years, I can assure you that is true.

When you are #1 in your market, all the traffic flows your way, because people make more money sending their traffic to you than they make keeping it to themselves.

When you are #1 in your market, you become the star. The default go-to person that everyone talks about.

When you are #1 in your market, you get treated to the best deals, approached by the best vendors, offered first right of refusal on the best joint ventures, and get the seat of honor at the head table. When you're #1 in your market, reaching out to an adjacent niche and dominating that one, too, becomes easier and easier.

When you're #10 in your market, you just hope your spouse's salary will cover the mortgage and groceries.

On Google AdWords, 2 percent of the advertisers get 50 percent of the traffic. Richard Stokes' book *Ultimate Guide to Pay-Per-Click Advertising* documents this. (Great book to study, by the way.) So you need to decide to be one of the top 10 percent players who share 90 percent of the spoils with Google.

Let me explain why this is important, and why you can't ignore Google.

Google is THE gold standard. Your ability to buy Google clicks is THE measure of your sales mojo. It is THE litmus test of your ability to be #1 in your market. Do you have the best sales machine? Can you be #1? Are you inching up on #1? Are you quickly becoming a contender? Or are you fading away?

Once you know how to do Google AdWords, then your ability to play there is where you find out exactly how you stack up.

THE THREE NICHE DOMINATION STRATEGIES OF GOOGLE ADWORDS

1. If you can afford to spend even one penny more than all your competitors to buy clicks, then sooner or later you WILL be #1. This is Jonathan Mizel's famous "Unlimited Traffic Technique." When you have the best sales funnel and conversion rates, you get easy access to *all* the traffic, not just some of it.

2. If you can't be the big fish in a big pond, be a big fish in a little pond. This is very big and very important. **This goes hand-in-hand with . . .**

3. If you can find a little pocket where competition is thinner and you *can* dominate, then you can **chisel your way in** to an overlooked market in Google AdWords. (There are millions of them right now and there always will be!) You can grow from there. Even if you're David facing off against Goliath.

Until every single person on Earth who searches Google finds the thing they are looking to buy, there's room for you.

I know what you're thinking: Yeah Perry, that's great. I get all that. But it's a Catch 22. How can I dominate a market if I can't get traffic? How can I get traffic if I haven't yet figured out how to dominate a market?

Every single piece of advice you get in the rest of this book falls under one of these three strategies. In the pages to come, Mike Rhodes, Bryan Todd, and I are going to take you by the hand and show you how. Google's job is to thin the herd. Our job is to make you fat.

How to Force Prospects to Choose Your Site
Make Them Buy from You, Not Your Competition

Google gets searched six billion times every day. That's 70,000 searches every second.

Google can bring thousands of visitors to your website 24 hours a day, 7 days a week, 365 days a year, whether you're taking a shower, eating breakfast, driving to work, picking up your kids at school, taking a phone call, sleeping, sitting on the commode, daydreaming, busting your butt to beat a deadline, chasing some customer, typing an email message . . .

And it can all happen on autopilot: 100 percent predictable and completely consistent, like clockwork.

Ten or fifteen years ago, an impossible dream; today, a reality.

And of all the different traffic sources you can buy (we wrote the world's most popular book on Facebook advertising, too), Google is the most steady, the most stable, the most predictable. If you want traffic 24/7/365, Google is unmatched.

Just think of the lengths to which we entrepreneurs, business owners, and sales people go just to get a company off the ground, just to get a sale.

I could recount in agonizing detail the *years* of my life I spent pounding the phone, pounding the pavement, making cold calls; renting trade show booths, going to no-show appointments, and booking meetings that were a total waste of time.

But not anymore. I don't go to them anymore; customers come to me. It's been that way so long, I'm very much used to it now.

They'll come to you, too.

Getting new customers is a real grind for a lot of people. It's the number-one obstacle to starting a new business. But all that can be a thing of the past. Instead of chasing customers, they can now come to you, all day and all night.

History has proved Google AdWords to be the biggest revolution in advertising in the last 50 years. Never before had it been possible to spend five bucks, open an account, and have brand new, precisely targeted customers coming to your website within minutes.

There are a lot of things you might want from Google. Maybe you're adding an online component to your retail operation, giving you steadier cash flow and deeper discounts from your suppliers. Maybe your payroll is going to get easier. Maybe your consulting business will be positioned better.

Maybe you're already getting traffic, but free listings are too unreliable. Maybe you've been successful selling on eBay, and now you want to play with the big boys. Maybe you've been futzing around with "social media," and you've finally decided it's time to make some money instead. Maybe you're a working mom, and you want to finally be able to come home.

If you're privy to the secrets of online marketing, all those opportunities will open up to you. You'll have fresh hot sales leads waiting for you in your email box every morning when you sit down at your desk. You'll have customers buying from you 24/7/365.

Instead of chasing customers, they'll come to you. Instead of trying to *guess* whether your next product launch will work, you can *know*. Why is this even possible? Because in the last decade, the very direction of business itself has reversed.

In the old days (remember the 1990s?), entrepreneurs and salespeople chased customers with phone calls, letters, and ads in newspapers. Now customers chase businesses on the web.

Back then you had a list of prospects you tried to get to buy. Now the buyers—millions of them—are trolling the web every second of the day, looking for businesses that can scratch their itch.

Ever heard Woody Allen's saying "80 percent of success is showing up"? The phrase takes on a whole new meaning in the 21st century. If you just *show up* on Google and its search partners, when people type in the right phrase, a starving crowd will bust your doors down to eat at your restaurant.

They'll fill every table and book the kitchen with orders. If they like the daily special and the dessert, they'll come back and eat again.

There's a big feast going on, *if* you show up.

Here you'll discover the secrets of showing up. Not just somewhere, but at the right places and times. In front of the right people. And if you're already advertising on Google, you'll learn how to cut your bid prices 20 percent, 50 percent, maybe even 70 percent or more.

This book is for:

- Online catalog and "mail order" marketers
- Local retail stores and service businesses
- Niche product marketers
- Home businesses run from spare bedrooms or basement offices
- Authors, speakers, consultants, and publishers
- B2B marketers collecting sales leads
- Nonprofits, churches, and charities
- Resellers, repair services, parts suppliers
- Online communities and membership sites

Google AdWords can help your business whether you're the little old lady selling quilts in Eastern Kentucky or the multinational corporation. You don't have to be a geek to do this; many of the best online marketers are nontechnical people who succeed simply because they understand their customers.

A lot of these success stories are from "invisible entrepreneurs." By invisible, I mean that their next-door neighbors have no idea what they do and probably just assume they're unemployed or something.

But they're running micro-empires from their spare bedroom. And they're in hundreds of industries, ranging from the mundane to the ridiculous to the outrageously specialized.

Some of these guys and gals are making *serious cash*. Tens, even hundreds of thousands of dollars a month. And they're not in "sleazy" businesses, either.

In this book I'm going to show you exactly how they do it.

> ## Google Gets Searched 6 Billion Times Every Day*
>
> Every search is typed in by a person who has an itch they want to scratch.
>
> *Source: Statistic Brain (www.statisticbrain.com/google-searches/), January 2014

HERE'S HOW TO MAKE SURE THEY FIND *YOU* AND BUY FROM *YOU.* NOT SOMEONE ELSE

Got a watch with a second hand?

Tick. 70,000 people just searched Google for something and went to somebody's website.

Tick. 70,000 more.

Tick. 70,000 more.

4,200,000 people a minute. Every minute, all day long.

All night long.

Here they come. 70,000 every second.

Are they finding your website?

Are they buying from you?

Or are they finding someone *else's* website and buying from them instead?

They could be finding you. They *should* be finding you. They *can* find you and buy from you. Many of them will come to your site, buy from you, and come back again and again, *if* you follow the simple instructions in this book.

Google AdWords can be the traffic monster that feeds your autopilot marketing machine and churns out a profit for you every day and every night, hitting the entire world up for customers while you sleep. Not just bringing you tire kickers but highly qualified buyers who are proactively looking for exactly what you sell right this very minute.

Buying from *you*. Not somebody else.

If the internet matters to your business, then no book you've ever bought has more potential to make or save you money than this one.

This book is written so you can blow through it, fast, and get going immediately on your course to make serious money with Google insider marketing tactics. That's the fun part: quickly implementing killer tactics that will flood your business with prospects and profit.

But there's a serious side, too. I've held nothing back here. So not only will you know how to play the Google AdWords game, you'll discover how to craft powerful marketing messages and hooks, bond with your customers, and dominate your market.

In this book you'll discover:

- Tragic, costly mistakes that almost *all* Google advertisers and online entrepreneurs make—and how to easily avoid them (including techniques Google itself *should* teach you, but doesn't).
- How to disaster-proof business startups and product launches, and pound the risk out of new ventures. (Most times you've only got one or two shots to nail it; why would you want to leave anything to chance?)
- Profiles of successful online businesses. Having coached hundreds of online entrepreneurs to success, I've accumulated a list of vital characteristics that separate winners from the losers, many of which defy normal "business school wisdom."
- How to create ultrapersuasive Google ads and web pages that not only convert visitors to buyers, but automatically improve with time, making it impossible for your rivals to catch up to you.
- The advanced (but simple) shortcut secrets of getting deep into your customer's head, so you know exactly where his hot buttons are, and how to punch them at will. Result: Customer loyalty that reaches fanatical levels, and a rabid customer base that eagerly buys almost everything you ask them to buy.

And if you're already advertising on Google, you'll get 30 percent to 300 percent more visitors, for less money than you're paying right now.

While many hard-core "let's get after it" types will mark up and dog-ear this book, you can really start seeing results *while* you're reading it. There are shortcuts you can get after tonight, and see results before you go to bed an hour later.

Your business can literally be better by tomorrow morning.

So strap on your crash helmet, because you're in for a wild ride. *Onward!* Stick with me, Mike, and my partner Bryan as we show you the secrets to online business success.

—Perry Marshall

P.S.: I've created an online supplement to this book with more than $85 worth of extended book chapters, audio interviews, information on specialized topics, and ongoing updates on Google's ever-changing rules. You can access it at http://www.perrymarshall.com/supplement.

P.P.S.: Here are some cool success stories I've gotten from my customers:

I first purchased Perry's AdWords guide about five years ago and just recently purchased the newest version.

That's about five years of Perry Marshall information and I've never once been offered a dream. I don't do AdWords advertising because I can't afford it.

But Perry never promised me that I could get rich using AdWords, i.e., he never tried to sell me a dream. I really appreciate that. Like he said, AdWords is not a business. It's a tool you can use to advertise your business and I don't know anyone that's more qualified than Perry Marshall that can teach you how to benefit from AdWords.

I can promise you this. This information will save you a lot of money and possibly even an arm and a leg . . . it all depends on what kind of fish you're swimming with.

—Roger Kelley, Decatur, AL

Since your last coaching call, we made the keyword matching changes as you recommended, and have the following to show you. Our overall CTR is 4.4 percent—our best ad is 12.4 percent and the worst one is a very respectable 3.1 percent!

—Simon Chen, The Eightblack Group, Melbourne, Australia

I've been a faithful Perry fan since I met him at a Dan Kennedy event about five years ago. I own most of Perry's products, I've been through the bobsled run twice and I attended a four-man intensive at his house last year.

Perry always tells it like it is. He's not like most of the "gurus" out there always trying to sell you their next product or coaching program. Perry gives us rock-solid advice on how to grow our business or how to sell more products. He repeats his solid advice over and over with no sales hype. That's why we love and trust Perry. That's why I've been a longtime customer and I buy everything he offers.

Recently I took a real job after being on my own for ten years. I'm now an online marketing/SEO analyst for a local software company. I'm managing their AdWords campaigns, which are over $20k/month worldwide.

Using what Perry taught me, I increased their CTR from just over 1 percent to over 6 percent in just one day. They're running three times more ads on the same budget and they're getting better qualified leads.

Think about using your knowledge managing AdWords campaigns as a consultant or for a company. There are tons of online marketing jobs out there right now and most pay over 6 figures a year. I never thought I could go back to a real job but I love

getting that steady paycheck and going home at 5 o'clock every day not worrying about keeping my business going. Plus I'm consulting on the side still so I'm making more than I ever have."

—TED PRODROMOU, SAN ANSELMO, CA,
AUTHOR, *ULTIMATE GUIDE TO LINKEDIN FOR BUSINESS*

Your AdWords guide is worth hundreds of times its cost. And the free advice in your marketing emails—one story in particular about the Wright brothers and Samuel Langley—has been absolutely priceless.

—PAUL DEL PIERO, AUSTIN, TX

I was getting about 2,830 clicks per month with Google AdWords at $1.06 per click. I've spent about 8 hours total reading your stuff and implementing it. Based on the results of my last few days I am on track to get 7,815 clicks in the next month and spend the same $3,000 a month . . . a savings of $23,400 per year, or $2,925 per hour for the 8 hours I have invested. This is without doubt one of the absolute best investments I've ever made and I haven't even started! And yes, I have done most of this while sitting at home in my underwear.

—KEITH LEE, TMS, KENT, WA

I'm telling everyone that your book is "required reading" if they want to market online. I actually read your 'Definitive Guide' in one day, and that evening started my first AdWords campaign. I now have four of them running, and the average click-through rate for all campaigns is above 2 percent. I also get well over a 3 percent CTR (some as high as 15 percent) on my more targeted keywords. This has increased the traffic to my sites tenfold in some cases, and has made my monthly revenues much more consistent (which is always nice). Best of all, I've never had a keyword shut down by Google for low CTR, and I've only done one round of "peel and stick" with my ads. I give all the credit to my recent AdWords success to you and your book.

—RYAN DEISS, AUSTIN, TX

I had spent almost 100k on wasted SEO firms & websites with no real reward. I discovered Perry on another podcast I was listening to & have learned so much in only

a year. I have just started employing his processes to Google AdWords and am reaping the benefits already. I appreciate your delivery of information & the lack of BS in your sales tactics to everyone.

You bring great info to the table so we do not have to sort through to find what is useful. It's simply amazing watching my Click Thru Rate go from 0.3 percent up to 48.0 percent in less than 30 minutes.

The most important part is, I AM BEATING THE COMPETITION in cost and better yet finding areas of "no competition." Thanks for such awesome marketing advice, your material is by far the most valuable I have purchased. Your concepts are working for me, and I intend on running this as a service for a lot of my web hosting clientele."

—EDDIE SYMONDS UPPER MARLBORO MD

WOW! I got a 500 percent increase in response . . . with just a quick "Band-Aid" fix. Can't wait to see what happens when I follow all of your suggestions."

—JENNY HAMBY, COPYWRITER AND SEMINAR MARKETING CONSULTANT, SEMINARMARKETINGPRO.COM, PLAINFIELD, IL

How to Build Your Own Autopilot Marketing Machine

We're not going to just teach you a handful of Google tricks. We're going to show you how to make the internet your slave. (Plus you'll find out why selling on the internet can be a lot simpler than most people think, because . . . only a handful of things really matter anyway.)

If you're at a party and tell folks you're starting an online business, they won't spare a bit of advice. They'll give you an endless list of things they think you need: dedicated servers, security certificates, iPhone apps, Facebook apps, pop-up windows, blogs, meta tags, streaming video, WordPress, SEO plug-ins, cascading style sheets (CSS), RSS feeds—all kinds of stuff.

(Are your eyes glazing over yet?)

Some of the things on that list will certainly come into play for you at some point. But people who are way smarter than you or I have blown hundreds of thousands of dollars before the first visitor even showed up and bought anything.

Big mistake.

Techno-wizardry is, for the most part, a distraction and a waste of time. So in this short chapter we're going to show you the moving parts you need and just how simple a thriving, profitable website can be.

IT ALL STARTS WHEN A PERSON SEARCHES FOR SOMETHING

Karli types in "homeschooling" at her computer and here's what shows up on Google:

On the top and right are the AdWords ads, which are paid. Running down the left are the free "organic" search listings.

She clicks on the ad near the top that says

6th–12th Homeschooling—Fully-Accredited & Most Electives
www.americanonlinehigh.com/
$31 Gets You Started Today

Or . . .

Karli is clicking around the 'net and she's at www.homeschoolcreations.com reading up on learning for preschoolers:

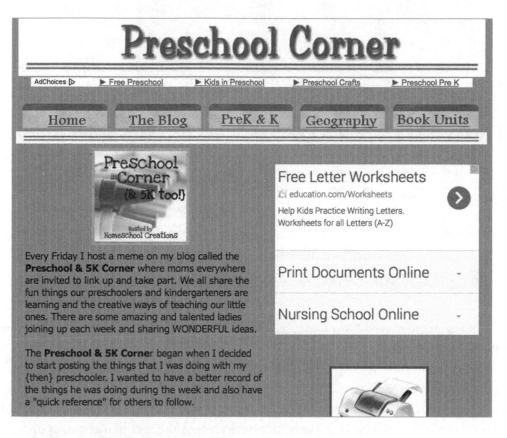

And she sees the ad over on the right that says

> **Free Letter Worksheets**
> education.com/Worksheets
> Help Kids Practice Writing Letters.
> Worksheets for all Letters (A–Z)

This ad is also served by Google through the AdSense program for website owners, to dozens, hundreds, possibly thousands of websites.

The ad sounds interesting. She clicks on the ad and is taken to this page:

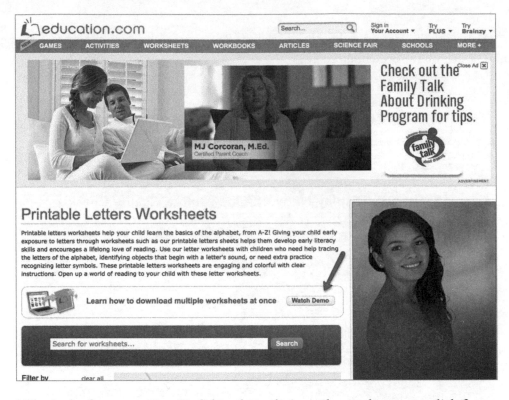

That's the first step. Now Karli has three choices: She can browse or click for more information, or she can leave. On other sites she may be given the option to buy.

There's a number of sites where the best thing to offer is information instead of a product up front. The way Karli gets the information is by entering her address to get a gift, sample, download, white paper, report, or guide. This specific offer is especially important if the problem Karli wants to solve is an ongoing area of interest, as opposed to a one-time impulse buy.

If this were a product for people with diabetes, for example, it would be a very good idea to collect Karli's email address, because if Karli is a diabetic, she's going to have diabetes next week and next year, not just today. Could be a valuable email list! Plus this gives you a chance to talk to all the Karlis on your list and get to know them better.

THE SEARCH PROCESS

In the course of Karli's search process, one of three actions will occur:

1. *She will buy something* (like a guide to homeschooling or a report with the latest on diabetes).
2. *She will leave.*
3. *She will ask for more information.*

If you have obtained her email address (by having her opt-in and sign up), you can invite her to come back to learn more about your information, products, or services.

That's what this is all about.

Anything that gets this done is good. Anything that complicates it or gets in the way is bad.

See, this is really simple. Futzing around with Flash presentations and 19 different ways to build a web page—all that stuff is beside the point. The point is: *Scratch Karli's itch and move the stuff from your shelf to hers, as quickly, easily, and simply as possible.*

Search vs. Display Network One-Minute Reality Check

Google's Search Network reaches people who actively go searching for a specific keyword phrase, whether they used Amazon, Ask.com or some other search partner site.

Google's Display Network (GDN) is the vast array of sites on the internet that display Google ads, from tiny mom-and-pop websites all the way up to CNN and the *New York Times*. We devote Chapters 17 and 18 to strategies for targeting GDN.

So which is better for your business? Google Search or Google Display?

Find out in just 60 seconds!

Take this short quiz and get an instant ScoreCard on how appropriate your business is for 1) Google AdWords for keyword search and 2) Google's Display Network. Your ScoreCard will also gauge the competition level and priority you should place on AdWords compared to other advertising opportunities.

It only takes a minute:

www.IsAWforMe.com

Your Mission, Should You Choose to Accept It

Your mission is to buy clicks for $1 and make $2 while Karli is on your website. Your mission is to make more money from your clicks than your competitors make from theirs. And if that means making 50 cents while Karli is on your website, going negative initially but then earning $1.50 back during the next three months, you've succeeded.

That's it.

The rest of this book is all about how to do this.

Most people don't realize how powerful the one-dollar-in, two-dollars-out mindset is in the grand scheme of things—and why Google AdWords is usually the most reliable, consistent place to make this happen.

What About Facebook? Facebook Ads vs. Google Ads

You may be wondering where Facebook fits into the equation. Facebook has matured from social media curiosity to robust source of high quality converting traffic.

Advantages of Facebook advertising: It's very good for businesses that sell art, culture, personality, experiences, entertainment, and fun. Results can be almost instantaneous and it's good for quick hits, fast bursts of traffic, and live events. Facebook traffic can be bargain priced if you really know what you are doing.

Disadvantages of Facebook advertising: It's never "set and forget." You don't really optimize Facebook the way you optimize Google ads, and it doesn't run 24/7/365. You constantly have to be coming up with new ads and promotions. Facebook is all about the next promotion, the next big idea, the next great thing.

Advantages of Google advertising: It's very good for businesses that sell solutions, components, results, details and work. It runs 24/7/365 and while it takes work to optimize, once it is optimized and working, it can be reasonable to maintain and produce steady results for months, even years.

Disadvantages of Google advertising: It's very competitive, success is usually not instantaneous, and Google itself can be bureaucratic and difficult to deal with.

How appropriate is Facebook advertising for your business? Score yourself on a scale from 1 to 10 in 60 seconds with our free tool at www.IsFBforME.com.

How well does Google Search fit your business? Google Display Network? Score yourself for Search and Display in 60 seconds with our free tool at www.IsAWforME.com.

Don't do Google *or* Facebook without getting a solid education first. If Facebook is for you, get our book *The Ultimate Guide to Facebook Advertising*, also by Entrepreneur Press.

If You Do This Right, It Can Literally Make You Rich. Here's Why . . .

My friend and legendary marketer Jonathan Mizel says, "Internet traffic goes where it's rewarded, respected, and paid for." If you reward and respect your visitors—and if you're able to pay more for them than everyone else advertising in your category—*then you can have as much traffic as you want.* The traffic will literally *seek you out.*

This is not an exaggeration. It's completely true. But traffic will only seek you out when it's profitable.

So you develop your Google campaigns, send traffic to your site, collect information requests, make sales, follow up with your customers, and do whatever you need to do, to make the whole process flow like water running downhill.

After your Google campaign is working is the time to focus on other marketing strategies. Then (and only then) do you go to all of the *other* traffic sources available to you, like Bing, banner ads, email lists, and affiliates.

As we'll discuss in other chapters, affiliates (people who send you traffic in exchange for commission on sales) can be a *huge* source of traffic. If your website doesn't pay, affiliates won't send you anything. But good affiliates can turn the tide in your favor, making you the dominant force in your market.

By following the steps in this book, you'll set yourself up to get massive amounts of traffic and your business will grow exponentially.

A FEW TOOLS YOU NEED IF YOU'RE JUST GETTING STARTED

Whether you're selling skin cream or ebooks or computer games or imported wood carvings, you need a handful of tools to be in business:

- A domain name
- A website with web pages
- An email broadcast/autoresponder service
- A shopping cart service
- A product to sell
- A Google AdWords account

The online supplement to this book (www.perrymarshall.com/supplement) has links to dozens of resources for getting these things done, plus additional tutorials and MP3 files. But here's a quick rundown of the most important stuff:

You can register a domain name at BulkRegister.com. Many companies can host your site inexpensively.

You can create your site with an online content management platform like WordPress.

An excellent email system is AWeber. You can queue up automatic messages that go out when people request information or buy. You can send email newsletters and announcements to your customers and prospects. AWeber also does a good job of getting your messages through the spam filters.

If you're just getting started, *do not* futz around with installing payment software on your server, etc. Go to a third party like 1ShoppingCart (1shoppingcart.com)—it has a great service that allows you to quickly set up order forms, take orders, process credit card transactions, follow up with emails, and manage your customer list.

If you're a more mature marketer, Infusionsoft is a complete e-commerce platform with customer and email management, autoresponders, and a shopping cart.

The product is up to you. You can use your Google ads and your website to learn about any market you want and decide if you want to stay in it.

The next chapter shows you how to quickly set up a Google account. Let's get it started, shall we?

Building a Google Campaign from Scratch
The *Right* Way

My friend Bill Yaccino stumbled into a little side business, officiating weddings. He was a pastor in his day job, and he got couples through referrals.

He and I were having lunch one day at Panera Bread. He says to me, "Hey Mr. Marketing Man, do you think I can find engaged couples on Google?"

"You bet," I said. "Get out your laptop."

Within ten minutes he'd created his first Google account. I said, "Let's make this really simple." I set his campaigns to "Google Search Only," geography to "Chicago Metro Area" and we chose just a handful keywords:

"wedding officiant"
[wedding officiant]
"chicago wedding officiant"
[chicago wedding officiant]

And we wrote a couple of ads and set a bid.

His website was hosted on one of those "instant web page" services and his landing page left a lot to be desired, but it was adequate for the time being. We pointed his ads to it. I gave him precise instructions about how to adjust his landing page for better conversions.

Obviously a keyword phrase like *wedding officiant* restricted to one metro is a very low-traffic niche. Nevertheless within days he was getting traffic and new gigs.

I don't know if he realized it or not, but the sheer simplicity of what we had just done (very narrow keywords, phrase and exact match only) was the key to a business that continued to bring Bill young, eager couples for years.

Not only was it a nice side business that generated extra income, but many of those couples sought him out for advice during the first months and years of their new life together. I give Bill credit for accomplishing one more thing most advertisers don't do: Bill turned that one click into a life-long relationship.

Not only that, Bill eventually created a network of wedding officiants all over the country, who mimicked his simple web strategy!

Ten minutes from right now, you too can have a Google campaign up and running, sending visitors to your website. The speed at which you can do new things and make changes in Google's system is stunning.

But speed can also be a trap. Sometimes people do rash things when they're in a hurry.

This is not a long chapter, but it conveys some seriously important concepts. Many have skipped these steps and landed on the PPC slagheap. So take a little extra time to go carefully through these steps. It'll save you a lot of money. You'll still have your Google campaign up and running in an hour or two—and it'll be set up better than 95 percent of Google campaigns on the web.

(Hint: If your ads are *not* better than 95 percent, they'll probably never see the light of day. It's not that hard to be in the top 5 percent, but you need to pay close attention.)

THE BEST WAY TO RESEARCH YOUR MARKET

What keywords are you going to use to reach your market? Answering that question the right way can spell the difference between success and failure. Ultimately you're out to hunt down the top *one or two keywords* that will bring you the most paying customers,

and tweak your entire sales process around that. That's what the most successful AdWords advertisers we know are doing now.

To find that bull's-eye keyword, or "keyword center," we're going to use Google's Keyword Planner, which you find under "Tools" in your AdWords account:

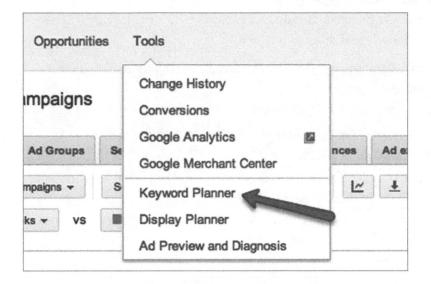

One of the huge advantages of AdWords is that it links you with people who are already "sold" on the concept that you are promoting. You don't have to talk them into anything—they're already on Google looking for what you've got. You just need to figure out the keywords *they* use to describe *what you offer*, so you can connect with them.

To answer this question, you need to describe what you're promoting as clearly as possible—and identify who wants to buy it. This is your ideal customer.

1. Define Your Perfect Customer

We recommend that you stop right now, pull out a piece of paper, and physically write down a one-paragraph description of your ultimate money-in-hand-and-ready-to-buy paying customer.

Those are the people who already know something about the type of product (or information) you sell or the service you offer. These people probably don't know about *you,* but they do know about your product. Often they have an immediate problem and have decided to go online looking for a solution. They may have already made up their mind about how they want to solve the problem. Now they're searching Google, trying to locate the product that fits their solution, and then buy it.

Your description may look like one of these, which we borrow from our friend Glenn Livingston, who teaches this bull's eye concept in powerful depth (at PerrySentMe.com):

- "My best prospect is someone who already believes in nonpharmaceutical and natural remedies for migraines and is actively searching for the best one to purchase."
- "My best prospect is someone who has already made up his or her mind to buy pottery via the web."
- "My best prospect already knows pay-per-click management services exist and is proactively searching to hire one."

Have this description physically written out and keep it there in front of you as you go through the keyword search process.

2. What Keywords Are Your Potential Customers Using to Search for Your Product or Services?

Head over to Google's Keyword Planner (you must be logged into an AdWords account to use this, but you don't need to spend any money yet), choose the "search for new keyword and ad group ideas" option and enter some phrases that you think reflect customers who are in that mindset. You can ignore the other three Keyword Planner options for now. We'll go into them in more detail in Chapter 6.

Let's take the migraine example. A starter idea would be "natural migraine remedies," because that would seem to specify people who are looking for a *natural* solution, something for *migraines* as opposed to more general issues, and *remedies* as opposed to facts or data or information:

Keyword Planner
Plan your next search campaign

What would you like to do?

▾ Search for new keyword and ad group ideas

Enter one or more of the following:
Your product or service

natural migraine remedies

Your landing page

www.example.com/page

Your product category

Enter or select a product category ▾

Google gives a decent size list on the "keyword ideas" tab. We can now go through the list keyword by keyword and compare each to our written customer description, choose the keywords we feel are a fit, and ignore the ones that aren't.

Yes, this is a subjective judgment, which is fine; you can make an educated guess about its relevance on a 0–10 scale. Is it a 1? A 5? a 9? If you feel it's less than 3, skip it as a keyword, for now.

You might collect a total list of no more than one to two dozen keywords. That's perfectly fine. It's a mistake to start out with too many keywords anyway.

3. How Many People Are Searching on This Keyword?

We're aiming to find the ultimate bull's-eye keyword here. We don't have to nail it down today, but this search narrows the playing field and makes the job easier.

For your one to two dozen keywords you can go with what Google's Keyword Planner already told you. Or you can take each one and do a further keyword search on it and add in totals from other variations that you believe would *fully match your written customer description.*

Note how many searches some of the variations get:

Keyword (by relevance)	Avg. monthly searches	Competition	Suggested bid
natural remedies for migraines	2,400	Medium	$3.11
natural migraine relief	1,600	Medium	$4.34
natural remedy for migraine	590	Medium	$2.42
natural migraine remedy	90	Medium	11.09
migraine natural remedies	260	Medium	$3.32
migraine remedies	6,600	Medium	$4.84
natural remedies for migraine	260	Medium	$1.70
migraine home remedies	2,900	Low	$2.64
natural migraine treatment	390	Medium	$2.48

The average number of monthly searches for each keyword is listed beside each keyword, as shown in the last image. However, the blue graph that you'll see in the

interface above this shows the average for the entire group of keywords. You'll want to consider individual search volume when choosing your top keyword(s).

4. How Much Money Are Advertisers Making off This Keyword?

You can judge this by how much the keyword costs.

We're looking for the keywords where the money is. The market has its own way of answering this. The maximum cost per click that people pay represents the upper limit of the money available in that market. Google gives you a suggestion right in the tool.

Now collect as many relevant keywords like this as you want, and then make an educated comparison among them to find the best fit for your profile. You're off to the best start when you've got 6 to 12 *tightly matched groups* of keywords.

And ultimately you're best off with that one single bull's-eye keyword. Glenn Livingston goes through this issue thoroughly at www.PerrySentMe.com.

HOW TO SET UP YOUR CAMPAIGN

To start your campaign, go to https://adwords.google.com, find the "Get started now" button, and sign up for an AdWords account. Once logged in, click the "Create your first campaign" button.

1. Select Your Campaign Type and Name

First, choose the campaign type—for now we highly recommend the "Search Network only" option (other campaign types are discussed in detail later in the book) and then give your campaign a name.

We also highly recommend removing the tick next to "Include search partners" for now (you can always change this later).

Campaign name: My first campaign

Type [?] | Search Network only ▾ | ⦿ **Standard** - Keyword-targeted text ads showing on Google search results [?]

Search Network with Display Select
Best opportunity to reach the most customers
s - All the features and options available for the k [?]

Search Network only
Google search and search partners
sting Ads - Ads promoting your product inventory erchant Center [?]

Display Network only
Google's network of partner websites
earch Ads - Ads targeted based on your website

Shopping
Best way to create Product Listing Ads
about campaign types

Online video

Networks [?] To choose different networks, edit the campaign type above or create a new campaign.

✓ **Google Search Network** [?]
☐ Include search partners

2. Choose the Geographic Location Where You'd Like Ads to Show

Next, decide how large or small a geographic area you want to target. You can choose whole countries, regions of countries, states or provinces, cities—even U.S. Congressional districts! You can also choose custom-designated geographic areas, such as latitude-longitude coordinates or the radius of a set number of miles or kilometers around a specific address. Click "Let me choose . . ." and then search for the most appropriate area for you:

Bid strategy [?] Basic options | Advanced options
○ I'll manually set my bids for clicks
⦿ AdWords will set my bids to help maximise clicks within my target budget

Budget [?] $ [10] per day
Actual daily spend may vary. [?]

You can likely leave the "Language" setting as whatever Google suggests, or change if needed.

3. Choose Your "Bid strategy," Set Your Daily Budget

We recommend (for now) changing the default "Bid strategy" to "I'll manually set my bids for clicks." This gives you more control and will help you learn AdWords at a greater level of understanding. You can always change to one of the many automatic options later.

Your daily budget is the maximum that Google is authorized to charge you per day. Chances are that you will hit that maximum most days. Google offers several payment options: "You can make payments before your ads show (manual payments) or make payments after your ads show, and have those payments made automatically (automatic payments). Some businesses are also eligible for a Google credit line (monthly invoicing)."

Set your daily budget so that if you screw up big-time, your checking account won't get emptied out. You can always come back and bump it up, but it's important to have a safety net.

4. Ignore the "Ad Extensions" Section for Now

This is an important part of any campaign, but leave this for now and add these when you get to Chapter 22.

Click "Save and continue."

5. Create Your First Ad Group and Write Your First Ad

We'll enter the "CRM Software" ad that we've written:

Now let's explain what we just did, and why.

More people click on ads when the *headline* includes the keyword they're searching on. So use your keywords in your headline when you can. You're limited to 25 characters here, so for some search terms you'll need to use abbreviations or shorter synonyms.

The *second and third lines* allow for 35 characters of text each. In most markets you'll be more successful if you describe a *benefit* on the second line, followed by a *feature* or *offer* on the third line. Later on you can test which order converts better.

Even though Google places the field for your *display URL*—the web address people see in your ad—below your main ad copy here, when your ad displays on the search results page, its URL will actually show up right below your headline. The display URL has to be the same domain as your site, though the URL itself doesn't necessarily have to be the specific landing page that you take people to.

The last line is your actual *destination URL,* or your specific chosen landing page. You can also use a tracking link here.

Here's the short version of your ad template:

> Headline—up to 25 characters of text
> 2nd line—up to 35 characters
> 3rd line—up to 35 characters
> 4th line—your Display URL

6. Insert Your Keywords Into the Keyword Field in Your Account

Paste in your keywords. We'll start with just one set, and we'll add plus signs (+), brackets ([]), and quotes (" ") to see precisely how many searches of each type we'll get. More on this in Chapter 5.

Note: When you're getting started, it's *not* a good idea to dump hundreds or thousands of keywords in. Start with a tiny handful of important ones and work from there.

7. Set Your Maximum Cost-Per-Click

Set your maximum price-per-click now (called your "default bid"), but realize this: Every keyword is theoretically a different market, which means that each of your major keywords will need a bid price of its own. Google will let you set individual bids for each keyword later. Don't set a bid for your Google Display Network (GDN) ad here: run that traffic through a different campaign.

If you can only afford $50 per day instead of $170, it's better to bid on low-cost keywords so that your ad can be seen by as many people as possible. Due to the limitations of any budget, if you're going after high-priced keywords, you'll exhaust your budget quickly and your ads will only be seen part of the day, rather than a full 24 hours.

8. Review Everything

Double-check your ad and your keywords to be sure they're the best possible match. Check your cost-per-click to be sure you get the positions on the page you want. Double check your daily budget to be sure you don't unwittingly drain your bank account right out of the gate.

9. Enter Your Billing Information

Your ads will start showing as soon as you confirm your payment information. Now you're set.

THINGS YOU CAN TWEAK RIGHT NOW

You can almost always improve on the number of clicks you'll get from the ad you've just written. As you'll see later, it's almost impossible to guess what is going to make people click; you need to let the visitors vote. So write a second ad you think can beat it, and go back into your ad group to post it:

CRM Software
www.crm1to1.com/FreeTrial
Manage 1000 to 10,000 Customers
30-Day Free Trial & 24/7 Support

Google will rotate this automatically against your first ad. After a few days or weeks, you can pick the winner and delete the loser. Results will come in faster if you test just two at a time.

You can also add more keywords to your list, adjust your cost per click or destination URL for individual keywords, create more ad groups and campaigns, and adjust your campaign settings to fit your style.

In Chapter 30 we'll give you some cool tips for getting more clicks and sales from your ads through smarter traffic management.

When you follow these steps, a campaign will grow that is unique to you and your customers. The success is yours, and so is the profit. It's your business, unlike any other, with your fingerprints and personality all over it. Yours alone. Nobody can replicate that.

THE MAGIC IS IN THE PROCESS

The most important thing you should know about a Google campaign is that it's not a single technique or something that you set up once and forget about.

We have clients whose Google campaigns seem to hum as if on autopilot, but the real power in Google AdWords comes from logging in every few days or once a week and making constant refinements that 2X, 5X, or 10X your traffic. The number of visitors grows even while your cost per click declines over time.

This doesn't take a lot of time—sometimes only a few short minutes each week. But you earn compound interest on those efforts because your profit margins get fatter as the traffic grows.

Hint: 90 percent of advertisers check their campaigns once a month or less. If you do it weekly, you're far ahead of the pack. And since 2 percent of advertisers get 50 percent of the traffic, those routine check-ins move you way ahead of the curve.

HOW TO SET YOURSELF UP FOR SUCCESS

Now you know how to build a small, basic ad campaign. The foundation for future success is laid by organizing larger groups and campaigns properly. In the next chapter you'll learn how to do that.

Meet Uncle Claude

If You've Ever Sold Anything on the Internet, This Man Is Your Uncle

Every field of knowledge exists because a handful of luminaries made ground-breaking discoveries and showed others the way. And there's almost always one who stands head and shoulders above the others.

In management it's Peter Drucker. In engineering it's Thomas Edison. In physics, Albert Einstein. In rock 'n' roll it's the Beatles. For saxophone players it's John Coltrane.

In results-driven advertising, it's Claude Hopkins (1866–1932). Whether you know it or not, if your website is generating a profit, it's because you've discovered something that Hopkins figured out, probably before the turn of the century.

Uncle Claude invented the coupon. (Did you know he created it so that advertisers could track their results?) He pioneered concepts like split testing, premiums, free samples, and mail-order

marketing. In fact, his book *Scientific Advertising* is so important we've included it in the online supplement to this book at www.perrymarshall.com/supplement.

In the rest of this book, we take Hopkins' ideas, which in the late 1800s took months to implement and test, and show you how to do the same thing, literally *10,000 times faster.* We've included choice nuggets of wisdom from him in many of the upcoming chapters.

Thanks to Uncle Claude, it's never been easier—or more *scientific*—to make a fortune in marketing.

Organizing Your Campaign
How to Pay Less and
Get More Clicks

During the first five years I taught Google AdWords, the most common problem I encountered was simply the messy Google account: all kinds of keywords, jumbled together, dumped into a single ad group with no rhyme or reason. The keywords didn't match the ads, or maybe only one of them did, and the rest of the keywords looked like Cyclops at a wedding reception. The ads didn't match the landing pages and the landing pages didn't communicate the company's USP.

I was astounded they even got any traffic at all!

Well that was years ago. Today, a campaign like that won't even see the light of day. The 2008 recession drowned everyone whose campaigns were a mess. The bare minimum requirements of a well-organized campaign today include:

- Narrow silos of keywords
- Ads that precisely match the keywords
- Landing pages that precisely match the ads.

We have done a *lot* of Google AdWords consultations, both through our coaching programs and with people who come to our site looking for help. Want to know what the number-one mistake people make still is?

Hastily built campaigns.

Badly organized ads and keywords cripple your Google campaigns and cost you a *ton* of money every single day: good, old-fashioned Google Stupidity Tax.

WHAT GOOGLE DOESN'T TELL YOU: THE WRONG WAY TO ORGANIZE AN ADWORDS CAMPAIGN

Starting out, it's a temptation to set up a campaign that includes everything but the kitchen sink, one that looks something like this:

Smith Telecommunications
Robust Solutions for
All Your Voice Mail Needs
www.smithtelecom.com

auto attendant
business telephone systems
call management systems
voice mail
voice mail equipment
voice mail service
voice mail systems

The plan would be to send all visitors to the homepage, which has a bunch of different options: links to services, equipment, Q&A, About Us, Contact Us, etc. So if we made a map of that AdWords campaign, it would look like this:

What's wrong with this picture?

Here's why this ad is destined to fail:

- There are too many different kinds of keywords in the same group. Every one of these keywords needs to be in its own group, *along with a list of very similar words and phrases.*
- The ad doesn't match the keywords, and it can't because there are too many different kinds of keywords in the group.
- "Smith Telecommunications"—or the name of almost any business—is a *lousy* headline. The clickthrough rate (CTR) is going to be very low, and the bid prices will therefore be higher. The ad is about Smith Telecommunications, not what the customer really wants.
- Your ads need to be about your customer—focused on what they're searching for!

THE RIGHT WAY TO ORGANIZE AN ADWORDS CAMPAIGN

Well-organized campaigns get results from the beginning and are easy to adjust and optimize. Over time this makes a huge difference. Here are a few simple steps you can take to organize your campaign.

1. Define Your Campaign

In a single Google account, you can have practically as many campaigns as you want. Some of these campaigns may be on a completely different topic, selling completely different services and sending traffic to a completely different website. In fact, if you have more than one website, you should have a different campaign for each site. A campaign is just a handy way to organize a number of ad groups, usually according to broad topic—for example, a specific type of service or product. So the first step is determining your campaign's focus.

2. Define Your Ad Group

Ad groups are the action centers within a campaign that contain clusters of keywords and ads together, grouped around a single theme. You can have multiple ad groups in a single campaign. How you separate out your *campaigns* is up to you. How you separate *ad groups,* however, is one of those things where there's a right way and a wrong way.

In a *perfect* world, you'd have an ad group with an ad written specifically for every single keyword. Since each keyword is different, each ad would be different, too. If you had 50 keywords, you'd have to write 50 ads and track them through 50 ad groups.

In the real world, that's kind of impractical. So you'll want to cluster similar keywords together with a single ad.

3. In Each Ad Group, Focus on One Type of Product or Service

If you want to advertise more than one product or service on AdWords, it's important to identify each item that you're marketing and whether they're related. Then differentiate each type of product under a different ad group.

- A person who searches for "voice mail *service*" needs to be taken to a page about voice mail service.
- In contrast, a person who searches for *equipment* needs to be taken to a *different* web page—one about voice mail equipment.

These are two entirely different topics. If people have to figure out where to go after they land on your web page, you're making them work too hard. You need to show them exactly what they were searching for.

Now if you structure your campaigns right from the beginning, it's a *lot* easier to make this work. Here's an example of how you can organize your ads and keywords:

4. Organize Related Keywords Together within an Ad Group

To do this, take all of your different keywords and use Wordtracker (http://freekeywords. wordtracker.com; www.wordtracker.com) to organize them into narrow "silos" of very tightly related terms. These silos should always be very narrow, like this:

Voice Mail Services	Voice Mail System	Auto Attendant
voice mail provider	voice mail systems	answering attendant auto system
voice mail service	voice mail systems for realtors	auto attendant voice mail services
voice mail service provider	telemarketing and voice mail systems	auto attendant
voice mail services	phone systems voice mail	auto attendant phone system
	home office voice mail systems	auto attendant software
	home office telephone voice mail systems	auto attendant system
		auto attendant voice mail
		phone auto attendant

5. Eliminate Negative Keywords

There's another step we need to take before pasting this into a campaign: Consider negative keywords. These are related terms that will cost you clicks without bringing you business. Here's a list of keywords that come from a search on *voice mail software*:

> voice mail software
> voice mail business software
> voice mail software for panasonic
> voice mail broadcasting software
> voice mail business software
> multiple voice mail software
> mac voice mail software
> multi line voice mail system software vru
> norstar voice mail software
> software to record voice mail
> free voice mail software

You might not want visitors who want something for *free*. Your company also has nothing to do with voice *broadcasting*, and you don't have anything for *MacIntosh* computers. So turn those into negative keywords by putting a minus sign in front of them. The above list now looks like this:

voice mail software

voice mail business software

voice mail software for panasonic

voice mail business software

multiple voice mail software

multi line voice mail system software vru

norstar voice mail software

software to record voice mail

-free

-mac

-macintosh > Negative Keywords

-broadcast

-broadcasting

When you set up your ad campaigns, each one of these keyword lists is going to go into a different group with its own set of ads.

6. Chop Out Irrelevant Keywords to Improve Your CTR Even More

Sometimes in your keyword collecting you'll inadvertently bid on terms in your keyword list that don't belong at all. This example is from a campaign that targets people who are searching on the subject of religion:

☐	●	mexican religion	$0.05	0	0 0.00%	$0
☐	●	religion and science	$0.05	0	0 0.00%	$0
☐	●	comparative religion	$0.05	0	35 0.00%	$0
☐	●	japanese religions	$0.05	0	1 0.00%	$0
☐	●	losing my religion lyrics	$0.05	0	0 0.00%	$0
☐	●	babylonian religion	$0.05	0	0 0.00%	$0
☐	●	spanish religion	$0.05	0	0 0.00%	$0

Most of the keywords here are irrelevant to what we were going after. They got zero clicks and nearly zero impressions. Of course, "losing my religion lyrics" takes the cake. We'll delete that keyword and then stick in the term "lyrics" as a negative keyword. We'll now get a higher CTR because now that big fat "0" is no longer bringing down the average.

SPLIT TEST YOUR ADS!

HUGE TIP: The key to long-term success on AdWords—and to keeping your bid prices down—is always testing two ads at the same time (referred to as split testing), deleting the inferior one, and then trying to beat the best one. Always have two ads running at the same time.

The Ads

We'll write two ads. Google will rotate them simultaneously. One will have a better CTR than the other; we'll later delete the inferior one, write a new one, and again split test those. Little by little your CTR will go up, up, up.

Voice Mail Software Make Your Communication Easier With Custom, Expandable Systems www.SmithTelecom.com/VMsoftware	← Headline contains your keywords ← 2nd line contains a BENEFIT ← 3rd line contains a FEATURE or OFFER ← 4th line: Display URL has a keyword in the subdirectory/VMsoftware that will help the CTR
Voice Mail Software For Any Business & Any Phone System Same Day Installation & Easy Terms www.SmithTelecom.com/VMsoftware	Same formula for Ad #2, but we're testing a different message. Notice that we capitalize the important words.

- We've generated a list of various keywords: Voice mail system, voice mail software, voice mail service, auto attendant, etc.
- We've used keyword research tools to drill down and generate many variations on these keywords.
- Each family of keywords goes into its own group.
- We rotate two ads at the same time, all the time, and constantly try to beat our best.
- When visitors click on the ad, they are taken to the exact page on your site that has a specific solution to their exact problem—not the homepage. No guessing or clicking all over the place to find what they want.

Here's another example of how to cluster keywords into groups and campaigns, for a variety of martial arts related terms:

How to Organize Your Campaigns and Ad Groups

	Campaign #1 Self Defense	Campaign #2 Martial Arts	Campaign #3 Fighting	Campaign #4 Security & Safety	Campaign #5 Protection
Ad Group #1	Women's Self Defense	Karate	Wrestling	Personal Safety	Self Protection
Ad Group #2	Defense Class	Tae Kwon Do	Grappling	Women's Safety	Women's Protection
Ad Group #3	Defense Video	Aikido	Hand-to-Hand Combat	Personal Security	Child Protection
Ad Group #4	Defense Tactic	Hapkido	Weapons Combat	Children's Security	Assault Protection

Do you want to make it easy to manage campaigns and match your keywords well to ads within each ad group? Organize your campaigns this way, and it will be. More importantly, you'll get more clicks.

Note: This can also be a sound way to organize campaigns for Google's Display Network (GDN). Just note that search campaigns *must* be separated from GDN campaigns in order to be effective. (More on GDN campaigns in Chapter 17.)

	Campaign #1a: Self-Defense (Search)	Campaign #1b: Self-Defense (GDN)	Campaign: #2a: Martial Arts (Search)	Campaign: #2b: Martial Arts (GDN)	Campaign: #3a: Fighting (Search)	Campaign #3b: Fighting (GDN)
Ad Group #1	Women's Self-Defense	Women's Self-Defense	Karate	Karate	Wrestling	Wrestling
Ad Group #2	Defense Class	Defense Class	Tae Kwon Do	Tae Kwon Do	Grappling	Grappling
Ad Group #3	Defense Video	Defense Video	Aikido	Aikido	Hand-to-Hand Combat	Hand-to-Hand Combat
Ad Group #4	Defense Tactic	Defense Tactic	Hapkido	Hapkido	Weapons Combat	Weapons Combat

Never, Ever, Ever Let Google Do This

Occasionally, high-spending customers (and sometimes small ones, too) get a phone call or an email from a Google rep, offering to "optimize your ad campaigns."

Many customers who had previously built their campaigns according to our precise instructions have taken up Google on its offer. There are rare, occasional exceptions, but in ten years almost all have reported to me that it was an unmitigated disaster. It cost one client in the UK about $50,000. Google may have built the greatest piano in the history of the world but that sure doesn't mean it knows how to play it.

The only way to truly understand the Google machine is by spending your own money. It has a funny way of forcing you to learn from your mistakes. Few if any Google employees have learned on their own dime, so they generally have no clue how to optimize a real-world campaign. (By the way, you should *never* hire someone to manage Google ads for you unless they can prove to you that they learned on their own dime.)

If you ever take up Google on any such offer, *do not under any circumstances let it touch the campaigns you built.* Ask Google to set up separate campaigns that run in parallel. Then compare the performance throttling the daily budget of each campaign. Restore the old ones immediately if the new ones are inferior.

Important tip: Do not pause display network campaigns; it resets the data. Use the daily budget tool to lower the traffic instead. Then you can easily restore the budget and original performance.

THE "PEEL AND STICK" STRATEGY: GET A HIGHER CTR JUST BY MOVING YOUR KEYWORDS INTO NEW AD GROUPS

The technique I'm about to show you is one of THE most important techniques you can learn in Google AdWords!

This is an old example from Google's previous interface, but it still illustrates the point perfectly. Look at this ad group and the fact that most of its keywords are getting CTRs of above 2.0 percent. Notice how some of these keywords could be headlines of their own:

Religion Run Amok	+ Create New Text Ad	Image Ad
7 Great Lies Of Organized Religion	1 of 21 Ads: View all below	
A Hard Look at Past & Present		
CoffeehouseTheology.com		

Delete | Edit CPCs/URLs

☐ Keyword	Status [?]	Max CPC Bid	Clicks ▼	Impr.	CTI
Search Total			5,106	605,222	0.8%
Content Total [?] — image ads			0	0	
Content Total [?] — text ads			1,843	1,270,376	0.1%
☐ what is religion			501	19,380	2.5%
☐ world religion			153	15,126	1.0%
☐ [history of religion]			123	5,424	2.2%
☐ jewish religion			107	2,017	5.3%
☐ [freedom from religion]			91	2,700	3.3%
☐ [anti religion]			86	2,713	3.1%
☐ [what is religion]			79	6,291	1.2%
☐ christian religion			77	7,787	0.9%
☐ "catholic religion"			69	7,759	0.8%
☐ world religions			67	4,778	1.4%
☐ "organized religion"			65	2,316	2.8%
☐ [world religion]			62	6,545	0.9%

We noticed that. So we did something about it. Pulled those keywords out of that list and came up with several brand new ad groups. Here's one:

Dark History of Religion	+ Create New Text Ad	Image Ad	
7 Great Lies Of Organized Religion	7,878 Clicks	0.3% CTR	
A Hard Look at Past & Present	Served - 100.0% [more info]		
CoffeehouseTheology.com	Edit - Delete		

Delete | Edit CPCs/URLs

☐ Keyword	Status [?]	Max CPC Bid	Clicks ▼	Impr.	CTR
Search Total			271	10,484	2.5%
Content Total [?]			7,607	2,295,102	0.3%
☐ history of religion	Active		150	6,431	2.3%
☐ [history of religion]	Active		100	3,314	3.0%

The CTR on [history of religion] jumped from 2.2 percent up to 3.0 percent. That's *an improvement of 36 percent,* with so little work!

But it gets better:

Organized Religion - 2005 7 Great Lies Of Organized Religion A Hard Look at Past & Present CoffeehouseTheology.com	+ Create New Text Ad \| Image Ad 1 of 2 Ads: View all below				
Delete Edit CPCs/URLs					
☐ Keyword	Status [?]	Max CPC Bid	Clicks ▼	Impr.	CTR
Search Total			189	3,753	5.0%
Content Total [?]			0	2,094	0.0%
☐ "organized religion"	Active		145	2,885	5.0%
☐ [organized religion]	Active		29	542	5.3%
☐ organized religion	Active		15	326	4.6%

That improved the clickthrough rate by 79 percent! Impressive. Plus, you'll notice that the keyword shows up not once but twice in the ad copy. That didn't hurt either.

Want a better CTR? Want higher positions on the page without paying any more per click? Want more profit in your pocket at the end of the month? This trick will work for you again and again. It's called *peel and stick.*

You take a high traffic keyword, *peel* it out of a group and *stick* it in a new one, with its own ad. It only takes a few minutes.

Almost everything you do to improve the structure of your AdWords campaign is some version of peel and stick. If you advertise all over the country, but you decide you need special ads for San Francisco, peel and stick is how you get the job done. You can optimize 95 percent of your marketing by peeling and sticking 5 percent of your keywords.

Why Peel and Stick Is So Simple, So Powerful

Sometimes after you turn on your traffic you'll discover there are keywords in your ad groups that get a lot more hits than you were expecting. *And* their CTRs, you're convinced, could be a lot higher.

Pause any keyword you find like that and stick it into a new ad group with a clever ad that matches it perfectly.

That's peel and stick. As simple as that. This technique can do wonders for your CTRs.

Why does it work so well? Very simply, it's because people are more likely to click on your ad if they see your keyword in the headline.

Want to improve your CTR by as much as 80 percent? Organize your keywords differently.

Super Important! "Stick Without Peeling"

Unless your campaigns are brand new and have little history, when you do peel and stick, I do not generally recommend that you delete the old keyword from the old ad group, or even pause it at first.

That's because you might "break" something that is working.

Instead, you should copy the old keyword into the new ad group, bid 10 to 20 percent more money in the new ad group, thereby "tempting" Google to favor the new ad group over the old.

Once you see the new ad group is working, you can back down the bid price of the old keyword and then pause it after the traffic has moved over to the new ad group. This protective measure is especially important for long-running Google campaigns.

More Easy-to-Follow Examples

Here are some ads that some of our associates ran for their businesses, with a sample of a few of the actual keywords they used. Best part is, they're far from perfect. They can be improved even more:

How to Sell Anything
Skills Your Competitors Don't Have
Powerful Secrets You Won't Believe
www.XYZ.com

 how to sell
 [how to sell]
 "how to sell"
 –marijuana
 –devil
 –soul

These negative keywords are kind of funny. You definitely don't want those searches!

Dentures to Be Proud Of
Free In-Office Consultation & More
For a Smile that Wins New Friends
www.XYZ.com

 dentures
 affordable dentures
 denture repair
 same-day dentures
 permanent dentures
 partial denture

How many clicks is "denture repair" or "partial denture" getting? If there are a lot, each of them needs peel and stick.

Power Supplies to Order
Custom Design Requests Welcomed
Any OEM Application, ISO 9002
www.XYZ.com

 power supply
 power supplies
 12 volt power supply
 5v power supply
 class 2 power supply
 ac power supply

Try a separate ad group just for "AC power supply."

A/C Transformers Qty 250+
For OEM Applications, ISO 9002
Custom 1-Day Quote, Fast Delivery
www.XYZ.com

 transformers
 power transformer
 transformer accessories
 power supply transformers
 power transformer tube
 –robots in disguise

Admittedly, the length of some of these search terms might make peel and stick a bit challenging, especially if you're trying to fit the keyword in the headline and be descriptive at the same time.

Toothache Relief, Finally!
Your Local Pain-Free Dentist
Improves Your Health & Much More
www.XYZ.com

 toothache
 toothaches
 toothache remedies
 toothache cure
 toothache relief
 toothache pain

If "toothache remedies" gets enough searches to make a difference, do peel and stick with it.

Day Trading Course
Develop Your Personal Schedule
Maximize Your Trading Potential
www.XYZ.com

 trading course
 [trading course]
 trading training
 [trading training]
 "trading books"
 commodities course
 futures course

If "trading training" is getting enough clicks already, pull it out and put it with a new ad. "Commodities course" and "futures course" belong in their own separate ad groups, no question.

If you organize your Google ad groups so that your keywords call out to searchers from your headline and ad text, you can get more visitors to your site, earn better positions on the page, and pay less money for your clicks.

Do you want to improve your clickthrough rate by 10 percent, 30 percent, 80 percent, or better and not have to pay a penny more per click? It's all in how you organize things.

As simple as this is—so simple that most people miss it the first time—it's the single most effective secret that has helped our customers get more clicks without paying a penny more.

For a look at a classic old-style ideal ad group that still serves as a good starter model for matching keywords and ads on Google search, visit www.perrymarshall.com/adwords/idealadgroup.htm.

Uncle Claude Sez

You are presenting an ad to millions. Among them is a percentage, small or large, whom you hope to interest. Go after that percentage and try to strike the chord that responds. . . . They will decide by a glance—by your headline. . . . Address the people you seek and them only.

Keywords
AdWords Success Starts Here

My friend, colleague, and client Matt Gillogly was running Google ads in real estate. As you might expect, real estate keywords are ferociously competitive, especially nationwide. He was looking for a competitive edge.

One night he was watching a real estate TV show and it occurred to him: "Hey, I bet a lot of people who watch this show are my perfect target customers, because they're amateur real estate investors."

He started bidding on the name of that TV show as a keyword. To his delight, he discovered, 1) yes, there's fair amount of searches for this show, and 2) yes, those customers buy!

It pays to be a little more resourceful than everybody else when you do keyword research!

Keywords are the heart and soul of AdWords. There are certainly other elements you need to understand in order to guarantee your success at pay per click (PPC), but fail to understand keywords and your business will tank. Guaranteed.

Many online marketers think of extra keywords like finding a few bucks under the car seat, add a few of them onto an existing marketing campaign to generate a little extra profit.

Not so! You need to be deliberate. Different kinds of keywords demand different strategies.

Keywords are your foundation. Get the right keywords in place from the beginning and everything that follows becomes that much easier.

Think about the number of times in an average day that you open Google in your browser and run a search. Maybe you're researching a work project. Maybe you're browsing for a cool new gadget. Checking football scores. Looking for that one "how to" video. Settling an argument over whether it's possible to sneeze with your eyes open. And so on.

Nearly everything we do online begins with a search. And that involves thinking up the best phrase that represents the problem we're trying to solve, the question we're trying to answer, or the itch we want to scratch. This is why keyword research is a step in PPC strategy that you cannot skip.

Let's say you run a website that sells the latest tablet computers. Imagine yourself in the shoes of someone who is about to search for tablets and places to buy them. What keywords would he or she type in?

This exercise isn't new. Marketers and salespeople throughout the ages have formulated winning pitches by figuring out what's going on in the heads of the people they want to sell to. Decades ago, Robert Collier famously said, "Always enter the conversation that is already taking place in the customer's mind."

Think about that. Too many business owners are trying to *create* a conversation in the mind of their customers, when what they should really be doing is figuring out the conversation that is *already there.*

None of us wants to be told what to think. But we love people who can echo exactly what we're already thinking and feeling. Stepping in to help customers get where they *already want to go* and do what they *already want to do* is where true PPC magic happens.

The amazing part is, before the internet, the conversation in a customer's mind was a private deal, a mystery you could only guess at. But in the Google age your customer opens his browser and literally *types his inner head conversation into the search bar!*

We may not be able to predict the exact keywords an individual is going to use, but 99 percent of the guesswork has been removed from the process. And, as we'll see later, absolute precision isn't necessary anyway.

So here's where we start: Imagine your ideal customer, and picture what it is they're likely to type into Google. Do that and you're the first giant step closer to constructing a highly effective PPC campaign.

HOW TO FIND THE MOST PROFITABLE KEYWORDS

By now you've likely figured out that once you start trying to predict the keywords your customers are using, you're going end up with a very, very long list.

Not to worry. The longer your list of keywords, the wider the array of customers you'll reach. That said, don't spend months trying to create an exhaustive list. We start by narrowing things down a little bit. You can find the audience that's most interested in your product or service by understanding the three major groups of online searchers:

1. *Browsers* are people searching for general information. It's usually hard to tell what exactly each person is looking for. One person might be doing research for a term paper. Another person might be killing time waiting for a bus. The vast majority of this group are not ready to buy and probably never will be.
2. *Shoppers* are definitely interested in your product but they're still at the research stage, checking out reviews and comparing prices. Some folks from this group will be ready to buy in a matter of days or even hours, but for others it may be weeks, months, or possibly never.
3. *Buyers* are typing with one hand and their credit card in the other. They know exactly what they want and the only barrier to making a purchase is finding the right place and the right deal.

So how do you tell which of these three groups a person is in? By studying the keywords that they enter into the search bar. As a general rule of thumb the more specific the search, the closer they are to the "Buyer" group.

Take, for instance, the three different types of people searching for televisions:

A browser will search for keywords containing just one or two words with no modifiers:

- TV
- Televisions
- LCD TVs
- 3D TVs

A shopper is a bit more specific, using modifiers that will help find sites containing greater depth of information:

- Samsung TV reviews
- Best Samsung TVs
- Samsung TV 42"
- Samsung LCD TVs compare

Finally, the buyer is very specific, often using the results of his previous research in the keywords.

- Order Samsung TV 42"
- Buy online Samsung 42"
- Samsung TV UE32F5500 buy
- Samsung TV UE32F5500 best price

If you're just getting started with your AdWords campaigns and budget is your biggest concern, it makes sense to target only the buyer group. These folks are the easiest to convert to customers. As your experience grows you can extend your reach to the shoppers and, to some degree, even the browsers as well.

So let's start with a group of buyers, and put together a first draft of our keyword list.

Step 1: Scour Your Website

Browse through your site and your entire product range and make a list of everything you sell. You probably know your product line pretty well. Step into your customer's shoes and assume he or she doesn't know your products by heart. Think of synonyms he or she might use. Then combine these with some of the common buyer keywords.

Sticking with our TV example, if one of your products is a Samsung LED TV, then you might come up with these keyword combinations:

- Samsung LED TV
- Buy Samsung LED TV
- Best Samsung LED TV
- Compare Samsung LED TV

Step 2: Sniff Out Your Competition

Take a look at your top competitors' websites. You'll almost certainly find a few phrases and expressions that you hadn't thought of. Add these to your list as well.

Step 3: Ask Your Customers

Do a survey. Have a casual phone chat with a few of your most recent buyers. Ask them specifically how they found your site and, if they can remember, the keywords they searched on in the process. Also quiz them about the kind of keywords they use in their searches in general. At this stage you won't hear a huge amount that surprises you but you'll definitely pick up a handful of new keywords or modifiers to add to your list.

Step 4: Ask Your Staff, Family, and Friends

This is an extension of Step 3. At this stage you may feel like you're scraping the bottom of the barrel. But that's the point—it's all about compiling as exhaustive a list as you can.

Step 5: Dive Into the Keyword Tools

For the most part, Google's keyword resource is good enough. (More on that in a bit.) As you gain experience, however, third-party tools will allow you to dig even deeper. This is especially true if you're managing PPC campaigns for clients.

There are plenty of software applications to choose from. SpyFu, AdGooroo, WordStream and Wordtracker are each helpful in their own way. Most keyword tools of this type work by figuring out what your competitors are bidding on and feeding the data back to you. There are limits to how accurate this supply of information can be. But they will give you keyword ideas you would otherwise have missed.

HOW TO GET THE MOST FROM GOOGLE'S KEYWORD PLANNER

If you've been diligent with the previous steps you should now have a long list of keywords. We'll use Google's Keyword Planner (an amalgam of two items from their old suite of tools—the "Keyword Tool" and the "Traffic Estimator") to add a few more, and then begin the refining process.

You don't need to be running PPC ads to use Google's tool, but you do need an AdWords account. If you haven't opened one yet now's the time.

The advantage of Keyword Planner comes from Google's massive storehouse of data that it uses to find you new keywords and to predict their cost and value.

Find the Keyword Planner under "Tools" at the very top of the AdWords page:

On the front end, the Keyword Planner presents you with four options to begin your research:

1. *Search for new keyword and ad group ideas*. Enter a keyword or a URL and Google will give you a whole of bunch of ideas to get you started.

2. *Get search volume for a list of keywords, or group them into ad groups.* If you already have a list of keywords, Google will give you an estimate of the number of people who are searching on each of these phrases each month.

3. *Get traffic estimates for a list of keywords.* This is similar to the above but will give you quite a bit more detail, including the estimated number of clicks a campaign on a particular keyword should give you, as well as how much you can expect to pay to use it.

4. *Multiply keyword lists to get new keyword ideas.* This feature takes two distinct types of keyword lists and combines them into one master list. For example, you could have one list of your products and a second list of all the various colors in which your products are available.

This may seem like a clever feature, but it's not a particularly useful one. The master list you end up with will contain scores of obscure keyword combinations that will receive little or no traffic. Google could penalize you for this by showing your ads less frequently or requiring you to bid more for your keywords.

Let's focus on "Search for new keyword and ad group ideas." Begin with a single broad phrase or word that describes your primary product, or simply enter your URL. (Try your competitor's URL too.) You have the option to select a category but this isn't strictly necessary at this stage.

Finally, click the "Get Ideas" button.

Google will respond with an avalanche of "Ad group ideas," each themed around a specific set of keywords. For example, if you entered "bed" as your keyword, you can expect to see one ad group for bunk beds, another ad group for queen beds, another for children's beds, and so on.

<div style="border: 2px solid #000; padding: 10px;">

Let Others Do Your Keyword Research for You

In addition to using your website URL or that of a competitor, you can also get some very interesting results by entering the URL of the Wikipedia page that's most relevant to your primary keyword. Once you've done that, enter that same Wikipedia URL at OpenSiteExplorer.org and you'll find a whole range of other closely related pages that you can plug into Google's Keyword Planner.

You can repeat this exercise using URLs from online directories, blogs, and even forums that are closely related to your main keyword. These are easy to find in Google by searching for your primary keyword along with the relevant modifier. For example, if you were looking for blogs on the subject of beds, search for: beds +blogs.

</div>

The default view at this point is "Ad group ideas," but after performing your search you'll see an alternate tab titled "Keyword ideas." Click on this and you'll receive a wealth of additional information on each suggested keyword.

Plus you'll also see a couple of features on the left-hand side, one called "Targeting" and the other called "Customize your search." We're going to use these to get Google's seemingly endless list of suggestions down to a manageable number.

Start out by using the "Targeting" options to refine your search:

Location

If you only service a specific country or region then this is where you specify that. If you adjust this option you'll notice that the statistics Google has provided on areas such as "Avg. monthly searches" and "Suggested bid" will change accordingly.

Languages

This is self-explanatory and is usually set to "All languages" by default.

Network

Do you want your ads to be shown only for searches on Google, or also on Google's search partner sites? When you're starting out, err on the side of choosing the simplest options, and then expand as you grow in experience and confidence.

Negative Keywords

Enter a keyword here and Google's suggestions will no longer contain that search term.

Once you've finished refining your list you can either download the keywords to add to your existing list, or import Google's list directly into a campaign. The choice is yours. Either way, you may still want to do some additional trimming.

PPC beginners frequently fall into the trap of assuming that keywords are all about volume and trying to hit every possible angle. In practice, having too many keywords is worse than not having enough. You want to find that "Goldilocks zone" where you have enough keywords to give you results, but not so many that you dilute your efforts and end up with overload.

If you're starting out, go for a minimum of 50 keywords and an absolute maximum of 250. (You can certainly have more than these, but let's keep things simple at first.)

So what do you cut and what do you keep?

Imagine that you're an archer looking at your target. The bull's eye represents the keywords that are right on the money and a near-perfect match for what you're offering. The ring just outside the bull's eye represents keywords that are still closely matched but not quite as exact. The next ring out contains keywords that are still good but are bringing you more shoppers than buyers.

When creating your first keyword shortlist, start with the bull's eye, and work your way out from there. The resulting list will provide you with an excellent starting point from which you will be able to run your first profitable campaigns.

> ### How to Zero in on the Profitable Keywords
>
> Another way to streamline your keyword list is to use Google's filter to focus on keywords that have medium or high levels of competition, or that have a minimum bid threshold of at least $1.
>
> Google's PPC program has been around long enough that if certain keywords have a very low cost of entry it's almost certainly because lots of other advertisers have tried to use them and struggled to make them profitable. By focusing only on fairly popular keywords, at least at this stage, you'll be able to exclude keywords that will be more challenging to convert into profit.

STEP UP YOUR GAME USING KEYWORD MATCHING OPTIONS

When you're ready to import your keyword list into Google, there's a final step to consider. And beware: skip this step and you'll burn through your budget in a matter of days, maybe even hours. Plus your conversion rates will be pitiful.

Remember, we're targeting buyers first and foremost. You've likely spent considerable time crafting your keyword list to focus on this group. But if you simply import those keywords into your ad groups as they are, you may unintentionally waste all your hard work.

Google provides matching options as a means to match your keywords with genuine, real world searches. This process is entirely in your hands. Let me explain.

1. Broad Match

If you don't tell Google how and when to show your keywords, it will default to this setting and show your ads for any search it considers relevant. This could include searches that use your keywords in any order, or don't even contain your keywords at all.

So if you enter your keyword into your list as

> formal shoes

with no punctuation or brackets, then Google could show your ads for any of these searches:

- What are formal shoes?
- Will formal shoes get me a better job?
- Buy shoes online
- Good work shoes
- Smart shoes for prom

Can you see the problem here? The first two searches are by browsers who are a long way from spending money. The next three searches are vague, and will pull in people looking for products you don't even stock.

The result? You're going to waste money on tire-kickers or you're going to get a very low clickthrough rate. If that happens, Google's "Quality Score" rules kick in, which could make your PPC campaigns far more costly to operate.

This is one of the biggest pitfalls new PPC operators fall into. It's Google's "Stupidity Tax." Broad-match searches generally get lots of impressions—and it looks as if something good is happening—but their clickthrough rates and conversions are usually abysmal.

The solution is simple. Google lets you input your keywords with some simple punctuation that more specifically indicates what kinds of searches you want to show for.

2. Exact Match

This option gives you total control. You'll get fewer impressions and fewer clicks overall, but you won't have to worry about wasting clicks on useless searches. Just enter your keyword with square brackets around it:

[buy formal shoes]

Ads connected to this keyword will now only show when people type in this exact keyword phrase verbatim. If a person searching enters a keyword phrase that includes any other words before, after, or in between, your ad won't show.

In the above instance your ad will show for this search:

buy formal shoes

But it won't show for any of these:

buy formal shoes online
formal shoes buy
black formal shoes
formal black shoes

Your ad also won't show if the searcher enters "buy formall shoes" with a misspelling. (Although you can choose the misspelling option—more on that in Chapter 16, "Campaign Settings.")

And that's why exact match is a two-edged sword!

You avoid wasted impressions at the expense of missed opportunities. To put it bluntly, people are weird: For all the effort you put into finding the most logical keywords to use, someone will use the word "purchase" instead of "buy" and you'll miss out on valuable traffic.

Which brings us to . . .

3. Phrase Match

Enter your keyword in straight quotation marks. People will see your ad when they type in the keyword in that precise order, but your ad will also display if they type in additional words before or after:

"formal shoes"

With this keyword your ad will show for all of the following searches:

formal shoes
buy formal shoes
formal shoes buy
purchase formal shoes
buy formal shoes online

However, it won't show for searches that insert anything in between the keywords or use them in a different order. For example:

shoes formal
formal black shoes
buy formal work shoes
formal mens shoes

Phrase match is useful because you get more impressions than with exact match but you still retain a level of accuracy.

You may *still* miss out on some opportunities, however. So Google thankfully gives you:

4. Modified Broad Match

This option behaves like broad match but you can specify that one or more of the words in your key phrase must always be present. Add a plus sign immediately before the non-negotiable word, like this:

+formal shoes

This keyword will show for any search that Google considers relevant but *only* if the person searching included the word "formal." This way your ads will show for all of the following searches:

buy formal shoes

ULTIMATE GUIDE TO GOOGLE ADWORDS

buy formal footwear
affordable formal black shoes
what are formal shoes?
formal shoe shop

But your ad will not show for:

buy work shoes
best smart shoes
buy black evening footwear
smart cheap black shoes

There's lots of flexibility with modified broad match but, as the above illustrates, you need to think carefully about which words to "anchor" using that "+" otherwise you could still wind up with some irrelevant impressions or miss out on some key opportunities.

In this example you might be better off with:

+buy formal shoes

Google knows what formal shoes are, so let them show your ads for searches related to the concept but restrict it to searches that contain the word "buy."

It all comes back to intent. What is the conversation taking place in your ideal customer's head? Most people who use the word "buy" in a search are looking for websites that sell the product in question and are ready to spend money.

Modified broad match offers a superb balance between flexibility and accuracy and is an important tool to learn to use well. However, when you first start out it can offer many opportunities for mistakes. The problems we identified with broad match can easily manifest themselves here if you put the "+" in the wrong place!

If you're feeling confident, give it a try. But if you're putting together your very first campaign, and especially if your budget is tight, start just with phrase match and pin down the most targeted searches for your product or service.

Matching Options and Single Words

WARNING: It's typically best *not* to use phrase match or broad match for keywords that consist of a single word. This will greatly limit Google's ability to understand your campaign's intent and you'll often end up matched with a very broad range of searches, most of which will be highly irrelevant. The result will be a high spend and minimal success.

YOUR QUICK ACTION SUMMARY

Keywords are the foundation of a strong AdWords strategy, but they're only the starting point. Don't obsess over building the perfect keyword list for your first campaigns. Good enough is good enough and, to be frank, the keyword list you have twelve months from now will probably look nothing like the one you have today. After you've spent a few months eliminating ineffective or costly keywords, finding variations of the winners, and reviewing your search query reports to see how searches are changing, your keyword list will have grown and evolved into something far more interesting, finely targeted, and profitable.

All journeys begin with a single step. Here's a quick review of what you need to do to get started:

- Set up your AdWords account.
- Brainstorm keyword ideas.
- Use Google's Keyword Planner to expand your keyword list.
- Refine the list with options and filters.
- Turn your keywords into phrase matches by wrapping them in straight quotation marks.

Uncle Claude Sez

The only readers we get are people whom our subject interests. Long or short, no one reads ads for amusement. Think of your readers as prospects standing before you, seeking information. Give them enough information to get action.

Niche Domination, Part 1
Chisel In Where the Chiseling Is Easy

We need to step away from the mechanics of Google AdWords for a few minutes and talk about *strategy*. Pay close attention to these next two chapters.

My friend and mentor Dan Kennedy spent years on the speaking circuit. Once he was in the "Green Room" for speakers with Norman Schwarzkopf, aka "Stormin' Norman." In the 1990s Schwarzkopf was a grand celebrity for having won Operation Desert Storm, taking Kuwait back from Iraq and stopping the armies of Saddam Hussein.

Dan asked Schwarzkopf, "Norman, what was the secret to your success? How did you become such an awesome celebrity overnight?"

He replied, "I only played games I could win. Desert Storm was a game we could win."

Contrast this with the War in Iraq, which in hindsight was a game nobody could win. Famous marketers and marketing gurus sometimes appear to walk on water. But what we really do is we find places where the water is denser than a human body and walk on *that*. We only *appear* to be defying gravity!

Picking battles you can win is one of the most vital of all marketing skills. And in Google AdWords, you can Chisel Your Way In where the competition is thick as thieves... or you can target niches where no one has decisively claimed the top spot, or the top player is weak or not paying attention. That's the best way to Chisel Your Way In with minimum resistance.

SIGNS A NICHE IS OVERLOOKED

1. Good niches almost always have advertisers. If there is a keyword for which you find no advertisers, odds are 95 percent that there is no money in that niche.
2. There is a major unmet need in that market. Sometimes it is very easy to tell. For example, people do search Google for "lemon scented hand soap" but as you can see here, almost none of the advertisers on Google specifically cater to it:

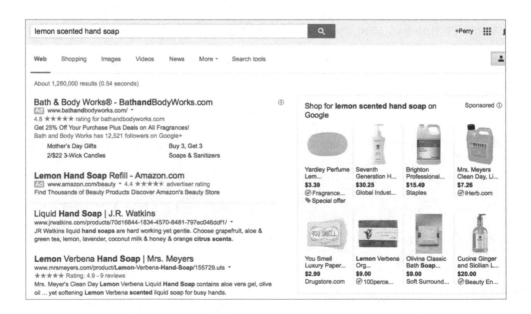

Admittedly, the "lemon scented hand soap niche" is small. But it is unclaimed. "Lemon scented soap" is bigger and is probably better. In these niches, it will not be hard to write a winning ad and landing page and become the big fish in the little pond. You might only sell ten units a month, but it's a good start. It is way better than getting your head handed to you on a platter by trying to compete in "hand soap."

3. There is a major unmet need in your market that is **not** readily obvious from keyword research. Glenn Livingston has devised a very easy, elegant way to find this unmet need. The following is adapted from Chapter 21 of *80/20 Sales & Marketing*.

THE 80/20 SURVEY TECHNIQUE FOR HYPER-RESPONSIVE INTELLIGENCE

Please pay close attention. This is one of the most important sections in this book! It will get you to the money in any niche faster than anything else I know. (You will also find an extension to this section in the online supplement for book buyers, at www.perrymarshall.com/supplement.)

Ninety-nine percent of marketers have absolutely NO idea how to use surveys. They think they're supposed to ask people what their most important question or need is, then just echo these needs back to them in priority order, kind of like a FAQ. But the problem with frequently *asked* questions is that they're also frequently *answered* questions.

Frequently Presented Needs Are also Frequently Catered-To Needs

In other words, all a standard survey does for you is identify the price of entry benefits for a market. It doesn't give you any way of distinguishing what needs represent the market gap or where you might position yourself with **point of difference benefits**.

Moreover, these surveys typically don't ask **why** the respondent is experiencing the frustration they're experiencing, which really castrates the purpose of doing the survey in the first place.

For example, it's infinitely more powerful to know that 40 percent of your prospects need a computer that boots up quickly *because* they're paid based upon per-unit productivity, rather, than just knowing they need a fast boot. In the former case, you don't know how to paint the mood and tone of your advertising, whereas in the latter you know it's all about the frustrations of per-unit workers.

Here's a simple way to fix this problem. Ask them not only **what** their single most important question or need is relating to your topic, but **why** they chose to look for

a solution today and **how difficult** it was to find a good one. Then score it using the protocol on the following page (which also takes into account each prospect's level of engagement).

THE 80/20 PROTOCOL

Send these three questions to your prospect and customer list; or recruit people via forums such as Twitter, Facebook, and other social media gathering places on your bull's-eye keyword; or ask on your landing page that's getting Google traffic from your target keywords:

- *The WHAT question*: "What's your single most important question about (keyword)?"
- *The WHY question*: "Why would it make a difference in your life to get a good answer for this problem or find a solution for your need? (Details, please.)"
- *The HOW DIFFICULT question*: "How difficult has it been for you to find a good answer for the above to date?" (Not at all difficult, somewhat difficult, very difficult)

So what do you do with this information?

Quick and dirty summary: You throw it into a spreadsheet. You discard the "not difficult" and "somewhat difficult" and you only keep the "very difficult." Those are the people who really have an itch that they can't figure out how to scratch.

Then you throw away the short answers and keep the long answers. What's left are your highly influential 5 to 10 percent who will actually give you money for a product that solves their problems. Their answers are literally a page out of their diary. And you'll know exactly what problems your product has to solve.

There's a much better approach, however, one that's much more precise. I have devised a simple scoring system for your survey, and you can download it at www.perrymarshall.com/supplement.

When you're done, sort your data by this score ("hyper-responsive score"), and look at the top 20 percent of responses. Or if you have thousands of responses, look at the top 5 percent instead: *These* are your most hyper-responsive prospects, and it's within those responses you'll find the most motivating language, needs, and your point-of-difference benefit.

To listen to a full-length interview where Glenn and I discuss depth-research techniques you can leverage in Google AdWords, please visit www.LivingstonReport.com.

I cannot tell you how powerful this is. I do "Livingston 80/20 Surveys" on my customers at least once every few months, and unless I'm having a stupidity spasm, any

time we go into a brand new product category or market. **The market will tell you what its unmet needs are.** *If there really is an unmet need, you will not have trouble getting people to take the survey.*

If you can't get people to take the survey, then there's no water in that swimming pool. Don't jump in it. Pick another market and go after that instead.

YOUR QUICK ACTION SUMMARY

Get feedback from your prospects before spending huge sums of money on product and web development:

- Send the three "what," "why," and "how difficult" questions to your prospects.
- Keep only the responses from people who indicated it was "very difficult" to find answers or help.
- Look at the top 20 percent of longest responses to see what your most rabid prospects had to say.

Uncle Claude Sez

Many things are possible in advertising which are too costly to attempt. That is another reason why every project and method should be weighed and determined by a known scale of cost and result.

Niche Domination, Part 2
Playing Games You Can Win

This chapter could make you millions of dollars and add years to your life.

When I first met Ed Rush, a former Air Force pilot, he was casting about trying to find his way in the world. He had recently left the secure, regimented world of the military. The ever-shifting, bloodthirsty world of self-employment was perilous and scary.

He and his wife were eating bologna sandwiches and ramen soup. She was hoping he would figure something out, hoping it wouldn't take him too long.

He was hoping he wouldn't be a miserable failure.

He tried all kinds of things. He was fascinated with leadership. At one point he sent me a CD of him giving a talk on leadership. I told him, "Ed, nice try, but leadership is way too competitive of a field and you have way too few credentials to make that fly."

He did some soul searching and he realized he knew something few others knew: How to become an Air Force pilot.

The odds are heavily stacked against anyone who wants to become a pilot in the Air Force. Ed had deep inside knowledge, he'd had a very successful career, and guess what: People were searching. And nobody selling information on that topic had the credibility he had. It was an under-exploited niche.

Ed told his customers: "I can't promise you'll get in if you take my course, but I can promise your chances will be much, much higher with my help than without it." He added a satisfaction guarantee and created a product.

He built a website and started driving Google traffic. That site went on to generate substantial income for Ed. He became THE dominant player in the "Become an Air Force Pilot" niche.

Ed's story is a perfect example of how you succeed with Google AdWords: You find an under-served niche where you have a strong unique selling proposition (USP), and you address the unmet need with your greatest strength.

Most people will say "Yeah, but in my market there already is an Ed Rush and he's #1. He's probably raking it in. Meanwhile, I'm sitting here at #20 or whatever the last position is. How do I make this work?"

Answer: You do **not** simply try to be a bigger, badder, more-mojo version of Ed. You do not go head to head. That is almost always doomed to fail.

Unfortunately, that is what most Google advertisers do. Most Google advertisers say "All I need is better ads, a better landing page, and a better offer, and then I can beat Ed and can be #1 instead of him." Well, yes, that is true, but there is almost always some additional element you will have a tremendously difficult time overcoming. For example, if Ed already has social proof, such as 100 glowing testimonials, and you've got 5, the next 95 testimonials are going to take a l-o-o-o-n-g time to get. And by then he'll have 150.

The way you chisel your way in is, you find a sub-niche that Ed does not serve. For example: "How to get accepted as an Air Force Pilot if you are an African American."

Now maybe the process is absolutely identical. Maybe there are no differences at all. Maybe your chances are exactly the same whether you're white or black. However, I doubt it's exactly the same. Even if it is the same, it doesn't matter. *If customers who are searching perceive it's different for an African American, then there's a market.*

Obviously you'd almost certainly have to be black in order to pull this off. If you're not black, you'll have to come up with some other angle. But the point is, this is a perfect example of locating an under-served sub-niche. If Ed is already the #1 Air Force training

guy, it's going to be very hard for you to replace him as #1. But if nobody is the #1 black Air Force training guy, it's very *easy* for you to claim that spot.

This is how you chisel your way in to Google AdWords!

Notice that what I just told you doesn't really have all that much to do with Google AdWords per se. Certainly it has a lot to do with keyword and market research, as I'll describe in a minute. But it has more to do with your USP and your offer.

And really it goes deeper than that. Stick with me because I'm going to explain one of the most powerful concepts in this book.

THE "WORKING STIFF TO $230 MILLION" NICHE DOMINATION STRATEGY

Richard Koch wrote the million-copy selling classic *The 80/20 Principle*. When I read it, very early in my AdWords career, it set my mind on fire. It altered the way I saw everything, especially AdWords. Suddenly I understood there are tiny levers everywhere that swing huge doors.

Eventually I wrote my book *80/20 Sales and Marketing*. Richard and I became friends. Richard wrote the foreword. He was already the 80/20 guy and I had little chance of displacing him. However, I used the same strategy I just described for Air Force pilot gurus, and decided to become the 80/20 guy for sales and marketing. That was a much easier battle to win—I just carved off an unclaimed niche, like settlers in the 1800s claiming their free 160 acres of farmland in Nebraska.

Richard Koch has a fascinating story. He started out in corporate consulting. He did stints at both Boston Consulting Group (BCG) and Bain Consulting, the company Mitt Romney is associated with. Though his time at those companies was frustrating and not outrageously successful (he quit before they could throw him out at BCG), he absorbed a *tremendous* amount of knowledge and insight from BCG's founder Bruce Henderson, as well as Bill Bain.

He left and formed another consulting firm, L.E.K. Consulting, with two ex-Bain colleagues. L.E.K. was enormously successful, because Richard combined the wisdom and experience of Bain and BCG with a completely new niche and business model, and smart partners.

L.E.K. prospered and Richard sold his stake in the company for $6 million.

After the sale of the company, and after taxes, Richard had $4 million left. That was 23 years ago. At that point, he became a consulting private equity investor. He used the vast experience and acumen he'd acquired in his consulting years to precisely define:

- What kind of companies to invest in
- Which niches to pursue

■ Growth strategy for those companies
■ When you should get in
■ When you should get out

In other words, exactly the same things you should be deliberate about as you maneuver in Google AdWords!

Richard began taking equity positions in small companies.

Over the last 23 years, he's applied 80/20 and focused his efforts on 16 select firms. Not 160. Just 16.

Half the companies Richard's invested in have gone on to be tremendously successful, selling for many times what they were originally worth. Half his investments have grown 5 to 50 times their size when he bought in.

This is how Richard Koch has grown his net worth from $4 million in 1990 to $230 million as of 2014.

Richard's asset base has grown an *average* of 19.2 percent per year for more than two decades. If you don't believe me, get out your calculator and do the math. $4 million to $228 million in 23 years.

■ Warren Buffett became the world's richest man on 20.3 percent per year . . .
■ Peter Lynch of the Fidelity Magellan Fund made just 29 percent annual returns . . .
■ And forget his $1 billion day—George Soros's Quantum Fund averaged just 30 percent annually . . .

How is it that Richard can consistently beat the market by double digits every year, year after year? How does he attain results within spitting distance of Buffett and the world's richest billionaires?

By the way, he's still 20 years younger than Buffett. He's not a mutual fund manager. He's not a corporate analyst. He's not a mathematician or "spreadsheet junkie" by any stretch of the imagination. He doesn't have a splay of six computer monitors with charts and market data blaring at him every day.

ALSO:

When a venture capitalist (VC) invests in ten companies, they expect seven to go belly up, two to do OK and one to explode to 10X. VCs are the fraternity that gave birth to Facebook and Google. Those guys make billions of dollars this way.

Even the best are lucky to bat 10 percent.

Yet Richard has invested in only 16 and hit pay dirt—*serious* pay dirt—on eight. Way too many to ascribe to luck.

So here's the question I have for you today:

HOW IS IT POSSIBLE THAT RICHARD KOCH BATS 50 PERCENT WHEN MOST VENTURE CAPITAL FIRMS ARE DELIGHTED TO BAT 5–10 PERCENT?

And that's not all, 'cause the icing on the cake is Richard spends, at most, one to two hours per day working on his business.

The answer is that Richard picks his winners based on three factors that he calls the Star Principle:

1. Your niche is growing 10 percent per year or more
2. Your company is #1 in its niche
3. If you are not #1, create a sub-niche and appoint yourself #1.

Opportunities that match these criteria are worth your time. They're the ones that are going to grow. You get an exponential return on your time and money with Star Principle companies.

I don't know if Air Force recruiting is growing 10 percent per year, but everything else Ed Rush did matched the Star Principle criteria. *That is why Ed was successful building a lucrative business with Google AdWords traffic.*

On the other hand, if you do not have a strong USP, if you are far from #1 in your niche, if you go into a niche where there is lots of competition and little to differentiate you from everyone else, or if you go into a niche that is shrinking (CD manufacturing for example) then all the AdWords techniques in the world cannot save you.

That's because even if 95 percent of the AdWords advertisers do a lousy job, which is usually the case, the 5 percent who know what they're doing will still beat you.

I've created a more in-depth tool where you can evaluate any product or market you're in or choose to go into. The tool scores your business on a scale from 1 to 200, with 100 being the threshold for Star Business status.

Go to www.StarPrinciple.com and get your score. You'll see a page that looks like this:

A Star Business is one with an overwhelmingly high chances of success, based on the ingenious formula in Richard Koch's book "The Star Principle." Richard used the Star Principle formula to grow his fortune from $4 million to over $200 million in 23 years, successfully taking 8 companies out of 16 to blazing success. His 50% success rate is unheard of in a world where Venture Capitalists are thrilled to bat 10%. Answer these ten questions and discover your score:

1) How much has your business grown in the last 12 months?.

○ Pre-revenue
○ Business is down
○ 0-10%
○ 11-20%
○ 21-99%
○ 100-300%
○ over 300%

2) Are you THE leader in your niche?.

○ No
○ Hard to Tell

The tool is free and doesn't require registration. Answer 12 quick questions and get your score in 60 seconds. If you wish, you can sign up for the report that explains the tool and your score in detail.

SUCCESS THROUGH ELIMINATION

Every major success I've had in business has matched up to the Star Principle criteria fairly well. A quick Star Principle test is now one of the first things I do when evaluating an opportunity or client business.

As entrepreneurs, we thrive on action, excitement, and adventure. Many of us become adrenaline and activity addicts. Most of us habitually say yes to everything. But the best thing you can do to ensure future success is say NO to far more opportunities, markets, and even keywords than you say yes to.

We go into even greater depth on the "success through elimination" principle in the online supplement for book buyers, at www.perrymarshall.com/supplement.

How to Write Google Ads
Attract Eyeballs, Get Clicks, and Earn Money

Your Google ads are an army of 100,000 tiny salesmen traversing the entire planet for you. And you only have to pay their salaries when the customers crack their doors open to listen to them.

Advertising is *selling in print.* That means the words you should use in your Google ads are the same words you use when you're on the phone or sitting across the table from a prospect, convincing him to buy something.

Before you try to write advertising copy, you should try to explain what you're selling to someone who might buy. And then . . . when they raise their eyebrows and lean forward, pay attention to what you just said.

My friend and mentor John Carlton, one of the highest-paid advertising copywriters in the world, spends weeks, sometimes months, researching his clients' products or services, going from person to person or business to business, gauging their reactions and questions. John learns what buyers really want and the certain turns of phrase that make or break the sale.

My own website sports a perfect example of this. My first lead generation offer was a CD called *Guerilla Marketing for Hi-Tech Sales People.* The title of this CD came about exactly as follows. I was walking a trade show floor wearing a "speaker" badge a couple of years ago, and people would ask me what I was speaking on.

I tried a few different titles: "21 Secrets of High-Impact Low-Cost Marketing". . . "The Cold Call Curse". . . "Advertising Strategies for Technical Sales". . . but the one that provoked positive reactions was "Guerilla Marketing for Hi-Tech Sales People." So that's what it's been ever since.

Those tiny Google ads succeed for exactly the same reasons. The only challenge is your limited space. The headline is 25 characters or less, and each line of the body is 35 characters. The website URL displayed in the ad can also be up to 35 characters long.

So those are your limits. And that's OK, because your goal is not complex: just be *clear, simple,* and *relevant.* Claude Hopkins understood this well:

> *Literary qualifications have no more to do with it than oratory has with salesmanship. One must be able to express himself briefly, clearly, and convincingly, just as a salesman must. But fine writing is a distinct disadvantage. So is unique literary style. They take attention from the subject. . . . Fine talkers are rarely good salesmen. . . . Successful salesmen are rarely good speechmakers. . . . They are plain and sincere men who know their customers. . . . So it is in ad writing.*

English majors and Ph.D.s (and even MBAs) generally suffer from severe marketing debilitations. In advertising, an academic education is more of a liability than an asset! You don't need to be a literary genius.

Google Ads are the language of the street, not the ivory tower. Speak to your customers in the language they respond to in everyday conversation, and they'll click.

GREAT HEADLINES: RIVETING TO YOUR CUSTOMER, DEAD BORING TO ANYONE ELSE

Just as in print advertising and on web pages, your headline swings the biggest difference in response. It's in that split second of reading your headline copy that your customer first makes up his mind whether or not you're really relevant.

Start with that keyword your customer just typed in and fit it into your headline. That will be the first signal to him that you're truly relevant. This means that you'll want

to create enough different ad groups that each of your major keywords can have an ad of its own.

Let's say that you sell custom power supplies. There's certainly more than one way potential customers might come looking for what you sell. They might search for "adaptors." They might search for "power supplies." They might search for "transformers."

So you'll go to your major keyword tool, such as Wordtracker or Google's Keyword Planner tool, and you'll come up with all the possible major variations and related terms for your market niche. Then you'll separate them out into smaller groups that you can match to specific ads. For example:

Custom Power Adaptors

www.xyzadaptors.com
Record-Speed Custom Production Time
Get a Full Quote in 1 Business Day

> adaptor
> adaptors
> ac adaptor
> power adaptor
> custom adaptors

Custom Transformers, Fast

www.xyzadaptors.com
Inventory Cost, Lead Time Advantage
Get a Quote in One Day or Less

> power transformers
> electrical transformers
> voltage transformers

Note: This ad group will need a strong set of negative keywords to block out traffic looking for Transformers® movie or toy information.

Power Supplies to Order

www.xyzadaptors.com
Inventory Cost, Lead Time Advantage
Get a Quote in One Day or Less

> power supply
> power supplies
> switching power supply

> dc power supplies
>
> ac power supply

These ads aren't very flashy, are they? They're not loaded with over-the-top language. In fact, to folks like you and me they're, frankly, boring. But that's okay. They aren't meant for the average guy on the street.

This particular company caters to engineers. It speaks the language that engineers would understand, relate to, and appreciate. It matches its audience just fine. And it gets a good clickthrough rate. (Too good, in fact.)

Use your major keywords in your headline, and create as many different ad groups as you need to do this with all of your biggest keywords. That's what makes the formula work.

YOUR AD TEXT: WHERE YOUR INNER SALESMAN COMES ALIVE

After your headline, you've still got a second chance to convince your customer even further that you've got what he wants and get more clicks. This is where your inner salesman comes alive.

There's a second secret that makes this work. Check out the difference between these two ads:

Popular Ethernet Terms	**Popular Ethernet Terms**
3 Page Guide—Free PDF Download	Complex Words—Simple Definitions
Complex Words—Simple Definitions	3 Page Guide—Free PDF Download
0.1% CTR	**3.6% CTR**

The second ad got *36 times* the CTR as the first! What happened? What was the secret?

Look closely at the two ads. They both have the exact same wording. There's only one difference between them. What is it? The first ad listed features and offers first, benefits second. The second ad listed benefits first.

This secret is just as true in long-copy print advertising as in those little thumbnail Google ads.

Features and offers are what your product has or what you're going to do. They describe it, what it includes, and how big or small or robust or thorough it is. Benefits, on the other hand, are the emotional payoffs your customer gets from using your product.

Define the Features

So the list of *features* for a book-and-video course you sell may include these items:

- 12 timeless principles
- 17 brief, easy-to-understand video tutorials
- 24 chapters, 222 pages of rock-solid content
- 64 full-color photos
- Helpful, easy-to-read charts and graphs
- Step-by-step tips and instructions
- Fascinating stories, anecdotes, and personal experiences
- Introduction by Malcolm Gladwell

Show Them the Benefits and the Payoff

But your list of *benefits* will tell your customer how she'll actually be helped by what you've written. Sometimes there's a little bit of crossover between these and the features:

- Achieve a 46 percent improvement in less than 30 minutes.
- Reach your goals in one fourth the time using the 80/20 principle described in Chapter 5.
- Apply any one these 12 techniques immediately, and see instant results.
- Catapult energy levels, convert fat into muscle, develop strength, endurance, and flexibility all at the same time.
- Discover how making *more* mistakes can be a strategy that builds your skills even faster.
- Get compliments from your friends as they ask you again and again (jealously), "What has *happened* to you?"

There's no way to pack all of this kind of content into a Google ad, granted. But the principle of dividing benefits from features is universal. Your Google ad is about benefits (emotional payoffs) more than anything else. And when you describe benefits *and* features both, it almost always serves you to put benefits *first*.

The second ad did exactly that. Switching the order gave us a 3,600 percent improvement! We know this because we tested it. Will it work this way in your market? That's for you to find out.

You don't have to be a poet or a master copywriter to convince your customer that he or she will get something of value. State your case simply and clearly, and test to see if putting the benefits up front and the features second will boost your response.

Test Your URL and Grow Your Ad's Effectiveness

The display URL is the second most visible element in your ad. If you're lucky enough to have a domain name that uses the exact keyword phrase people are searching on, you're virtually guaranteed a high CTR. If you can *buy* such a domain, you could potentially double your CTR.

Regardless, with your existing URLs we recommend you test other variations like these in your display URL, including use of keywords as subdomains (which replace the "www") or subdirectories (which are always followed by the "/" slash), and capitalization within those subdirectories:

- www.healyourmarriage.com
- www.healyourmarriage.com/forgiving
- www.healyourmarriage.com/ForgiveHim
- forgiving.healyourmarriage.com

THE "GOLDILOCKS THEORY": WHY THE BEST ADWORDS ADS ARE NEVER OVER-THE-TOP

We thought we'd get ultra-creative one day, and we wrote up an in-your-face ad that would shock Google users into clicking. We were just sure it would work. After all, the number-one worst thing you can do is bore the hell out of people, right?

Here's what happened. It's the second ad below:

D.I.Y. Sales Leads
www.perrymarshall.com
Don't hire telemarketers
Make prospects chase you instead
42 Clicks | 1.0% CTR

Escape Voicemail Jail
www.perrymarshall.com
Get Customers to Chase You Instead
with Savvy Guerrilla Marketing
20 Clicks | 0.3% CTR
Deleted

We thought it was great. Our customers didn't. This happened again and again, and we learned a valuable lesson: Google searchers do not generally respond to hype. Nor do

they respond to messages that are too plain. What works is something in the middle—intriguing, yet not pushy. Swipe ads from *Cosmo*, but do it with caution.

Andrew Goodman, the author of *Winning Results with Google AdWords*, calls it the "Goldilocks" principle. Not too hot; not too cold—you want the temperature to be *just right*.

Avoiding the Google "Slap"

Here's an ad that was very bold, *and* performed well at first . . .

> **Prospecting Sucks**
> www.perrymarshall.com
> Make B2B clients call you first
> with smart guerrilla marketing
> 1.1% CTR

> **Disapproved**

. . . until Google's editor saw it and *disapproved* it. Google didn't let us use inflammatory words like "Sucks" or "Hate." We did get away with the word "stinks," however:

> **Prospecting Stinks**
> www.perrymarshall.com
> Telemarketing Annoys People
> Guerrilla Marketing is King
> 1.3% CTR

More Rules of the Road

Our friend Richard Stokes and his team over at AdGooroo.com share some examples of affiliate ads that perform stellarly on Google and therefore get solid positions and low bid prices and which get served well above 95 percent of the time on searches. Here are a couple:

> Keyword "FTD fruit baskets":

> **Fruit Gift Baskets, FRESH**
> capalbosOnline.com/Since-1906
> Always Fresh! Register & Save 5% on
> Every Order. Nationwide Delivery.

Keyword "fashion sneakers":

Fashion Sneakers & Shoes
www.zappos.com/Fashion-Sneakers/
Upgrade to Free Overnight Shipping
By Ordering One Item of Clothing!

Why do these work?

- Both include the keyword phrase in the ad's headline.
- Both make careful use of exclamation points.
- The second has an implicit call-to-action ("Upgrade to . . .").
- Each word is capitalized, and the first ad makes use of all caps.
- The second ad makes careful use of the word "Free."
- Specific, concrete numbers are put to use wherever possible.

FOCUSING YOUR ADS TO SAVE $$$ ON CLICKS

Your Google ads are an army of hardworking salespeople whose job it is to bring as many of the best prospects possible to your website. But you don't want just anybody. You don't want tire kickers; you don't want the looky-loos. You want genuinely interested people.

After all, you have to pay every time they click.

What to Do When a High CTR Is Not Your Goal

Sometimes you find yourself in a very crowded marketplace attempting to single out only a small percentage of people who you know are a real fit for what you offer.

That was the case with the adaptors example we showed you earlier. The business we were promoting provides custom-built electrical adaptors, converters, and transformers for high-tech original equipment manufacturers, and only deals in large-quantity orders.

You can imagine how many different types of people go looking on the internet for adaptors or converters or transformers in any given day. Even after we've used negative keywords (which we talked about in Chapters 4 and 5) to filter out the searches that we don't want—such as Transformers® toy robots or online dollar-to-yen currency converters—we've still got people searching for the same terms we're bidding on who aren't looking for what we offer.

The guy who's just looking for a replacement power adaptor for his personal IBM laptop, for example. He's not our man.

So it's up to our Google ad to filter out the rest of that traffic, to get as many *good* clicks as possible but as few of every other kind. The more is not the merrier.

Connect with Your Niche Customers

The key is being clear and specific. We're going to write an ad that addresses precisely the type of customer we're after:

AC/DC Converters for OEMs
xyzadaptors.com
Qty 250+, Rapid Custom Production
1-Day Quote & Overnight Delivery

This ad won't win any awards for high CTR or stunning copy, but it knocks out three criteria: 1) it's for people wanting *custom* design, not off-the-shelf, 2) it's for OEMs (original equipment manufacturers) only, and 3) it's for orders of 250 units or more.

A lot of people are going to see this ad and pass it up. And that's okay. All we want are clicks from people who match these criteria. The ad will do its job.

Again, there's no black magic. Just tell your story. Be clear, be straightforward, interesting, customer-centered, and, most importantly, relevant. Sell on the computer screen just like you'd sell in person. And people will see that you're for real, and they'll click and buy.

IF THE GUYS AT THE BAR WILL BUY IT, YOU'VE GOT A WINNING AD

John Carlton tells the story of the highly paid, highly sought-after copywriter who writes sales letters aimed at blue-collar men. Before he delivers a project, he takes the draft down to the neighborhood bar, buys a round of drinks for all the guys, and then reads them the letter. Then he gets their comments.

They chime in and tell him to tweak this, fix that, and change the wording here or there. But he knows he doesn't have a winner yet until one specific thing happens:

One of the guys in the group asks where they can get what the letter is offering.

That's when he knows he has a sales letter that's working. That's when it's ready for press. He's moved them from being critics to being buyers and they don't even realize it.

Take your copy—your Google ads, your sales page, your direct mail pieces, your email blasts—and test them in other environments, other venues, with friends or out on the street. When people are salivating over what you offer, then you've got a winner.

Uncle Claude Sez

The purpose of a headline is to pick out people you can interest. You wish to talk to someone in a crowd. So the first thing you say is "Hey there, Bill Jones" to get the right person's attention.

So it is in an advertisement. What you have will interest certain people only, and for certain reasons. You care only for those people. Then create a headline which will hail those people only.

We pick out what we wish to read by headlines, and we don't want those headlines to be misleading. The writing of headlines is one of the greatest journalistic arts. They either conceal or reveal an interest.

Chisel Your Way In
With Bionic Google Ads

"Most people think they've tested 20 Google ads but they really just tested 2 ads 10 different times."

—Dr. Glenn Livingston

Roundtable member Ben Gorelick was on the hot seat in AdWords Copywriting Express (www.perrymarshall.com/awce) where we re-wrote ads for him. His old ads were "decent":

Rock Climbing Courses Develop Climbing Skills Rapidly School in Picos de Europa, Spain www.rockclimbschool.com	Course	–	☐ Approved	20.61%	160	2,490	6.43%
Rock Climbing in Spain Immersion into World of Climbing Adventure in Picos de Europa, Spain www.rockclimbingguideschool.com	Spain	–	☐ Approved	7.71%	47	931	5.05%
Rock Climbing Learning Develop Climbing Skills Rapidly School in Picos de Europa, Spain www.howtorockclimb.com	Learn	–	☐ Approved	12.24%	71	1,479	4.80%

In our AdWords Copywriting Express course, I led him through a deliberate creative process, via the "Swiss Army Knife Formula." I forced him to answer the question: *Are you really selling rock climbing? Or are you selling something else? If so, what is the something else?*

He does sell something else. You can tell from his new ads what that "something else" is:

12.33%	**10.23%**	
Mountaineering School	**Which do you choose?**	**Work sucks?**
Born. College. Job. Marry. House.	1) Go bowling & have beer with Bob.	I unzip my tent.
Kid. Retire. Die. Want More?	2) Climb Mountains in Patagonia.	What's your commute?
PatagoniaMountaineeringSchool.com	PatagoniaMountaineeringSchool.com	PatagoniaMountaineeringSchool.com
12.04%		**8.74%**
Mountaineering School	**9.46%**	**Alaska Mountaineering School**
Fluorescent Lights are Killing You.	**Mountaineering School**	6 day Mountaineering Program?
Be More Than a Warm Corpse.	That Weak, Sniveling Voice in Your	What is this, kindergarten?
PatagoniaMountaineeringSchool.com	Head Begs You to Quit. Climb On.	AlaskaMountaineeringSchool.com
	PatagoniaMountaineeringSchool.com	
10.87%	**9.37%**	**8.66%**
Alaska Mountaineering School	**Hardcore Expeditions**	**Masochist Spa**
6 day Mountaineering Program?	A 76 y/o Climbed Everest Last Year.	Free mud facial: crawl in the mud.
Does your Mommy drop you off, too?	Here's a Trip your Granny Can't Do.	Tanning: It's called BEING OUTSIDE.

Notice the huge jump in clickthrough rates!

The marketing on his website—his autoresponders and everything else—is already consistent with this message, and fast growing more so. He is now on a steep vertical climb. If he stays on the path he's on, by the time his competitors figure out that he's kicking their asses, he's going to be so far out ahead of them that it's going to take **a lot** of energy to catch up; 80 percent of them won't stand a chance.

They'll still be selling rock climbs by the pound and he'll be selling a thrilling life adventure.

Notice how he doubled his CTR. He tells me his cost per conversion has plummeted by at least 30 percent and he's not even close to done with all the "obvious" changes that this shift demands. This one change grew his business by over $100,000 last year.

How did Ben write such outrageously fun ads with such ease? You're going to find out in this chapter.

When you get into the rhythm of Google AdWords, you find yourself writing lots of ads. Soon you find out that once you achieve a great ad, it can be really tough to beat it!

This short chapter will arm you with new tools that help you bust out of your creative ruts. **This chapter will empower you to write better and more powerful ads than ever before.** It's especially important if you're an advanced player.

Most people find one decent ad formula that "works" and just refine it. It becomes a rut. They get stuck. But you can do so much better. Not only can you Chisel Your Way In where you could not before, you can preempt others from doing the same to you. Today I'm going to show you 2 of 10 powerful ways to rocket your CTR with *emotional power*.

SIX DIFFERENT VERSIONS OF ONE AD

That's what happened with this example below: six different versions of a "How to Write a Book" ad, but same formula for each one.

You test adjectives, verbs, URLs, commas (ad #1 is the "little comma that could," which got an 8 percent CTR boost), and that's great. But 99 percent of people miss dozens of completely different, superb **hooks** they could use. You can approach your customers from a completely different, surprising direction.

And as your campaigns develop, you become more and more afraid to boldly experiment because you don't want to hurt your overall CTR and drop in the rankings. So you stay stuck.

The following is an example of a very successful ad campaign that is also stuck in a rut:

1.	2.	3.
How to Write a Book, Fast	How to Write a Book, Fast	How to Write a Book, Fast
14 Days from Start to Finish	14 Days from Start to Finish	Get the Job Done in 14 Days or Less
Unique, Step By Step Program	Unique, Step By Step Program	Unique, Step By Step Aff. Program
Write-A-Book-Faster.com	Write-A-Book-Faster.com	perrymarshall.com/WriteABook
4.	5.	6.
How to Write a Book, Fast	How to Write a Book, Fast	How to Write a Book, Fast
Finish Your Manuscript in 14 Days	14 Days from Start to Finish	Get the Job Done in 14 Days or Less
Unique, Step By Step Program	Unique, Step By Step Aff. Program	Unique, Step By Step Aff. Program
Write-A-Book-Faster.com	perrymarshall.com/WriteABook	Write-A-Book-Faster.com

I invented a reliable tool that breaks you out of that rut and consistently gets high CTR's. It's called the Swiss Army Knife Formula, and it has 17 "blades." In this chapter I give you the two most powerful blades, which all by themselves are sufficient to catapult you past your competition.

Here's an example of four ads that used the Formula. Each ad is *completely* different from the others (#2 had been my control for two months) and each commands a very high CTR:

Darwin vs. Jerry Falwell They're Both Wrong. Discover the Real Evolution Story www.CosmicFingerprints.com	Approved	13	87	14.94%
New Theory of Evolution Evolution in the Information Age And Proof of an Intelligent Design www.CosmicFingerprints.com	Approved	13	94	13.83%
If ID Isn't Science, Darwinism Isn't Either. Both are Religions. More Here- www.CosmicFingerprints.com	Approved	10	79	12.66%
Hi, my name is Doug. Can't stand creation 'science'. But evolution is kind of depressing www.CosmicFingerprints.com	Approved	8	65	12.31%

The second ad was my original control. It took months of traditional Google ad refinements to arrive at this ad. The other ads are hot off the press, created with the Swiss Army Knife Formula. All completely different, all with double-digit CTRs.

PROBLEM: "There's only a few things I can think of to say and it's really hard to not sound like everyone else in my market."

SOLUTION: There are literally **thousands** of things you can say, even in a tiny Google ad, which means there's **no such thing** as a market you can't break into, or do better in—even if you've been stuck with the same control ad for three years.

Use this Formula to generate fresh new ideas for . . .

- Google Ads
- Facebook Ads
- Headlines
- New landing pages to test
- Completely new ways to tell your story

Testing new ads becomes simple and formulaic. No more combing through huge swipe files looking for something you might be able to use. These are simple formulas you can apply instantly.

Blade #1: All the Different Relationships that Exist Between Your Customers and Five Other Types of People and Things

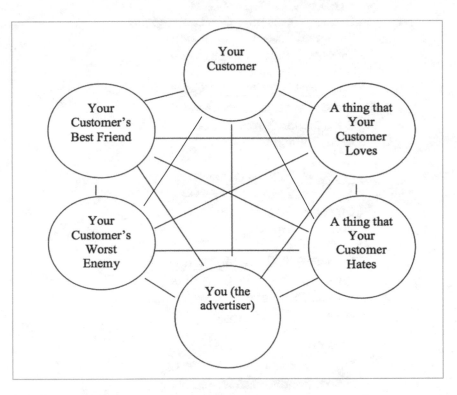

This picture shows 15 different relationships: Your customer and the thing she loves; your customer and the thing she hates; your customer and you, the thing your customer loves and its relationship to her worst enemy, and so on.

Most ads are about something the vendor sells or some really obvious problem related to the keyword. If we're writing an ad for the keyword phrase *bad marriage*, **the ads you see here are very predictable.** Which is pretty typical in almost any market.

Sponsored Links

Marriage Separation?
Spouse wants out? Don't do anything
before you see this solution now.
www-MarriageSeparation.com

Rhonda Kelloway, LCSW
Need **marriage** counseling?
Call Rhonda Kelloway Today.
www.RhondaKelloway.com

How To End A Marriage
Avoid the 21 biggest mistakes. Let
Dr. Reena show you step-by-step.
end-**marriage**.29p.com

Restore A Bad Marriage
What You Can Say, Do & Avoid
So You Can Save Your **Marriage**.
www.SaveTheMarriage.com

Celebrate Your Marriage
First rate destinations, World Class
Entertainment, Biblical Teaching.
www.celebratenet.com

The Swiss Army Knife Formula gives us all kinds of new ad hooks. The #1 thing the prospect hates may be constant fighting:

Bad Marriage=Constant Fights
Don't Go To Bed Angry
14 Minute Video will Calm Your Mind
www.AngryMarriage.com

Your best friend (at one time anyway) was your husband, and the #1 enemy is his lover:

Who is your husband with?
Is he sleeping with "her" right now?
Get revenge & a smile on your face
www.BadMarriageRevenge.com

How about an ad that's about the wife's worst enemy (the other woman), *and* the thing your customer hates the most (constant fighting):

Nasty Fight: The Other Woman
Sick of being compared with "her"?
Change the Game. Free Report
www.BadMarriageReport.com

How about an ad that's about the wife's worst enemy and her best friend (in this case her children):

The Other Woman: Step Mom
How will you feel when
Your children call her "mommy"?
www.BadMarriageReport.com/prevention

See how much emotion you elicit when you focus on the relationships between key players in your customer's drama? This is P-O-W-E-R-F-U-L.

I'm not promising you that every ad you write will smack the ball out of the park. I guarantee you that will *not* happen. However, you'll find a fraction of your Swiss Army Knife Formula ads achieve breakthrough.

Blade #2

Blade #2 is using three different kinds of imagery:

- Visual
- Auditory
- Kinesthetic

You rewrite your ads around pictures, sounds, or physical sensations in your prospect's body. Most people process information one of these ways more than the others.

Visual:

Other Woman Photographs
Will you see her with your children
in family portraits?
www.TheOtherWoman.org/Bad_Marriage

Auditory:

"I Hate My Other Mommy"
What will your little boy say
The day she moves in?
www.TheOtherWoman.org/Step_Mom

Kinesthetic:

When He Caresses Her
Do you feel sick on the inside?
Hope and healing here
www.TheOtherWoman.com/Community

So far we've just worked with two blades, which for 99 percent of markets will be enough for you to evolve from "pretty competent competitor" to lean, mean, fighting machine. There are 15 more blades. If you wish to go deeper with the Swiss Army Knife Formula, you can access a video tutorial at www.perrymarshall.com/supplement.

Now you have a systematic method to leapfrog to completely new, fresh ads on command. Go back through this chapter. Start by doing a Blade 1 exercise on your own business for your own customers, then write some ads. Test the ads in your Google account. Don't wait for tomorrow—do it today. Put the Swiss Army Knife Formula to work today and watch your CTRs and your conversions skyrocket.

Ads That Pass the Test
Editorial Guidelines and Split Testing

Today I want to tell you a dirty little secret.

A few years ago, Google started slashing and burning Google accounts by the thousands and tens of thousands.

I myself had almost ten thousand customers who lost their business overnight, because Google banned thousands of keywords, even entire Google accounts. Two days after the very first "Google Slap" I had 3,800 people (!) sign up for a teleseminar on "What the **** just happened to my Google account?"

That was only the first of a long series of purges, which mostly targeted affiliates and people in "edgy" businesses like alternative health and business opportunities.

Another customer of mine sold equipment that enabled you to add water injection to your car engine, which can increase fuel efficiency by 15 to 20 percent. Google banned his account because of all the problems they had with unscrupulous vendors selling mostly ebooks on the same topic.

What is this all about?

Certainly some of it is Google responding to customer complaints and seeking a quality search experience. But there's another ingredient: The long arm of the law.

In 2011, Google was fined $500 million by the U.S. Justice Department for selling ads to Canadian pharmacies that were illegally advertising cheap drugs to U.S. customers. In the government's opinion, Google was culpable and responsible for the actions of its advertisers.

That, combined with other government crackdowns, has tallied up over a billion dollars in fines. In the U.S. government's mind, why go after tens of thousands of rogue operators when you can put one bullet in the head of a behemoth? Uncle Sam punishes Google for the sins of its AdWords customers.

This is why Google seems passive-aggressive and bureaucratic. This is why you sometimes can't seem to get a straight answer from Google about editorial guidelines. Google itself doesn't know what's going to get it in hot water. So all they can do is try to avoid taking business that's going to get it in trouble.

So if you're in business opportunities, weight loss, alternative health, medicine, alternative energy—any "edgy" category where 1) customers are in a lot of pain or have extremely pressing problems, 2) unscrupulous operators tend to play, and/or 3) markets are regulated or frequently subject to crackdowns by Attorney Generals and complaints to the Federal Trade Commission—advertising on Google is going to be a dicey proposition.

Just last week, one of my best customers, John, who sells health supplements, got banned again, probably for the tenth time. His investors decided they were tired of the agony/ecstasy roller coaster with Google, and pulled the plug.

This chapter outlines how to stay in Google's good graces. Then at the end I offer some more urgent advice that you'll be wise to take seriously. Especially if you're like John, the health supplement vendor I just told you about.

FOLLOW THE EDITORIAL GUIDELINES AND KEEP GOOGLE HAPPY

Over the years Google has refined its policy on what is and isn't acceptable in an ad. Although most of it is common sense, it has still resulted in a fairly lengthy list of dos and don'ts, which can be found on Google's AdWords Policy Center page:

AdWords Policy Center

Welcome to the AdWords Policy Center. Here you'll find the requirements for advertising with Google AdWords. Our advertising requirements can be summed up by Google's Advertising Principles shown below. To promote a safe and positive experience for our users, each ad is reviewed based on these advertising principles.

User Experience
Advertising should provide a positive experience to users.

Safety and Security
Advertising should be safe for all users.

Accurate Ads
Advertising should be accurate and truthful.

Transparency and Privacy
Advertising shouldn't violate users' trust or privacy.

Restricted Products and Services
Advertised products and services should be legal and safe for all users.

Trademark, Copyright, and Counterfeit
Advertising should comply with laws and regulations.

Google's Brand
Advertising should be compatible with Google's brand decisions.

For past and upcoming policy changes, please see the AdWords Policy Change Log.

Advertiser Claims

If you're going to advertise with Google, you have to be smart about what you're claiming. It comes down to three words: truthful, accurate, and up-to-date. Sure, there's some subjectivity here but, as long as you do your level best to stay within the spirit of these particular rules, you shouldn't run into problems.

This is good common sense and good marketing sense: a clear connection between the text of your ads and the content on your website. If, for example, your ad offers a discount, it should be easy to find on your website. If your ad mentions special pricing, it should be no more than two clicks from your landing page. Any call-to-action in your ad should be immediately evident on the landing page.

If you claim to be the "world's greatest" or the fastest or smallest or cheapest or most expensive or whatever, you must back up your claim with proof. This isn't just a good way to stay in Google's good graces, it's good marketing. Put on your skeptic hat. How do I **know** that you are the fastest, smallest, or cheapest? Have you proven it, right there on the web page? Or provided a link or reference verifying that it is so? This is extremely important. More so for your prospective customers than Google's staff!

If your ad refers to pricing, it has to comply with local regulations. This can vary from country to country. If you're unsure of pricing regulations in your region, visit the AdWords Policy Center page.

Relevance, Clarity, and Accuracy

"Relevance" and "accuracy" refer to how well your ad copy matches what's on your landing page. "Clarity" covers a wider variety of sins you'll need to avoid, including:

- Missing lines of text
- Excessive spacing
- "Extremely bad grammar" (This is Google's exact wording, implying that they'll allow a modicum of imperfect grammar.)
- Generic call-to-action phrases (such as "click here" or "+1").
- Using characters for anything other than their intended or usual meaning. For example, the greater-than ">" symbol is fine if you're using it to indicate that something actually is greater than something else. But you can't use it as an arrow.
- Words in all-capitals
- Bad spelling
- Repetition. For example, "Buy! Buy! Buy!" would be flagged as unacceptable.

Follow the above guidelines when you build your ads and you'll be fine 99 percent of the time. Still, be sure and visit the AdWords Policy Center page and review their directions.

SYSTEMATICALLY GROW YOUR CTR WITH SPLIT-TESTING

Split testing is not new. History's first split tester was likely a forward-thinking stone-age real estate agent testing the difference between signs that said "Cave for Sale" and "Buy Cave Here."

However, the world's first split-testing maniac *we* know of was E. Haldeman-Julius, a multimillionaire of the 1920s and one of the largest publishers in the U.S.

Haldeman-Julius's empire was built through the sale of little blue books that covered all manner of different subjects. Close to 2,000 different titles were produced during his reign as a publishing magnate. He had a unique selling method, which illustrates why he was so successful: He would purchase full-page newspaper and magazine ads where he would list up to 200 of his available blue book titles. For just one dollar, readers could select 20 titles from the list and have them mailed out directly.

That sales technique was unique enough as it is. But what really set Julius apart is that he used this approach to split-test the titles of his books: If a particular title was selling poorly, he would simply change its name in future ads and watch to see if this generated more sales.

The difference in sales simply by changing the title on the cover was often striking. *Gautier's Fleece of Gold,* for instance, only sold around 6,000 books. Changing the title

to *A Quest for a Blonde Mistress* resulted in sales of nearly 50,000. The title *Patent Medicine* only sold a few thousand copies, but changing it to *The Truth About Patent Medicine* tripled sales.

The most striking example is no doubt *The Art of Controversy,* which only sold a few hundred copies. When it was renamed to *How to Argue Logically,* it went on to sell 30,000!

In this we see the method, and the power, of split-testing. Note that everything about the content and jacket design of Haldeman-Julius's books remained the same. The *only* element that changed was the title. As the numbers show, that alone meant the difference between a flop and a best-seller.

It's a pretty good bet that Haldeman-Julius would have adored Google advertising. In his day, split-testing took ages: Once a title change was conceived and selected, it would be weeks, maybe months before the new ads went to print, purchase orders came in, and the staff could total the resulting sales figures. PPC is a whole new world by comparison: You can set up a split-test and begin running ads in a matter of minutes. You can pick a winner in a matter of days, sometimes hours.

The lesson here? As a new AdWords advertiser, make this commitment to yourself: Every new ad group you ever create will have two ads. Once you've set up an ad group with ads to run against each other, just keep an eye on their performance. Once you have a clear winner, pause the losing ad, and write a new one to test against the winner.

Eight Winning Headlines

If you're short on ideas for different ad headlines to test, here are the eight most popular title prefixes from the E. Haldeman-Julius's empire for you to borrow from:

1. How to . . .

2. The Art of . . .

3. The Little Secret That . . .

4. The Truth About . . .

5. The Facts About . . .

6. The History of . . .

7. The Story of . . .

8. The Key to . . .

SEE IN ADVANCE HOW YOUR ADS WILL LOOK ON THE PREVIEW PAGE

If you want to write great ads, don't try to reinvent the wheel. The simplest, clearest, and most truthful ads are almost always the ones that end up winning in split tests.

For inspiration try Google's Ad Preview tool, which lets you see how your ads will appear on search pages. It will also show the ads your competitors are running. Go to the "Tools" section of your AdWords account and select "Ad Preview and Diagnosis."

From there, simply enter your chosen keywords to see which ads are running.

Sure, you could just visit Google in your browser and perform a search. But the Ad Preview and Diagnosis tool allows you to select different versions of Google, different languages, different locations, and even different devices to see which ads are targeting different profiles.

DISAPPROVED ADS

You'll jump through all the hoops, follow every guideline you know of, and still end up with one or more of your ads disapproved by Google. Such is life for the AdWords advertiser.

Don't worry, it's not the end of the world. You just need to find out the reason for Google's disapproval and then take the steps to fix it.

Disapproved ads are flagged in the Status column of the Ads tab. A message next to your ad will say "Disapproved" and next to that you'll see a speech bubble that you can hover over to reveal the reason for the disapproved status.

You may need to revisit Google's AdWords Policy Center page for clarification. Most of the time, however, the problem is one of the following:

- **Problem:** The ad has breached one of Google's "Editorial Guidelines."
 Solution: Rewrite the ad and resave.

- **Problem:** The page that your ad's URL points to doesn't exist (commonly known as a 404 error).
 Solution: Recreate the page or change the URL on the ad so it points to a working page.

- **Problem:** Your site has been suspended.
 Solution: This is a more serious issue that will probably strike multiple Ad Groups simultaneously. You'll want to contact Google as soon as possible to find out the cause. You can call the toll-free number from your within your account, you can complete the contact form at http://support.google.com/adwords/contact/approvals, or you can look for the cog icon in the top right-hand corner of the page, select Help, and fine the online chat feature. (This last option is usually the best solution as, in my experience, the staff that manage the online chats seem to be more qualified to help with this particular problem.)

Some People Never Have These Problems at All

If what you sell is "boring"—if you sell hydraulic presses, or industrial chemicals, or shipping containers, or lawn care—you will probably never have *any* of these problems. 80 percent of the people who run afoul of Google's rules sell things that are in some sense controversial.

Google Can Be Opaque

To be frank, Google sometimes simply will *not* tell you what you need to do to be OK or to get your ads approved. I suspect that the real reason for this is that if they help you too much, a U.S. judge may consider them complicit in your "scam," even though you are not in any way, shape, or form, a scammer. In some categories, you're guilty until proven innocent.

Jerry Ellefson of PPC Renegade (www.ppcrenegade.com) will, for a fee, walk "gray area" advertisers, or advertisers who've been slapped or banned, through an approval regimen. He does this based on deep inside knowledge and connections to Google's risk management process.

There is a hidden advantage to this. The advantage is: The red tape thins the herd so the spoils are divided among a much smaller number of winners who can brave the bureaucracy. If you can solve this, the rewards are great.

There is also a huge lesson in this. At the beginning of our Bobsled Run coaching program, where we walk people through the whole process from first click to final upsell, I warn students: "If one year from now you're getting 90 percent of your traffic from Google, I have failed to do my job. The real goal is to use Google as the anvil that you test your traffic on, so you can get lots of forms of traffic to convert. Then you go to Facebook, email lists, affiliates, SEO, and offline traffic sources. You diversify so you are no longer dependent on Google. Then, and only then, do you have a 'real' business."

Uncle Claude Sez

The uninformed would be staggered to know the amount of work involved in a single ad. Weeks of work sometimes. The ad seems so simple—and it must be simple to appeal to simple people. But behind that ad may lie reams of data, volumes of information, and months of research.

So this is no lazy man's field.

The Winning Method the World's Smartest Marketers Stole from the Wright Brothers

The boneyard of modern civilization is littered with "great" marketing ideas that never got off the ground.

Think of the billions and trillions of dollars companies spent developing products, only to find out that their products weren't what people wanted in the first place.

Let's *not* assume you're a corporation with billions of dollars to spend. Instead let's assume you're a regular person who quit a cushy job to pursue an entrepreneurial vision. As you calculate it, you've got to start making a profit in six to nine months or else you'll run out of money.

If that's you, then you can't afford to make a mistake. You can't spend three months developing a product and later find out in month six that the product has to be totally redesigned. That'll kill your business and send you back to the J.O.B. with your tail between your legs.

Let's make sure this never happens to you.

How can you prevent this? By testing your product idea and even your website itself on the cheap, using Google, *before* you've spent a lot of money on it. With the internet, you can find out if a product idea will succeed or fail for a few hundred to no more than a few thousand dollars.

If you do this, you will be sure that the product you develop will be well received.

HOW THE WRIGHT BROTHERS' SAVVY TESTING METHOD MADE THEM "FIRST IN FLIGHT"

The year: 1903. The place: a houseboat on the Potomac River, USA.

Just weeks before Wilbur and Orville Wright were to fly the world's first airplane at Kitty Hawk, North Carolina, Samuel Pierpont Langley, a well-funded engineer and inventor, was launching an airplane of his own—with the assistance of an entire staff.

Langley's assumption: Put a big enough engine on the thing, and it will fly. He focused all his effort on that one project: creating an engine powerful enough for the plane to go airborne. On October 7th, 1903, Langley tested his model for the very first time.

The plane crashed immediately after leaving the launch pad, badly damaging the front wing.

Two months later, just eight days before the Wright Brothers' successful flight, Langley made a second attempt.

This time the tail and rear wing collapsed completely during launch.

Langley was ridiculed by the press and criticized by members of Congress for throwing away taxpayer dollars on his failed projects. (Can you imagine the cynicism? I'm sure many sneering reporters believed that nobody could or would ever fly.) Disillusioned by the public response, Langley abandoned his vision.

Wilbur and Orville Wright, meanwhile, had a completely different approach: build a glider that would glide from a hilltop with no engine at all. They focused their energy on balance and steering. Power was almost an afterthought. Only after the glider worked by itself would they try to put an engine on it.

After three years of tedious experimentation the glider was working well, so they commissioned bicycle shop machinist Charlie Taylor to build them an engine. It was the smallest engine he could design—a 12-horsepower unit that weighed 180 pounds.

And on December 17, 1903, at Kitty Hawk, North Carolina, Wilbur and Orville Wright made history.

The Wright brothers changed the world and became famous historical figures, while few have ever heard of Mr. Langley. Their approach of making the plane fly *before* applying high power was the winning idea.

> *Langley had spent most of four years building an extraordinary engine to lift their heavy flying machine. The Wrights had spent most of four years building a flying machine so artfully designed that it could be propelled into the air by a fairly ordinary internal combustion engine.*
>
> —*Smithsonian* Magazine, April 2003

> *Skill comes by the constant repetition of familiar feats rather than by a few overbold attempts at feats for which the performer is yet poorly prepared.*
>
> —Wilbur Wright

Samuel Pierpont Langley died in 1906, a broken and disappointed man.

PEOPLE WHO TEST, FLY. PEOPLE WHO RELY ON BRUTE FORCE, DIE.

You don't want to die a broke and disappointed person. You want to die rich and famous.

Or at least rich, right?

Then there is a direct comparison between the Wright brothers and your career as an internet marketer.

The search engine is the motor. Your website is the glider.

A motor without a good set of wings does you no good. When you put an engine on a glider, you have a plane. When you feed traffic to a website that can "fly," you have a business.

And as smart marketers like "Uncle" Claude Hopkins have known for over a century, you get the wings to work through careful, systematic testing.

This is not a new concept. For more than 100 years, smart, savvy marketers have followed these time-tested principles of proven good sense, and made their dollars go many times further.

In 1923, Claude Hopkins said:

> *Advertising and merchandising become exact sciences. Every course is charted. The compass of accurate knowledge directs the shortest, safest, cheapest course to any destination.*

> *We learn the principles and prove them by repeated tests. . . . We compare one way with many others, backward and forwards, and record the results. . . .*

Advertising is traced down to the fraction of a penny. The cost per reply and cost per dollar of sale show up with utter exactness.

One ad compared to another, one method with another. Headlines, settings, sizes, arguments and pictures are compared. To reduce the cost of results even one percent means much.

So no guesswork is permitted. One must know what is best.

Building a business online doesn't have to be guesswork. It's not a crapshoot. It's a *science*. Wise men and women before us have taken the risks, tested the limits, learned the hard lessons for us, and laid down a clear path that we can follow with confidence.

Whether your business is all online, or only partly so, the foundation remains the same: Start small, test carefully, make modest improvements, get deeper insights into your market, test some more, and you'll *know* that your business is going to grow.

This well-worn path builds a sales process that works. And when you have a persuasive website, you have a glider. Just like the Wright brothers, all you need to do is put a lightweight engine on it and you can fly.

Add Google traffic the smart way and you've got a business that soars.

Google AdWords can bring you a lot of traffic, and that traffic is valuable to the extent that your website can convert the traffic to leads and sales.

When you're getting started, Google is like a lightweight engine that you can turn on and off instantly. You can test your glider safely without crashing, killing a potential joint venture partnership, or blowing a wad of money.

MARKETING MISERY: *NOT* NECESSARY

Thousands of people go to bed every night wondering *Why? Why can't I make any sales? Why can't I earn any real money at this?*

This is not necessary, but it's a lesson that the scorched dotcoms in 1997–2000 learned the hard way. They were like Langley. They focused on the engine instead of the wings. When it didn't take off, they just poured more gas into the engine. When that didn't work, they put it on a rocket launcher and forced it up into the air.

You don't have the time or the money to pour into product ideas and sales messages that, in hindsight, were "almost right." Your spouse won't let you blow the grocery money or college savings on a lark.

Reality is a great teacher, if you let it speak its piece. The people who click on your ads will tell you what they want, if you ask them. They'll show you what they want, if you watch them.

Uncle Claude Sez

The time has come when advertising has in some hands reached the status of a science. It is based on fixed principles and is reasonably exact. The causes and effects have been analyzed until they are well understood. The correct method of procedure has been proved and established. We know what is most effective, and we act on its basic law.

Once a gamble, advertising has become, under able direction, one of the safest business ventures to undertake. Certainly no other enterprise with comparable possibilities need involve so little risk.

"Deep 80/20"
It's Not What You Think . . . and I Can't Tell You How Profitable It Is!

This chapter will teach you the highest leverage skill that currently exists in marketing.

What I'm about to share is so incredibly important, it would be criminal to not devote a whole chapter to it. It's critical. Master this chapter and you'll work less, make more, be more focused, and feel less guilty about everything.

The 80/20 Rule, aka the Pareto Principle, says:

1. 80 percent of what you get comes from 20 percent of that you do: Small effort, big reward.

2. 20 percent of what you get comes from the other 80 percent that you do: Big effort, small reward.

Most marketers have heard about 80/20. Most *think* they know what it is. Most people who "know about" 80/20 do not actually understand it. I just was like everybody else. I *thought* I understood 80/20. Turns out, I did not understand it at all!

A true, in-depth understanding of 80/20 is literally one of the top ten most powerful marketing skills. "Deep 80/20" is right up there with getting website traffic, writing ads, developing USPs and building lists. But here's the thing:

All good marketers understand traffic, copywriting, USPs, and list building. But far less than 1 percent of marketers understand Deep 80/20. Read carefully because it will reveal all kinds of places where you are leaving money on the table.

Deep 80/20 is one of the main reasons you are reading *this* book right now and not someone else's. Back in 2003, AdWords was brand new and nobody fully understood how to make it work. It was a strange beast. Deep 80/20 was how I figured out AdWords in the first place. It still is.

I experienced a huge 80/20 epiphany reading Richard Koch's classic *The 80/20 Principle*. Suddenly, I saw layers and layers where before I'd only seen the surface. Eventually I expanded on this and wrote *80/20 Sales & Marketing*. Today I'm going to give you a quick, chapter-sized sample of Deep 80/20. Pay close attention.

BACK WHEN I THOUGHT I UNDERSTOOD 80/20 . . .

When I worked a job as sales manager, I heard about 80/20. I printed out a sales report from QuickBooks and went through it with my calculator. Yep. Sure enough: 80 percent of our sales came from the top 20 percent of our customers, and the other 80 percent of our customers generated the other 20 percent.

Dimitri liked to call me all the time. He would always nitpick about our software and he didn't buy much. Dimitri was near the top of my time-suck list and near the bottom of my money list. That 80/20 exercise made me realize he was chewing up time he didn't deserve. But my thinking stopped there. I didn't think much else about it, and moved on.

A few years later, reading Richard's book, a torrent of insights flooded my brain. I'm going to share them with you—and show you how to specifically apply 80/20 to Google ads so you spend way less time, get more done, sell more, and make more money.

80/20 APPLIES TO JUST ABOUT EVERYTHING YOU CAN MEASURE IN A BUSINESS

Sources of incoming phone calls, sizes of commissions for sales people, sizes of customers, physical location of customers, popularity of products, and quantity of

each type of product defect can all benefit from applying the 80/20 principle. And yes, AdWords stuff too: keywords, impressions, ads, conversions, visits to web pages. Just about every metric in this book obeys 80/20.

This means four fifths of everything is trivial and only one fifth really matters. This is a huge time saver. But that's only the tip of the iceberg.

80/20 ISN'T JUST TWO GROUPS, I.E., "THE 80" AND "THE 20"

It's actually a stunningly predictable *power law* that you can put on a graph. 80/20 says: If you have a column of data, and you know just one or two things, like the number of items and the total, you can predict with scary accuracy how they're all going to stack up. Here, I'll show you.

Let's say the newspaper says, "Southwest Airlines, the 167th largest company in the U.S. with revenues of $15.7 billion . . ." Guess what: You already know enough to size up the entire Fortune 500.

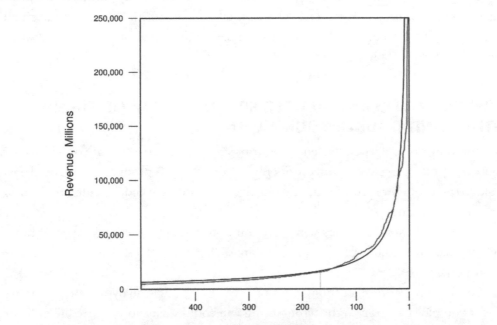

If you only know that Southwest Airlines is company #167 in the Fortune 500 with $15.7 billion revenue, you can accurately predict the sales of the other 499 companies on the list. This graph shows 80/20 theory vs. actual data from the Fortune 500 report.

If you know how big #167 is, you automatically know how big #300 is and how big #100 is and how big #50 and #10 are, plus or minus 25 percent. You also know the total revenue of the group as well. That's how reliable 80/20 is.

This is tremendously useful, and *very* powerful for marketers. You might be leaving a million dollars a year on the table . . . and you don't know it! Now in less than five minutes, it'll expose holes in your product line or pricing strategy. I created a tool called the 80/20 Curve (www.8020curve.com) and it accurately predicts where you're missing opportunities.

THERE'S AN 80/20 INSIDE EVERY 80/20!

80/20 still applies to what's left after you peel away the bottom 80 percent. Not only does 80 percent of your money come from 20 percent of your customers, but 80 percent of the 80 percent comes from 20 percent of the top 20 percent.

That means **4 percent of your customers create 64 percent of your income**. That's $80/20^2$. And it's still true of the top 4 percent: **0.8 percent of your customers deliver 52 percent of your income**. That's $80/20^3$. It keeps going until you run out of people.

This means you can extract huge amounts of money from tiny groups of people. Or keywords. Or ads or web pages. This is because 80/20 is an infinite repeating pattern. It's "fractal"—micro or macro scale—it's the same pattern over and over. There is *always* an inequality. Most people underestimate how great it is.

YOU CAN OVERLAY MULTIPLE 80/20S ON TOP OF EACH OTHER AND DOUBLE YOUR MOJO

Not only do you get 50 percent of your business from 1 percent of your customers, you may get 25 percent of your profits from 1 of your 250 products. You could easily make 10 percent more profit by pampering five big customers and fattening the margins on that one product.

The information age offers you more things to fix, optimize, and pay attention to than you could possibly attend to in a lifetime. That's why 80/20 has never been more important.

You have reams of data spilling out of AdWords, Google analytics, etc., 24 hours a day. If you pay attention to the wrong thing you could waste your entire life polishing turds.

To give you an idea how universal the 80/20 Curve is and how many boundaries it transcends, let me show you a few quick examples:

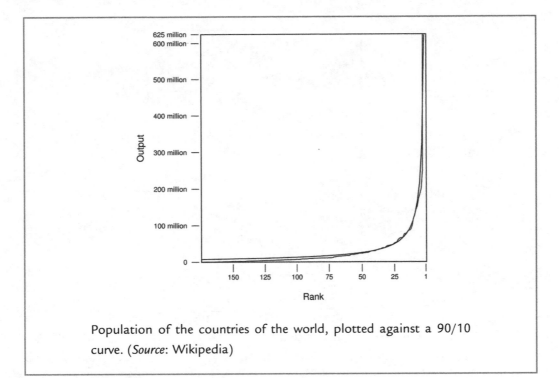

Population of the countries of the world, plotted against a 90/10 curve. (*Source*: Wikipedia)

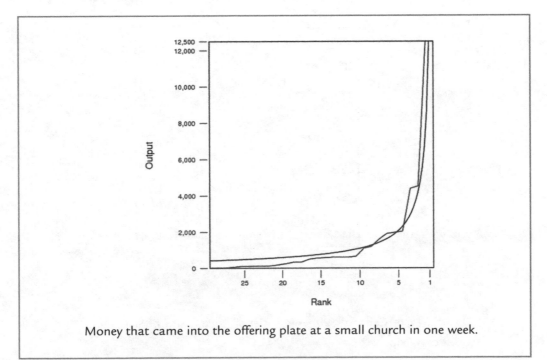

Money that came into the offering plate at a small church in one week.

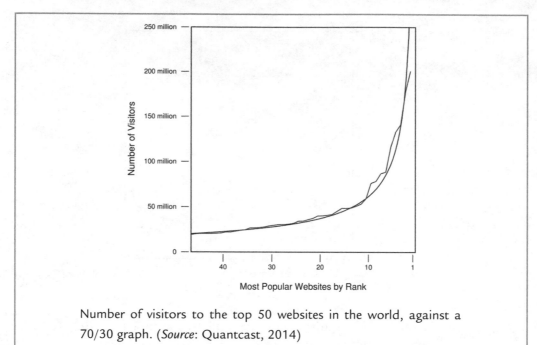

Number of visitors to the top 50 websites in the world, against a 70/30 graph. (*Source*: Quantcast, 2014)

Land area of Canada's 20 largest islands, against an 85/15 graph. (*Source*: Wikipedia)

80/20 isn't just a business rule of thumb, it's a law of nature. So now let's look at how 80/20 works specifically in Google AdWords.

As you saw in the examples above, the numbers "80" and "20" are not carved in stone. Sometimes it's 70/30, sometimes 60/40, 90/10 or 99/1. Keyword lists are very consistently 95/5. Take a look:

Keyword	Clicks	% percent of Ad Group
[how to write a book]	4,317	60.3%
how to write a book	1,452	20.3%
"how to write a book"	679	9.5%
"how to write a childrens book"	142	2.0%
how to write a children's book	112	1.6%
how to write a good book	92	1.3%
free how to write a book	61	0.9%
learn how to write a book	41	0.6%
how to write a fantasy book	30	0.4%
how to write a book proposal	26	0.4%
how to write a non-fiction book	24	0.3%
how to write a childrens book	23	0.3%
how to write a fiction book	22	0.3%
how to write a self help book	20	0.3%
tips on how to write a book	20	0.3%
how to write a book in 14 days	13	0.2%
how to write a nonfiction book	12	0.2%
how to write a chapter book	12	0.2%
how to write and publish a book	10	0.1%
how to write a picture book	9	0.1%
how to write a text book	9	0.1%
how to write a business book	9	0.1%
instructions on how to write a book	8	0.1%
how to write a murder mystery book	8	0.1%
how to write a book about my life	6	0.1%

This ad group has 25 keywords, but more than 80 percent of the traffic comes from two of them. Notice that the top three keywords are just match type variations of "how to write a book."

80/20 IS WHY "PEEL AND STICK" IS SO POWERFUL!

The 95/5 keyword pattern is universal. Peel and stick is simply recognition that since 5 percent of your keywords generate 95 percent of your traffic, you can optimize 5 percent

of your keywords by peeling them out and sticking each one into its own unique ad group.

You get 95 percent of the optimization by doing 5 percent of the work!

Peel and stick is the single most important AdWords skill next to split testing. That's because it allows you to happily ignore up to 95 percent of the stuff in your ad campaigns!

This isn't only true at the keyword level. It's also true at the campaign level. One of my Google accounts has 41 campaigns and 995 million impressions. The #1 campaign has 617 million impressions. One campaign generates a third of the exposure. That campaign has 28 ad groups and 80 percent of the traffic comes from the top 11.

The account in total has 3.1 million clicks and 2,857 ads (yes, we've tested a TON of ads!). The #1 ad has 303,000 clicks. One ad out of 2,857 generated 10 percent of the traffic. Five ads have gotten more than 100,000 clicks.

You could say the purpose of my two thousand ads was simply to arrive at a dozen killer Google ads, the supreme winners that generated half the traffic. And you would be right.

80/20 also describes:

- How many clicks your ads get in each of the 11 ad positions on Google search (the top 3 premium spots get 80 percent of the traffic)
- Traffic from placements on the Display Network
- Conversions from placements on the Display Network (top conversion sources will be different from top traffic sources)
- Visitors by city or state or country
- Conversions by city or state or country (top conversion sources will be different from top traffic sources)
- Clicks on the various ad formats and sizes
- Traffic to each page on your website
- Sales for each page on your website
- How many page views you get from the people who click on to your site
- How much time your visitors spend on your site
- How much money your buyers spend with you
- How many times your buyers buy
- How frequently your buyers buy
- How long customers stay loyal to you

The 80/20 pattern is truly everywhere. 80/20 radically changes how you manage your campaigns and your business. It means that most impressions, most clicks, most ads, most keywords, most ad groups, most web pages, most prospects and most customers *simply do not matter very much.*

It also means that a *few* impressions, a few clicks, a few ads, a few keywords and ad groups and web pages and customers determine almost everything!

When you start, your job is to throw just enough spaghetti against the wall to *start* to see where it is *starting* to stick, then immediately channel your efforts into improving what is working. This is why it's so important to build your business on what people actually do and actually want, so you're not steering a parked car.

PERFECTIONISM CAN GET IN YOUR WAY!

People who are good at AdWords usually have a perfectionist streak. That's what makes them good at it. Your perfectionist streak *likes* the idea of coming up with the best possible ad, of doing split tests, of putting up the best possible landing page, etc. You're constantly improving and your job is never done. You can always make it better and that's exciting.

But perfectionism has a dark side. The fact is, if you don't ignore most of what goes on in your Google campaigns, you'll never have time to focus on the few things that are actually working.

This is true in all aspects of marketing. Yes, I know, you've got a 1,000 page website and you'd love to give the whole thing a facelift. But in actual fact, 75 percent of your business is generated by three of those pages and no matter what you do to the least visited 800 pages on your site, it won't make a bit of difference. You have to set hard limits on your perfectionism. Otherwise you perfect the wrong thing.

The real power of 80/20 comes when you make it three-dimensional. Your ads are showing on 15,000 placement sites, but 50 percent of your traffic comes from 10 of them. You have 20 landing pages but 75 percent of your leads come from one of them. You have 86 ads but 20 percent of your sales come from one of them.

You copy your best ads and you do peel and stick for each of those placement sites. You also copy your best landing pages and make unique pages just for them.

Then you optimize. The ideal ad and landing page for each site is going to be different. So you start split testing ads and A/B landing pages. It is not unrealistic to expect that even if you already did a good job testing before, that this new level of refinement could double your sales.

Those 10 placements were sending you 50 percent of your traffic and since you doubled your conversions, now your whole business has grown 50 percent. And you did it with ten minor changes. See the image on page 120.

You can also peel and stick geographical locations—*but only do it for the highest-converting cities*. If San Francisco is a great city for you because it's 1 percent of the U.S. population but 10 percent of your sales, then you create a campaign just for San Francisco. You might use unique ads and color schemes.

But the problem is, San Francisco gets way less traffic than the whole U.S., so it takes longer to test. You can't test as many things. So you do your color scheme tests just on 250 x 300 pixel banners (which usually get a lot of traffic). Whatever works on those, you just apply to all the other banner sizes. You don't bother to split test the less-common 970 x 250 size because one test would take six months; this saves you a ton of money in design fees and you'll still make good decisions 80 percent of the time.

Visually, it looks like this:

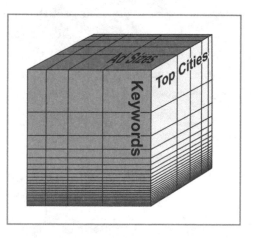

An inevitable consequence of 80/20 is that you sometimes feel like all your eggs are in one basket. And yes, there will always be a few baskets that have a lot of eggs. Warren Buffett says, "Keep all your eggs in one basket, but watch that basket closely."

The biggest "too many eggs in one basket" mistake people make is only advertising on Google. If only I had a dime for every customer who was going great guns, then got his ads disapproved or his account banned. Yes, do Google, but do Facebook ads, too. Do direct mail, too. Do LinkedIn ads, too.

THE MYTH OF THE LONG TAIL

Chris Anderson wrote a book called *The Long Tail: Why the Future of Business Is Selling Less of More*. He explained that the internet had made it possible for books that only sell 10 copies a year to stay in print forever, whereas in the old bookstore model, obscure titles wouldn't have a prayer.

Those 10 copies a year, on a graph, are the "long tail"—the millions of items that receive little attention and would never make it in the bookstore.

Anderson makes a very valid point, and it's why so many tiny little tribes and niches now have a voice on the internet. The phrase *long tail* is very useful because it's simply the left side of the 80/20 curve.

But you *must* be careful about the long tail. Received wisdom is that you can get lots of traffic from "long tail keywords," keyword phrases such as "how to write a murder mystery book."

Frankly that is just wrong. The phrase "how to write a murder mystery book" got eight clicks in two years. Yes, you should try to be a big fish in a little pond. But you can't be any kind of fish in a puddle. This keyword phrase is not worth anybody's serious time or attention, and while it may add a tiny amount of incremental revenue, it's completely trivial in the grand scheme of things.

On the other hand, if you can dominate just *one* high-traffic, high-conversion keyword, you can generate leads and sales for years. *If you can improve one keyword's ad by 10 percent, you might get a $100,000 per year raise.*

That means there's a right way and a wrong way to do "long tail." The wrong way is to just dump thousands of keywords into a campaign. The right way is to deliberately choose to be a big fish in a little pond and become the king of a small *niche* that has been overlooked.

There are thousands and thousands of such niches. The indicator is not that there aren't advertisers and bidders; rather, it's that nobody in a niche has a really great USP and the customers are itching for something more.

The common belief about the long tail is simply wrong. The offline world is generally 80/20, but many things online are 90/10, especially online. Ten percent of the search engines (Google) get 90 percent of the searches. Ten percent of the auction sites (eBay) get 90 percent of the auctions.

Yes, the internet has made it possible to sell ten copies per year of some obscure book written in 1913, but it's made it even more possible for Malcolm Gladwell to sell millions of copies of *The Tipping Point*.

Winners win big on the internet. My hope for you is that you'll be the Big Kahuna in your market, the #1 player, the alpha dog. And when you do, it'll be because you ignored 80 percent and got 1 percent exactly, precisely right.

SOME 80/20 RULES OF THUMB

I strongly recommend you pick up a copy of my book *80/20 Sales and Marketing* because it will take you much further on this journey. Meanwhile, some handy 80/20 rules:

- One-fifth the people will spend four times the money. If you have 100 customers who bought a $100 product from you, 20 of them will buy a $400 product. Four of them will buy a $1,600 product. 80/20 virtually guarantees this will be true.

- One percent of the work you did last year earned 50 percent of your money. The only people who normally see this with perfect clarity are straight commission sales people, but it's true for pretty much everybody.

- "Average" is seldom important in Google. Your average keyword, average ad or customer barely matters at all. A few of your keywords, a few of your ads, and a few of your customers matter a lot.

- Top 20 percent factors—the people and things that make the most difference— usually send signals ahead of time. If you ask a survey question, a casual buyer will often answer with a sentence fragment. A hot buyer will talk to you on the phone for 45 minutes.

Archimedes said, "Give me a lever and a place to stand and I will move the world." With AdWords, you have a lever. With a great product and USP you have a place to stand. Just know that 80 percent of your levers will get you nowhere and 20 percent will make you rich.

Get Perry's book, *80/20 Sales and Marketing* at www.perrymarshall.com/8020.

Vanquish the Thickest Competition with a Killer USP

Michael Strickland of Boulder, Colorado, runs a company that ships cars across the country. He enrolled in our "Bobsled Run" training course, our 12-week, hands-on, first-click-to-first-sale marketing funnel improvement lab. Like many people who take this course, he assumed we were just going to go "ninja" to the nth degree on Google ads.

Sure, we did do that, but on the very first live small group session, I asked him, "Michael, what is the reason why I should ship my car with *your* company instead of any and every other company out there?"

Michael didn't have a solid meaty answer to my question. Sure, he ran a good company and they delivered quality and good service and all that. But it was a deer-in-the-headlights moment, because he didn't have a definitive answer.

My response was, "Michael, you *must* create a great answer to that question." So we started building his unique selling proposition (USP) together. Two weeks later, Michael emerged with a powerful new USP and his "Damage Free Guarantee," which you can see on his website today at www.ShipACarDirect.com.

That was the tipping point of Michael's business. His sales doubled in six months. Yes, all his experiments and optimization of Google ads were helpful and necessary. But his ads didn't light on fire until his USP was solid. Once he had a terrific answer to "Why should I buy from you?" customers started responding, and the business went supernova.

The business ventures that fail the fastest in the marketplace are the ones that have no USP. The businesses that have their USP crisply and clearly defined acquire customers and grow.

What is a USP?

It stands for *unique selling proposition*. It's the "thing" that makes you unique in the marketplace—it's what customers can get from you that they can't find anyplace else. You can also call it your "unique selling position" or "value proposition."

Having a clear USP gives you a clear response for these questions:

- How are you unique?
- In what way are you different from your competitors?
- Why should I buy from you, rather than from someone else?
- Why should I care at all about you or anything you sell?

The term came from Rosser Reeves (1910–1984). He was a pioneer in the use of television ads, and he wrote *Reality in Advertising*, one of the most sought-after advertising books of the last century. (Try finding a physical copy of Reeves' book anywhere for less than $100.)

His message on USPs was simple:

- Your ad has to have some way of clearly saying, "Buy *this* product, and you will get *this* specific benefit."
- Your promise has to be one that your competitor cannot or does not offer.
- Your promise has to win over new customers.

You see, a USP is worthless if it doesn't *actually convince people to buy from you*. USP is the knife-edge of your chisel. A power USP empowers you to "Chisel Your Way In" anytime, anywhere. If you're not getting enough traction, sharpen your USP.

In this chapter I'm going to give you a method for defining your USP. And I'm going to give you a simple approach for how to test elements of your USP in your Google ads and find what gets you the strongest response.

THE SIX ESSENTIAL ELEMENTS OF A POWER USP

Any time you're communicating with a prospect you can appeal to any one of these, or all of them together:

1. You're unique because of the **buyer** you serve.
2. You're unique because of **what you sell.**
3. You're unique because you have an unusual **angle**.
4. You're unique because of what your product or service **does not do**.
5. You're unique because of the **time frame** around your offer.
6. You're unique because of how you **guarantee** your product.

How many of these elements are already true of you? Or: What can you change, shift, or alter in your business so that any or all of these elements *become* true of you?

We'll explore these one at a time, with examples of how each one might look in a Google ad.

You're Unique Because of the Buyer You Serve

Your business gets traction when you zero in on a niche. Maybe you target people of a specific demographic—a certain age, gender, income level, or religious or political leaning. Or maybe you solve a very specific kind of problem—a rare health issue, or a peculiar type of software malfunction. Maybe you cater to a particular hobby. If you're in B2B, there might be a specific narrow vertical you serve, or a particular stripe of business owner. Maybe you only work with companies of ten employees or less.

In extremely rare cases you could be unique because there's *no limit* to who you serve. For example:

> *My hiring and recruiting system is unique because it works for virtually any position in any business, anywhere—from the ecommerce business in the UK to the information marketer in Chicago to the nursing station in the Australian outback.*
>
> —Nancy Slessenger, Vinehouse.co.uk

Test the unique-buyer approach in your ads. Whether you serve a unique demographic:

Meet Singles Your Age
We're an over-50 dating site
made for older singles.
beyond50.com

Or you help people with a unique struggle:

Beat Procrastination

If you've tried everything else &
failed, my method is for you.
pjeby.com

Or you focus on a unique niche:

Proven ROI Web Design

Results-accountable website design
uniquely for ecommerce businesses.
trueroiwebdesign.com

You're Unique Because of What You Sell

Do you offer a service where others only offer a product? Do you offer a product where everyone else is selling services?

Are *you* the thing for sale, as a skilled technician, consultant, coach, or performer? Are you the entertaining or compelling personality that makes the business what it is?

If so, beat your drum. Having a story to tell will instantly separate you from the herd. Perry has made a name for his business by telling his unusual story:

"How an Inexperienced 29-Year-Old Punk Ignored All the Usual
'Marketing Wisdom'—Grew a High-Tech Business 2,000 percent in
4 Years, and Sold It for 18 Million Dollars!"
(www.perrymarshall.com/b2b-marketing/high-tech-sales/)

Test the "unique thing for sale" in your ads. Here are some examples.
A product for sale, instead of a service:

Clogged Drains?

Skip the plumber. Fix the problem
for good. This ships in 24 hours.
xyzdrainmagic.com

You for sale, with a unique story:

Social Media Done Right

Canada's only social media expert
running his own 8-figure business.
camediapower.com

You're Unique Because You've Found an Unusual Angle

There are so many "angles" you can use to separate yourself from competitors. Here are just a few:

- You promise a unique and specific outcome.
- You have a noteworthy track record.
- You have an unusual level of quality.
- The experience of doing business with you is one-of-a-kind.
- You offer a unique payment plan.

This ad celebrates a track record:

Iron-Clad Backup
A record 7 years without a system
failure. Reliability you crave.
abcbackupsystems.com

You can use acronyms and proprietary labels for products you sell and methods you use that get results. That approach always gets people to sit up and take notice. This business owner does just that. Try testing a similar concept in your ads:

Jazz Mandolin Made Easier
Unlock the "mystery" of jazz with
our one-of-a-kind FFcP method.
jazzmando.com

You're Unique Because of What Your Product or Service Does Not Do

We call these "negative promises." They're just as powerful as positive promises, often more so.

Maybe there's some unwanted ingredient or feature your product doesn't have. Maybe there's a bad result you prevent. Maybe there's some prerequisite for effectiveness that your product lets users bypass. Maybe your product avoids cost or waste.

This example ad captures the "negative promise" concept perfectly. Try testing one like it for your business:

Reduce Carpel Tunnel 50%
No office visits. No physical
therapy. No painful surgery.
ctstherapysolution.com

You're Unique Because of the Time Frame of Your Offer

You can promise results *within* a set amount of time or *for* a set amount of time. The question is, how specific can you actually get? The more explicit you are, the better your ads will perform.

> **Fast Corn Relief**
> Corns gone in 5 days or money back.
> Easy-to-use Kit.
> cornssolvedforgood.com

> **Install 1 MegaFilter and**
> Keep your home free of pollen &
> allergens for 6 full months.
> supermegafilter.com

Ads that use specific number symbols perform better. It's practically an ironclad law. There are two reasons why: 1) the brain processes the number symbol faster than written words, and 2) numbers make your message *specific*.

Prospects love promises that are specific, clear, and unmistakable. Claude Hopkins explains:

> *The weight of an argument may often be multiplied by making it specific. Say that a tungsten lamp gives more light than a carbon one and you leave some doubt. Say it gives three and one-third times the light and people realize that you have made tests and comparisons.*

You're Unique Because of How You Guarantee Your Product

Give your offer an "or else." A penalty to you if you don't deliver. Refund your customer's money. Replace your product. Redo your service.

Test a guarantee in your ad like this:

> **I Get You the Right Hire**
> Or I redo the entire recruiting
> process, any time within 1 year.
> vinehouse.com/recruitment/

The more ballsy and specific you make it, the more your prospects will sit up and take notice:

- "Double your money back"
- "Triple your money back"
- "Your money back plus $1,000"

■ "We'll refund your money *and* pay our competitor to come in and give you a replacement."

Combine your "or else" with a specific time promise, and your message has power. How's this for a specific, ballsy promise?

Our Plumber Comes on Time

If we're not on time we pay you $5
per minute late, up to $300.
benjaminfranklinplumbing.com

A Killer Strategy for Generating Sales Leads

Are you trying to "chisel your way in"? Your business must have a great USP— and so should the very first offer you use to attract attention. For decades, direct marketers taught you to offer free reports and white papers. "Free report: How to cut your back pain in half in 15 minutes or less."

Those still work, and perhaps to an extent they always will. But the amount of value you have to offer to get someone's email address, to get them to raise their hand, has risen exponentially as the web has matured. That "free report" strategy is tired at best, obsolete at worst. Many times it simply does not stand out at all. Everyone has a free report. Everyone has a free video. You can see that by scanning your competitors' ads.

A much less common strategy that works quite well is what I call the Disqualification Approach: Offer some kind of tool built to help many of your visitors figure out that they are *not* your customer. Let me explain.

When we wrote the first *Ultimate Guide to Facebook Advertising* a few years ago, I was concerned that most people who bought the book would eventually figure out Facebook was not for them. At the time, Facebook's ad platform was primitive and Facebook was not even appropriate for 60 to 80 percent of businesses at all. (That has since changed). I didn't want people buying my book and giving it two stars on Amazon because their ads were a failure.

So we created a tool, www.IsFBforMe.com. It scores people from 1 to 10 based on ten easy-to-answer questions. After they get their score, they can enter their email address to get a customized report that explains their score.

A Killer Strategy for Generating Sales Leads, continued

If people get a score of less than 6, we tell them to not even bother with Facebook.

This works extremely well. It gets lots of sales leads for us and they're qualified sales leads, because most of them are people with high scores. The fact that we actively push people away who are not good customers adds tremendous credibility when we tell someone "Yes, indeed, you should invest in Facebook advertising and education."

When you build a tool like this, if it doesn't disqualify a significant number of people who use it, the tool is wrong and your sales pitch is wrong. As I preach in my book *80/20 Sales & Marketing*, sales is first and foremost a DIS-qualification process. Most people are not right for you. So get rid of them at the outset.

A Disqualifier Lead Generation Magnet Helps You Write Better Ads

Which of these ads would you rather click on?

Facebook Ads are Hot
Discover the Secrets to Mastery
Free Online Training Video
www.perrymarshall.com/facebook

Or

Is Facebook for You?
Before (!) You Squander Time & Money
Take This Free 60 Second Quiz
www.IsFBforMe.com

Consider these two ads in terms of the **offer.** Which offer is more appealing? Which one promises you the most immediate gratification and appeal? This is a huge aspect of Google ads. It would be very rare for a training video to go viral, but our IsFBforME.com quiz went viral; in fact, many bloggers and authority sites happily recommend it.

Ultimately the offer your ad describes is more important than the words you use to describe it. What does your customer *get* by clicking on your ad? And how fast do they get it? How fast will it make a difference in their life?

This deserves serious thought, and most of all, serious experimentation!

Your mission: Test as many of these concepts in your Google ads as you can find the time for. Some will completely tank. Plan on it. But somewhere among these USP concepts will be a new winning ad and a new, proven way for you to approach your prospects, regardless of what media you use.

That is how you hammer out your USP in the crucible of the marketplace.

Uncle Claude Sez

A person who desires to make an impression must stand out in some way. Being eccentric, being abnormal is not a distinction to covet. But doing admirable things in a different way gives one a great advantage. So with salesmen, in person or in print. . . .

There is refreshing uniqueness, which enhances, which we welcome and remember. Fortunate is the salesman who has it.

Conversion Tracking
How to Know Where Every Penny Is Going

Following gut instinct can kill your PPC results. In this chapter we'll show you how to make decisions with hard facts, by setting up your first conversion tracking program right the first time, and how to use a thank-you page to welcome new customers and create upsells.

A few years ago, before Google's conversion tracking was as sophisticated as it is today, my team and I had determined that a certain keyword was a great target keyword for us. We fed $15,000 a month into that ad campaign for years.

I brought on a new marketing manager, Jack Born. Jack did more conversion tracking, and one day he called me.

"Hey Perry, you know that ad campaign? I don't think it's bringing you any paying customers. I think you're only getting tire kickers from that keyword."

This was totally counterintuitive. We were getting lots of email signups and, in fact, lots of customers.

Jack said, "I carefully connected the dots and I don't think this is the thing that's paying your bills. Let's pause that campaign and see what happens to our sales."

So, with fear and trepidation, we paused $15,000 per month of traffic.

Sales did not change one iota.

Dang. We must have spent $300,000 on traffic that wasn't even converting at all.

Ugh! Ever wish you could get $300,000 back?

Well . . . if you're not tracking conversions from click, to sales lead, to sale, then odds are 80 percent of your traffic is NOT converting to sales, and you don't know it.

If that's the case, you might as well find out right now!

What's the difference between a novice airplane pilot and a veteran? Ask any expert and they'll tell you: A beginner relies on sight and gut feeling, while an experienced professional relies on instruments.

This is counterintuitive. You might think experienced pilots with thousands of hours of airtime would reach the point where they could ignore instruments and fly on instinct. Quite the opposite. Novice pilots are unfamiliar with the complex range of cockpit instruments and are naturally inclined to use their basic senses. Veteran pilots, on the other hand, know your senses can deceive you, and so can your gut. The instruments are far less likely to give you faulty information.

Marketers have the same challenge. How do you know which of your advertising dollars are going to come back with friends attached?

Those of us who have been doing advertising the longest are by far the most vulnerable. We sit down to write a new ad or create a new offer, and we think we know what will get clicks, what will sell, and what won't.

But forecasting markets and predicting buyer behavior is near impossible. Worse still, knowing which keywords, ad groups, and campaigns are bringing us the best paying customers can be an opaque black box.

Truly experienced marketers create campaigns with the understanding that nobody knows what truly works until the target audience has cast their vote. And nobody knows which advertising dollars are creating the best return until we've looked at the hard data.

Google gets this. Their conversion tracking tools are engineered such that you have to guess what's working and what isn't. The "instruments" in the AdWords interface let you measure every last bit of prospect and buyer activity in precise detail. With this in place even the smallest business can go head-to-head against large competitors knowing exactly where their advertising dollars are having the greatest impact.

Google's conversion tracking can break down your numbers and tell you where each conversion came from. It can even show you the journey your visitors took to find you. Most importantly, it shows you where the waste is.

Do you want to know how to see exactly where your dollars are going? This chapter will show you. We'll start by looking over the options you have available, and then we'll walk you through a specific example of how this works.

THE FOUR TYPES OF CONVERSIONS YOU'LL WANT TO TRACK

For every business owner, "conversion" can refer to a variety of different actions that a prospect or customer takes. Some are more valuable than others:

- To a blogger it might be a visitor reading at least three posts.
- To a service provider it might be a visitor picking up the phone or completing a registration form.
- To an ecommerce site owner it might be a visitor making an online purchase of $100 or more.

Google makes it easy to track all of these. There are four essential types of conversions you'll want to monitor.

1. Track When Someone Lands on a Particular Page

This includes the person who sees your thank-you page after completing your newsletter signup form, or the buyer who arrives at your download page after purchasing your software.

This is the most common type of conversion tracking and the most basic. It's worth knowing how to set it up. We'll give you an example later in this chapter on how to do just that.

2. Track When Someone Calls You After Seeing Your Ad or Visiting Your Site

According to one survey, 70 percent of mobile users at some time or another have seen an advertiser's phone number on a Google results page and called it.

Putting your phone number in a Google ad is a strategy that works, especially if your number is "click-to-call." Best of all, it's easy for Google to track.

To learn how to set up phone-call tracking, you can review the section on ad extensions in Chapter 16, "Campaign Settings," and Chapter 22, "Supercharge Your Clickthrough Rates with Ad Extensions." Nevertheless, there are some additional tracking options we'll share with you here.

One option is to swap your regular phone number for a Google forwarding number. That way any time a person calls the forwarding number you get credited with a conversion, whether they saw the number in your ad or on your website.

This is only available in certain countries, but if you're able to take advantage of this you get access to better reporting. You can even specify to Google that only calls of a certain length will count as a conversion.

A second option is Call-on-Site. It's relatively new. With this feature a mobile user can see your phone number on your site and click on it to call you, and you get credited with the conversion. You keep your current phone number and Google tracks your clicks and calls. (It does require you to add a piece of code to your website.)

Either of these options is excellent. You may also want to try some third-party tracking options. Ifbyphone and Mongoose Metrics (are examples of these and are popular in the U.S. There are other good call-tracking services available that you can find by searching online.

3. Track When a Person Downloads Your Software Application

If your have an app on Google Play or the Apple App Store, Google can track downloads and count them as conversions. To set this up, find the URL for the download page of the app store you want to use, and make that the destination URL of your ad.

4. Track Conversions that Happen Offline

What if your primary business model involves calling leads and closing the sale over the phone? Google now has Offline Conversion Tracking, which lets you connect sales back to your AdWords accounts.

Imagine you discovered that 80 percent of the leads who arrived from AdWords ad groups A, B, and C converted to a sale, but only 5 percent of the leads who came through ad groups D, E, or F ended up buying. Just think of the leverage that would give you.

With this kind of conversion tracking you can know in advance which leads are most likely to become customers. That could save you huge amounts on your Google spend, and it could save your sales team tremendous amounts of time and effort.

Offline conversion tracking is a bit involved, but the effort is worth it. Read about it here: https://support.google.com/adwords/answer/2998031.

HOW TO SET UP CONVERSION TRACKING THE RIGHT WAY

Let's say you run a site where a visitor can fill in a form and get a free brochure. We'll walk you through how to set up your Google account to track that.

Step One: Conversion Category

First, you want to tell Google what kind of conversion you want tracked. Click the "Tools" dropdown at the very top of your AdWords page and select "Conversions." On the resulting page, click the big red "+ Conversion" button.

Google will ask you to name your conversion and indicate what the source will be. Choose a name that tells you what the conversion is (e.g., "Opt in for brochure") and select "Webpage."

You'll then be asked to choose one of the following categories:

- Purchase
- Signup
- Lead
- View of a Key Page
- Other
- Download (for tracking app downloads only)

In this instance, "Signup" and "Lead" are probably both applicable, but "Lead" is probably a little more relevant.

Step Two: Conversion Window

This indicates how many days or weeks you want Google to keep tracking the user after they click the first time. The default is 30 days. That's more than adequate for this exercise. If a person clicked on your ad but hasn't opted in for your brochure in 30 days' time, they're probably not worth following. Unless you have a very good reason for needing a different conversion window, leave this on the default setting.

Step Three: Conversion Count

Do you want Google to count all conversions in total, or only unique conversions? In other words, if a person clicks on your ad and then makes a purchase from you every day for the next three days, do you want this to be recorded as one conversion or three?

This will depend on the type of online business you operate. An ecommerce site owner, for instance, will usually want to keep track of every specific product purchased. He would select "All Conversions." On the other hand, an information marketer who provides PDFs for download may be more interested in simply knowing the total number of individuals who download one or more items. She would choose "Unique Conversions."

If you're not sure, go with "All Conversions." You still get data for both types. (If you select "Unique Conversions," you get less data and you can't change your mind later on without having to delete and recreate the conversion from scratch.)

Step Four: Conversion Value

If you're not running an ecommerce site you may be tempted to skip this one. Google will let you do so. But please don't. Setting a conversion value right from the beginning, for every conversion tracking program you set up, is going to make your data far more valuable in the long run.

Don't think of this as dollars. Think of it as a points system that rates the relative value of the different types of conversions that exist within your business. You might, for example, assign 50 points for a conversion that involves a visitor downloading a brochure, but 100 points if they complete a "please call me" lead capture form.

If your site is very basic and only offers one conversion action, then you can simply set the conversion value as 1.

Understanding Converted Clicks

In early 2014, Google's terminology changed. If you've been away from AdWords for a while and you're just coming back to it, or you're reading blogs and online tutorials that use the old terminology, it's worth noting the new labels.

"One Per Conversion" and "Many Per Conversion," are now called "Converted Clicks" and "Conversions," respectively.

This naming convention is easier to understand. "Converted Clicks" simply means the number of unique clicks that turn into one conversion, and "Conversions" means the total number of actions made by all of your visitors added together.

When it comes to reporting and sifting through your data, setting a conversion value is vitally important. You'll thank us later.

Note: If you're an ecommerce site owner you can set conversion values to adjust automatically based on the revenue of each product sold. Talk with your Google AdWords rep and your web developer if you want to go this route.

Step Five: Install Code

You're ready to install the code on your website that will allow Google to track your conversions. You can choose between installing it manually, in which case Google will give you a snippet of code to place on your key pages, or you can enter the email address of your web developer and Google will send the code there, along with instructions.

If you're not comfortable handling this part of the process and you don't have a web developer, you can find a freelancer or ask one of the many talented PPC practitioners in Planet Perry to handle this for you, such as in the private Mastermind group, www. perrymarshall.com/mastermind.

Important: The most reliable way to keep conversion tracking running smoothly is to ensure that your conversion action always results in your visitor being directed to a separate page that has a unique, static web address.

What do we mean by this? If you want visitors to complete a lead capture form, don't let your web developer talk you into using some fancy Ajax-style onsite messaging that keeps the user on the same page or generates a dynamic URL. Run the other way!

In our current example, once your visitor completes the lead capture form, you want them to be redirected to a unique thank-you page that has an ordinary static URL. If you

create multiple landing pages, each with a lead capture form, you can have one thank-you page for all of them. Or you can have a different thank-you page to go with each one.

Either way, simpler is better. This is the only way to ensure that your conversion tracking doesn't break further down the line, and that you don't end up making decisions based on bad data.

Your Thank-You Page: A Great Tool for Upsells

Thank-you pages are important and not just for conversion tracking. They also keep your visitors happy. Nobody likes an opt-in form that shoves the user off to another unrelated offer without acknowledging and thanking him or her for taking the action. Or worse, one that dumps the person unceremoniously back on the homepage.

Only a small percentage of your visitors actually put up their hand, so to speak, and indicate that they might be interested in doing business with you. Maybe between 5 and 10 percent. Treat these people with care and respect. A well-designed thank-you page that expresses appreciation for their interest is a great way to get your relationship with them started off on the right track.

You might provide the person with relevant information about what next steps to take. You could give them your contact information. Now might be a great time to ask for that Facebook like or Google +1. Maybe even post a short thank-you video.

FLY AUTOPILOT WITH CONVERSION OPTIMIZER

Once conversion tracking is in place, the quality of data you receive will blow your mind. You'll know which landing pages are effective and which ones aren't. You'll know which ads are most profitable, and even which keywords pull in the most affluent clients.

And just like the veteran airline pilot who spots something surprising on his instrument panel, sometimes you're going to see data that totally contradicts your expectations. You may discover that the ad with the best CTR has an awful cost per conversion, while that one ad with the low CTR that you've been thinking of shutting off is actually giving you the most profit.

How you use the data to improve your results is up to you. However, once conversion tracking is set up and working, you have the option to use Google's Conversion Optimizer (GCO).

This is a feature where Google adjusts your bids on the fly, so as to hit a specified cost per action (CPA), or cost per conversion.

If you have a lead generation site and your conversion tracking reveals that you're paying $70 on average for each conversion, you can use GCO, have Google take over the bidding for you, and try to improve that figure.

Go to the Settings tab in your specific campaign and click to edit the Bid Strategy section. You should see an option called "Focus on conversions (Conversion Optimizer)."

You can manually set your CPA or you can take Google's recommendation. GCO then goes to work.

Be realistic with your expectations. If you're averaging $70 per conversion, Google will recommend starting with a CPA of roughly that amount. If you ignore this and set your target CPA at something silly like $20, plan on being disappointed. The trick is to select a target CPA that is only slightly lower than your current average. As Google succeeds in hitting that target, you can gradually work your CPA down.

It can be a bit nerve-wracking the first time you try this. Monitor your results carefully.

But note: Google is pretty good at this, primarily because of the massive volumes of data they employ to make this work. In fact, with a little steering from you, Google Conversion Optimizer can bring tremendous amounts of traffic with remarkable ease, especially in big markets.

Also note: Before you become obsessed with dramatically driving down your CPA, remember this golden rule from Dan Kennedy:

The winner is not the business that gets the cheapest leads. The winner is the business that can afford to pay the most per lead.

There's nothing wrong with paying less for your conversions. Profit is a worthy goal. But sometimes you want to grow your market share, even your market. It's possible to your cost per conversion by a few dollars but your lead volume as a result. That may be the best strategy to lock in market share and secure long-term profit for your business.

Just be sure you have the resources to handle the increase in customers!

Display Conversion Optimizer and Numbers that Work

A version of GCO, called Display Conversion Optimizer, is also available on the Google Display Network. We'll cover this in more detail in Chapter 18. In both cases, the feature becomes available to you after you've recorded 15 conversions in a 30-day period.

Nevertheless, Google performs better if you wait until you have a more substantial set of data and results to work from. We recommend getting at least 100 conversions recorded and measured before you dive into this feature.

TAKE ADVANTAGE OF ANALYTICS

On a final note, if you're also a Google Analytics (GA) user, you can connect your AdWords conversion tracking with your GA account. This saves you from having to install additional code on your site, and it gives you some measuring options that aren't available through conversion tracking alone.

For example, if you own a blog and your goal is for a visitor to read three pages on their visit, this is simple to set up in Analytics.

There are some caveats, though. Analytics uses different methods for counting conversions, so your GA numbers may not perfectly match those in your AdWords account. Analytics also has a bit of a built-in delay: as little as 24 hours and as much as two to three days.

GA is worth considering but it's best not to rely on it. We prefer to use AdWords as much as possible and only use GA goal tracking if there's a special kind of setup that our regular conversion tracking can't handle.

YOUR QUICK ACTION SUMMARY

Google AdWords is the pinnacle of direct marketing. But you cannot use it effectively if you don't first enable Conversion Tracking.

- Select your Conversion Category (most likely "lead" or "purchase").
- Choose your Conversion Window, Count, and Value.
- Install the Conversion Tracking code on your website, or delegate this to your web developer.
- Review your data to improve your AdWords results.

Uncle Claude Sez

Never be guided in any way by ads which are untracked. Never do anything because some uninformed advertiser considers that something right. Never be led in new paths by the blind. Apply to your advertising ordinary common sense

The only purpose of advertising is to make sales. It is profitable or unprofitable according to its actual sales. It is not for general effect. It is not to keep your name before the people Treat it as a salesman. Force it to justify itself. Compare it with other salesmen. Figure its cost and result. Accept no excuses, which good salesmen do not make. Then you will not go far wrong.

Take the opinion of nobody who knows nothing about his returns.

Campaign Settings

Once I did a consult with a customer who was buying tons of traffic and spending a small fortune. As far as anyone could possibly tell, he had chosen superb keywords. People who searched on those keywords bought, but he was spending tons of money and getting no sales.

The reason he asked for the consult was, he couldn't seem to find his ads anywhere, even though Google said he was in position three!

What was going on?

I started investigating. Turns out he'd somehow switched his campaigns from "United States" to "All Countries." His *average* position was three, but he was

actually number one in Pakistan and number 42 in the U.S. He probably wasn't number three anywhere.

Sure, there was lots of traffic from Pakistan and India and a dozen other countries. But none from buyers with credit cards and valid shipping addresses.

One quick fix and problem solved. Just like that.

Fact: *Changing one small setting can radically alter the profitability of your campaigns.* For better *or* for worse.

But wait a minute, you say—a Google campaign has dozens of different little settings you can tweak or alter! How do you know how to launch a new campaign with the exact right settings in place?

We've already shown you how to create a new campaign from scratch. This chapter introduces you to a host of strategic bells and whistles and how to set them up right.

THE PERFECT SETTINGS FOR A NEW CAMPAIGN

Within your AdWords account, head over to the Campaigns tab and find the "New Campaign" button.

You'll get a lot of different options thrown at you, but we'll show you here what the main settings are that you need to focus on. And don't worry—you can adjust or reset any of these settings later on.

Campaign Type

You have four options for new campaigns:

1. Search network with display select
2. Search network only
3. Display network only
4. Shopping

If you're a first-time user, then start with the second option, "Search network only." This is the most straightforward approach and is the area you should be looking to master before branching out into other areas of Google's networks.

Choice of Networks

We've dedicated all of Chapter 25 to Google's Search Partner Network. For now, turn this off so that your ads will only show on Google's main search pages, such as Google. com, Google.co.uk, etc.

Location

As tempting as it may be to broadcast your ads across the entire world, it's much easier to start with a single location and expand from there as your clickthrough rates and conversion rates improve. Choose the single country that represents your main target audience. Or, if you're a local business, choose the town or city that you serve.

Language

The "language" of the user is dictated by the language that their browser is set to. Again, don't try to reach the world with your first campaign; choose the main language(s) of your primary market only. If, for example, your market is the UK, then choose English. If it's Canada, go for both French and English.

Bid Strategy

The default option is "I will manually set my bids," and this is the setting you should start with for now. You can look over the advanced options later.

Default Bid

This option allows you to tell Google the maximum amount you're prepared to pay for a single click. This is tricky, especially if you're just starting out: You may not yet be 100 percent settled on an answer to this question. You can and will adjust this multiple

times over the coming weeks and months, so don't worry about trying to find the perfect number. Just pick a sensible starting point. For many people that will be around $1 per click.

Daily Budget

Google has a very specific goal: They want to spend 30.4 times your daily budget each month. This is a fact. Sure, your daily spend will be a bit higher on some days and lower on others, but by month's end it will even itself out.

Again, you can change this setting later. So choose what you think is a sensible starting point that won't melt your credit card. We encourage our students to start with $10 per day. That ensures that their overall spend won't exceed $304 per month until they're ready to increase their budget.

MORE SETTINGS TO SAVE YOU MONEY AND INCREASE CLICKS

Once your campaign is running you can adjust any of the above options. You'll also find some additional settings that are available to tweak.

Delivery Method

You have two options for how you want Google to spend your daily budget:

- Standard (spreads your ad spend out over the full 24 hours)
- Accelerated (starting from 12:01 A.M., show your ads quickly, even if this means hitting your daily budget before sunrise)

"Standard" is usually the best option because, unless you have a very high daily budget, "Accelerated" may result in your ads being paused quite early in the day, causing you to miss your opportunity to reach people. Your best customers may, for example, only go online in the evening.

Scheduling

The most common use of scheduling is to turn off your ads at certain times of the day, even whole days of the week. That's a powerful money saver if you know that there are certain times where you'll burn through your budget if you let your ads show.

However, we recommend you leave this setting alone to begin with. While your number of impressions and clicks may vary quite a bit depending on the time or day, conversion rates are usually consistent. Once you've gathered a significant amount of data on your campaign, then and only then, would you have good reason to make adjustments.

You can also use this setting to specify an end date for your campaign. This is useful if you sell a product or service that's only relevant to a specific time of year, such as now shovels, lawn mowers, or Valentine's Day-themed gifts.

When to Leave Ad Scheduling Alone

A common mistake among AdWords users is to assume that people only shop and buy from them at certain times of the day or week, and to set up aggressive ad scheduling in their account to show ads only at those times.

If the call-to-action on your landing page is to telephone your business, and that line is only open during office hours, then it may make sense to set the scheduling to only show your ads between 9 a.m. and 5 p.m. However, if you're selling online and can take orders 24/7, leave ad scheduling alone. Traffic volume may ramp up from early morning and slow down late at night, but conversion rates will generally remain consistent.

It will depend on your market, but if anything, conversion rates are *higher* during the evening as people are casually surfing on their phone or tablet during TV commercial breaks and taking advantage of the downtime to catch up on their online shopping.

Ad Delivery

Google wants some amount of control over the split-testing you do. If they see an ad getting significantly more clicks than another they'll want to show it more often. This is understandable; they get paid for the clicks. But that isn't helpful for you as a conscientious PPC marketer who stays on top of your ad performance, frequently runs multiple split-tests, and wants control over the process.

Here are your options:

- Optimize for clicks. Google will calculate the winner of a split test as quickly as possible and begin showing the better-performing ad more frequently.
- Optimize for conversions. This is only an option if you're using conversion tracking, a subject for another chapter.
- Rotate evenly for 90 days and then optimize.
- Rotate indefinitely.

> ## Why Google Lumps Users Together
>
> Google has lumped desktops and tablets into the same category. You can't specifically target mobiles and tablets anymore. Why? The market is changing, they say. New creations such as "phablets" (a mid-sized device halfway between a phone and a tablet) and "Google Glass" are proof, they say. Google would rather PPC users target customers in other ways, such as by location, interest, and age.
>
> The best PPC geniuses are control freaks. By definition. Take away more of their control and they'll fight you.
>
> Conversions from tablets are *considerably* different from desktops. Within AdWords there's not much you can do anymore to address this, other than turning all of your mobile targeting off. We wish it were different.

We recommend you choose the last option: rotate indefinitely. It's the only way to be sure that each ad you split test gets an equal amount of traffic. It makes for truer winners and losers. The other options are well-intentioned, but they can sometimes skew the data. Rotating your ads indefinitely means it will take longer for you to get a demonstrable result, but it's necessary if you want to get the maximum possible return on your PPC investment.

Keyword Matching Options

If you're running campaigns that target exact match or phrase match keywords, this setting lets you tell Google how to handle plurals, misspellings, and other close variants. If you're a beginner, leave this setting on the default. Tweaking it is only required at a very advanced level.

MOBILE SETTINGS: WE SURE WISH WE COULD DO MORE

It used to be possible to create a campaign that exclusively targets mobile users. That's no longer the case. You can remove your ads from mobiles entirely or you can adjust how focused your campaign is on mobile devices. You can't do much else beyond that.

There's good news, though: It's possible to adjust your level of ad presence on mobiles. Mouse over your ad and a dropdown box will appear. Click it and choose "Edit":

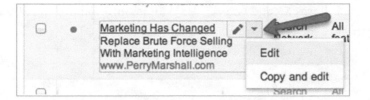

From there you can check the "Mobile" box below your ad copy, which tells Google you would prefer to have this particular ad shown on mobiles.

Google may still show these ads on desktops and tablets as well—but this will give an ad greater weight toward mobile users.

There's a catch with this feature, though. It only works if you have at least one other ad in the ad group marked with the opposite setting. In other words, if you have two ads in an ad group and you select both of them as preferred for mobile, then both ads will continue to be shown on all devices as Google decides is appropriate.

Why does this matter? If you're running a split test with your ads and you're specifying certain ads as mobile-preferred, you'll want to have the same number of ads in that ad group with the box unchecked. Otherwise your numbers will be skewed.

As of this writing, there's no other way around this.

UPPING YOUR GAME WITH BID MODIFIERS

Here's a new method of adjusting your bids based on geography, time, device, and more.

Device

By default, your maximum bid will be the same across all devices, but here you can tweak your bid for mobile devices, setting it anywhere from 90 percent less up to 300 percent higher. For example, if your maximum bid was $1 and you set the Mobile Bid Modifier to -50 percent, then your maximum bid for mobile clicks would be $0.50. If

your maximum bid was $1 and you set the Mobile Bid Modifier to +200 percent, then your maximum bid for mobile clicks would be $3.

This setting makes it possible for you to opt out of the mobile network altogether. Just set the Mobile Bid Modifier to -100 percent and your ads will only show on desktops and tablets going forward.

You may be wondering if there's a way to turn off ad serving on desktops and tablets and go mobile only. There isn't, sadly. The closest you can get to that is to start with a low bid and then set the Mobile Bid Modifier to +300 percent and hope that moves the needle in the direction of being mobile-only. This probably will work.

Geography

It's not at all unusual for some regions, or even countries, to perform better than others. In fact, it's normal and you should expect it. Skilled AdWords practitioners sculpt the geography of their campaigns to target hot customers and eliminate others. With this bid modifier you can increase and decrease bids by area.

If your CPA in Chicago is $50, but in Florida it's $150, try decreasing Florida bids between 30 to 70 percent and increasing Chicago bids 40 to 80 percent. And whereas the device modifier only allows you to increase bids by up to 300 percent, all other bids, including geography bids, can be modified by up to 900 percent.

Time

Don't confuse this with ad scheduling, which allows you to turn off ads on specific days or during specific time periods. The time bid modifier doesn't turn your ads on or off, but it does let you adjust your bid up or down for certain hours or days.

How Are My Mobile Ads Performing?

If you're unsure whether or not removing mobile ads is a good idea, then visit the AdWords "Campaign" screen and use the "Segment" dropdown option to see your results on different devices.

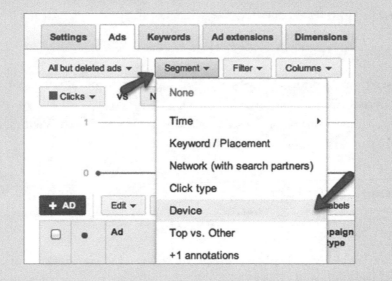

For each of your campaigns this will show statistics for desktop computers, mobile devices, and tablets. If you have conversion tracking turned on, you'll also be able to see your cost per action (CPA) for each device. If the tablet CPA is high, there is little you can do about it, but if your mobile CPA is at the point where it's hurting your profitability, then set the Mobile Bid Modifier to –100 percent.

Let's say you find that your conversion rates are great on Wednesdays but terrible on Sundays. Simply increase Wednesday bids and decrease Sunday bids. Your ads will show in higher positions for the former and lower positions for the latter. That will affect the number of clicks you receive as a result.

Just like with the geography bid modifier, the maximum increase you can set is 900 percent.

RISKY! BEWARE OF BID STACKING

This could seem technical, but it's important that you're aware of this effect, even if it isn't necessary to understand it precisely.

As the name suggests, bid stacking is what happens when you activate more than one bid modifier at a time. If you're not aware of this before you start playing around with this advanced feature, you can end up paying considerably more for clicks than you intended.

If, for example, you modify your bid up by 10 percent for people living in London, and also modify your bid up 10 percent on Wednesdays, when someone from London clicks on your ad on a Wednesday, then Google will apply *both increases* to your spend. Here's what that would look like:

Regular bid is $5.

- User from London (+10 percent) clicking your ad on a Tuesday (no modifier) increases your maximum bid to $5.50.
- User from London (+10 percent) clicking on your ad on a Wednesday (+10 percent) increases your maximum bid to $6.05.

Got it?

The same applies to decreasing bid modifiers as well. If your regular bid is $5 and you bid up 10 percent for London dwellers and down 20 percent for mobile users:

Regular bid is $5.

- User from London (+10 percent) clicking on your ad via a desktop device increases your maximum bid to $5.50.
- User from London (+10 percent) clicking on your ad via a mobile device (-20 percent) decreases your maximum bid to $4.40.

Let's try one more. Grab a calculator and see if you can work out the answer yourself. Regular bid is $10.

Bid modifiers are down 25 percent for mobile users, up 200 percent for users from Florida, and up 20 percent on Tuesdays and Thursdays.

What would be the bid for a mobile user from Florida, clicking on a Tuesday? (The answer is at the end of this chapter.)

FLEXIBLE BID STRATEGIES: CAUTION!

There are a few more advanced campaign settings that can be found in the "Shared Library" section in your AdWords account.

Each of these is a method by which Google can raise or lower your maximum bid as they see fit. Does that sound disturbing? It won't be if you proceed with caution and monitor your results carefully to ensure you're getting an ROI that justifies it.

1. *Maximized Clicks.* Google automatically adjusts your bids to try to maximize the number of clicks you receive. You still need to set a maximum budget, but Google then has free rein to adjust your bids in whatever fashion it believes will deliver the most clicks. If sheer traffic is more important to you than conversions or measurable results, this could be worth testing. Otherwise, steer clear.

2. *Target Search Page Location.* Google adjusts your bid based on whether you indicate you're looking merely to get onto the first page of search results or to the very top of all results. Be cautious with this one. Getting to the top of the page can be expensive. Be aware that you're giving Google the power to spend your money.

3. *Target Cost Per Acquisition.* If you're using conversion tracking (which we covered more fully in Chapter 15) you can select this bid strategy to enable Google to try to maximize your conversions while still hitting your desired CPA. You set your target CPA dollar amount and Google then decides when to show your ads, who to show them to, and how much to charge you per click in order to reach your goal.

4. *Enhanced Cost per Click (ECPC).* This is arguably the safest of Google's flexible bid strategies. It's a good place to start. You select your default bid as usual, but Google increases or decreases the bid based on the likelihood that a particular click will lead to a conversion.

5. *Target Return on Ad Spend (ROAS).* This is another option if you're using conversion tracking, but this time the strategy is to hit a target ROI. This means you're going after a *conversion value* rather than a total number of conversions.

Note that strategies 3 and 4 above can only be applied to campaigns and ad groups, whereas strategies, 1, 2, and 5 can also be applied to individual keywords.

YOUR QUICK ACTION SUMMARY

Google's new approach to mobile targeting can be frustrating, but the new range of flexible bid strategies and bid modifiers has opened up a whole new level of control for you that's worth exploring.

- Create a new campaign and select your settings carefully.
- If you have an existing campaign, review your settings and take a look at some of the advanced settings that are available.
- If you're ready for some advanced strategies, review the bid modifier and flexible bid strategies facilities, and try one of them out.

* Answer from page 154: Maximum bid would be modified from $10 to $27.

How to Get Your Ads on Millions of Websites with Google's Display Network

In this chapter we're going to show you how to reach 93 percent of internet users through a single network, how to get your ads in front of YouTube and mobile app users, and how to tap into Google's inside knowledge of pretty much everyone. Plus we'll show you a simple campaign offer that can help you dominate your niche.

A year or two after AdWords began, Google started selling ads on its Display Network. At the time, the ability to advertise on a search engine was new and exciting. Search ads were the hot commodity. The prospect of selling only to people who had just searched for what you sell was cocaine.

Display advertising was more akin to billboards and magazine ads, so we viewed it with suspicion. "This is just a money grab by Google." (When I catch myself saying that, it usually turns out to be a half truth.)

I had a site, www.coffeehousetheology.com, which I was advertising on the Search Network. One day I *accidentally* turned on the Display Network. Sheer accident. The very next day I noticed something:

I got 100 opt-ins instead of yesterday's 15!

Which Is Better for Your Business? Google Search or Google Display? Find Out in One Minute!

Take this short quiz and get an instant ScoreCard on how appropriate your business is for 1) Google AdWords for keyword search and 2) Google's Display Network. Your ScoreCard will also gauge the competition level and priority you should place on AdWords compared to other advertising opportunities.

It only takes 60 seconds:

www.IsAWforMe.com

At first, I didn't even know why! I sifted through my account and finally figured out what had changed. All those new signups were from Display Network traffic!

The site was about spirituality. People are vastly more interested in spirituality than their search activity on Google would ever suggest. Many topics are like that. A person may rarely search for it, but if you put the right ad in front of them, they'll stop what they're doing and listen to you.

Google Display Network (GDN) is perfect for such topics. For mass-appeal consumer offers, GDN can deliver *tremendous* volumes of traffic. GDN can be potent for B2B and small niches as well. GDN proved to be tremendously effective for that project, getting me hundreds of thousands of opt-ins and millions of visitors for a bargain price.

If you wanted to see your ads on CNN's website, how would you do that?

You could try the traditional route: Check that your budget has room for the tens of thousands of dollars you'd expect to spend. Make endless phone calls, engage in dozens of email conversions, battle through the layers of gatekeepers and decision-makers until you reach the person who has the authority to discuss the advertising opportunity with you. Finally, assuming you managed to agree to terms and have your content approved,

line up behind all the other businesses who also want their products and services featured on CNN's high-traffic website.

Actually, you don't need to do any of that.

Just log in to your AdWords account, load up the Display Planner, create a campaign that targets CNN—choose a specific page on their site if you like—and then decide how much per click you're willing to bid for the privilege.

It's that simple.

That's the power of GDN. Extend your AdWords campaign beyond mere search pages and you have access to *more than two million websites* that have agreed to place Google ads.

In the years since introducing the program that website publishers know as AdSense, Google has become one of the largest advertising networks in history, connecting publishers and advertisers from all corners of the globe.

At its simplest level, it's a beautiful system:

- A website owner (the "publisher") produces content and is eager to make money from the traffic that his site commands.
- He places code on his website, similar to an invisible box, which Google can use as they see fit.
- People (the "advertisers") pay Google to place their ads on his site, in the invisible boxes.
- Google shares a portion of that income with the publisher.
- The publisher doesn't know exactly what ads will appear on his site, but he trusts Google to properly screen and manage the advertisers. As a result he avoids having to spend huge amounts of time looking for advertisers and managing clients on a one-to-one basis.

As an AdWords user, whether you were previously aware of this or not, you have access to the entire GDN, and you can add it to your PPC campaigns with just a few clicks. However, just like the rest of your Google PPC campaigns, the difference between a stunning ROI and complete failure is how well you understand the options available to you and how well you prepare and implement your strategy.

This chapter is an introduction to GDN. In Chapter 18, we'll dig deeper into the subject.You will also find extended materials on my website at www.perrymarshall.com/supplement.

DISPLAY VS. SEARCH

The most obvious difference between GDN and Google's Search Network is the range of locations available to you on which you can advertise. The search network only

gives you access to Google's sites, and only to people who are proactively searching for information. By contrast, GDN gives you access to every kind of site imaginable, reaching people who are expressing all manner of different interests.

Just how huge is GDN? It connects you to more than two million sites. The number of individual web pages you can target reaches into the billions.

From small blogs and forums receiving a few hundred visits per day to internet titans like CNN, TripAdvisor, and LinkedIn, the audience tucked away in GDN is mind-boggling.

And that's *before* you factor in YouTube videos and mobile apps!

There's also a less obvious but more important difference, namely, the mindset of people who see GDN ads. People go onto Google's Search Network proactively looking for information. They see your ads as a potential solution.

In stark contrast, people who see GDN ads are *not* searching for your information—they're just browsing a website that interests them. They may see your ad as an interruption, in much the same way that people see commercials on television and radio.

That doesn't make the GDN useless, it just requires a different approach—what some people refer to as "interruption marketing." You present an enticing offer that is so engaging that viewers will feel compelled to stop what they're doing and give your ad a healthy moment of attention.

If the Google Search Network is like playing checkers, then GDN is chess. They both involve strategic thinking but while the latter requires more thought before each move, it offers vastly more options to win!

IS GOOGLE'S DISPLAY NETWORK WORTH THE EFFORT?

GDN is *absolutely* worth the investment of your time and effort. It allows you to:

- *Reach 93 percent of internet users through a single network.* Chew on that a bit. You have access to virtually the entire gamut of internet users through a single portal. As we discussed in the opening section of this chapter, this is infinitely more practical than trying to negotiate with individual websites and corporations one at a time.

- *Target specific groups of people with very specific interests.* The early days of GDN were a little scattershot, but Google has worked very hard at making its network more organized and its matching system more precise.

- *Use more creativity in your ads.* GDN ads are more than just text. You can craft image ads, which are great for branding as well as creating very eye-catching campaigns. Expandable ads are also available, which activate when viewers hover their mouse cursor over your image for more than two seconds. You can also get

away with more creativity in general than you can in search, since the context is so much wider.

- *Reach the mobile and tablet market.* In the Apple and Google app stores are countless free programs that are monetized through GDN. If you want to reach a younger, technologically savvy audience, this is an excellent venue.
- *Generate an impressive ROI.* This is the best news of all. Many advertisers skip the GDN because they don't understand it. Many who do use it don't do so correctly. But if you tackle GDN with the right strategy, you can dominate your niche at a fraction of the cost of advertising on the Search Network.

Yes, generating a profit from GDN takes more time and commitment than regular Search-based PPC work, and you should expect your budget during the first month or more to be predominantly spent on testing and tweaking your campaigns. But once you've got this sorted, the results can be spectacular.

One of our students uses GDN to generate *conversions* in a particular niche for just two cents a piece. On most regular Search Network campaigns you can't even buy a single *click* for that price!

HIT THE BULL'S EYE BY CAREFULLY CHOOSING YOUR TARGET

The more relevant and targeted your GDN ad, the better your ROI will be. The difference between a carefully targeted campaign and a poorly targeted one can be astounding. One of our clients hired a so-called "PPC expert" and burned through $15,000 to generate just three leads. This client came to us, and after a single week spent improving their targeting options, we cut their costs to just $15 per lead.

When GDN is Absolutely Vital

As amazing as the GDN can be, if you're new to PPC there's no shame in leaving it be until you've mastered the search network first. GDN is most helpful to folks who already have a very good range of PPC campaigns running and are satisfied that they're maximizing their effectiveness on search. For them, GDN is the next natural step in extending their reach. If you're not at that point yet, not a problem. You can come back to this idea later on.

That said, regardless of your level of experience, *everyone* can and should use the GDN for remarketing campaigns. More on that in Chapter 24!

In another example, a client came to us spending $200 per conversion (which was still profitable for them); within three months we had this down to $34 per conversion. So much healthier.

Google provides you with four different options for selecting your place in the GDN.

Managed Placement Targeting

With this option you enter the web address of the sites where you want to advertise. If those sites are available, Google will show your ads there. You can even target a specific area on a site. For example, you can select www.nytimes.com which will give you access to the entire New York Times website, or you can specify www.nytimes.com/pages/technology/ which will limit your ads to the technology section.

This is a good option if you want a lot of control, but it greatly limits your reach. Google doesn't publish its entire list of partners so you'll need to research what's available and you'll inevitably miss some prime opportunities. Even if you spend days or (more likely) weeks handpicking a hundred sites, you'll only be reaching a fraction of the sites Google has access to.

Topic Targeting

Google categorizes all of the sites in their network under various topics. Using this option, you can choose broad or narrow categories of site on which to show your ads. There are about 2,000 topics to choose from. You can view these in your AdWords account or at https://developers.google.com/adwords/api/docs/appendix/verticals.

The more specific and drilled-down a topic you choose, the better your targeting will be. For example, "Arts & Entertainment" is extremely broad, but you can drill down to "Arts & Entertainment > Entertainment Industry > Recording Industry > Record Labels" for terrific precision.

Keep in mind that by using this method *you aren't targeting people who work in those industries, but rather people who are interested in these topics* and who visit sites on these subjects. Many of those people could become your customers.

Keyword Targeting

Topic targeting is an easy place to begin, but it's still quite broad. For even better results, target by keywords.

There's a board game produced by Hasbro called *Taboo,* where the object is to explain a concept to your teammates and have them guess and say a particular word. The fun challenge is that you're also given a list of five words that are "taboo"—i.e., you're not allowed to use them as part of your explanation.

For instance, if the word you're trying to get your teammates to guess is "dog," the taboo words you can't use might be: pet, friend, bone, bark, and woof.

Keyword targeting is a bit like *Taboo,* but in reverse: You give Google five or more words and they figure out the concept. You can actually choose up to 20 keywords, and from those Google will go find webpages that fit.

Let's say you're a vendor of Chicago Bears branded clothing. You want to advertise on GDN and use keyword targeting to find sites to sell on. If the only keyword you give Google is "bear," you're going to have problems. Google won't know what to do with it. They might assume you mean Bear Grylls, teddy bears, Care Bears, the Right to Bear Arms, or any of a host of other things.

But if you play *Taboo* in reverse and also give Google clue words like "football," "gridiron," "1985 Super Bowl champions" and "NFL," Google is going to do a much better job of matching your ads to pages that show content relevant to the Chicago Bears football fans you're targeting.

Sometimes one keyword is enough. If you just gave Google the words "Chicago Bears" that would probably suffice. But in most cases you'll want to add a few additional words to make your intention more clear and give you a broader reach.

Behavioral Targeting

This option focuses on individual visitors rather than their location or associated keywords. Google knows volumes about its users, including their favorite sites, the videos they watch, the items they purchase, the types of emails they receive, and more. They combine this information to create a fairly accurate profile of each user's personal interests.

For example, if you visit lots of sports-related sites, Google will rightly assume that this is a topic you care about. And if most of those sites are about golf, Google will assume golf is your favorite sport and add it to their profile of you.

This may sound a bit scary, even invasive. You can see a snapshot of Google's profile of you at http://www.google.com/ads/preferences.

Gmail, Behavioral Targeting, and Your Privacy

Google also uses behavioral targeting to show advertising inside people's Gmail accounts. Google claims that for privacy reasons no human ever reads the content of your emails. However, their software is capable of picking out keywords in your messages in order to show relevant ads to you.

What's interesting about this targeting method is that your ads will be featured to people who Google believes would have an interest in your business, regardless of the site they're visiting. A person could be on a site that sells clothes, but if her profile indicates an interest in tennis and you sell tennis equipment, your ad could appear right there on the clothing site.

DISPLAY PLANNER AND ALL THE CLEVER WAYS YOU CAN BID

Just like the Keyword Planner for Search (see Chapter 6), you can use Display Planner for researching keywords and GDN targeting options. Start with a single "seed" keyword or URL and Google will provide you with some suggested places to start, including:

- Keywords that may be suitable for a keyword-targeted campaign
- Recommended topics for contextual targeting
- Recommended "interests" for behavioral targeting
- Suggested sites for your advertisements
- Suitable YouTube videos and mobile apps

Play around with some of the options, but before you commit to the creation and activation of any ad groups, think carefully about the bidding options that are available.

Cost Per Click (CPC)

This is the default option. You're surely familiar with it by now. Set the maximum bid you're prepared to pay for each click and, when someone clicks on your ad, Google will charge you a figure up to and including that sum.

Cost Per Thousand Impressions (CPM)

Here you pay a set amount for Google to show your ad 1,000 times, regardless of the number of clicks you receive. This is good for brand awareness, but if you need the clicks for your campaign to be profitable, CPM is rarely effective. It's just too easy for your budget to blow up and leave you with nothing to show for.

Cost Per Action (CPA)

This option is only available to you if you've already been using Google Display Network for a period of time. You need at least 15 conversions in a 30-day period to give Google enough time and data to know what sites and contexts will give you conversions.

Once Google approves you for CPA, Google will adjust your cost per click based on what they know about the person making the click. If Google thinks the person is a good

candidate with a strong likelihood of converting, they'll charge you more. If they think the candidate is a poor match they'll charge you less or even hide the ad entirely.

Be aware that with this option you're putting a lot of control into Google's automated hands.

Note that CPC vs. CPM vs. CPA are all *different ways of slicing the world*. Broadly speaking, you can carve out an advantage for yourself simply by bidding differently than most of your competitors. Each of these options has its own pros and cons, but once you develop skill and familiarity, you can make it work for your situation.

Mission Critical: Conversion Code

Never begin any PPC campaign without first being sure that your conversion code is set up and measuring results properly. If you're not getting accurate feedback, you can't improve anything. See Chapter 15.

SELECTING GDN OFFERS

No one ever goes to a non-Google website hoping to see Google ads. If you're advertising on GDN, by definition your ads will be shown to people who are concentrating on something else.

That doesn't mean your ads have to be an interruption or an annoyance. For the most part people accept advertising as part of the fabric of the internet, television, radio, and print. At worst, we simply tune ads out.

Some commercials go viral and become very popular. People share them on social media and seek them out on YouTube. Super Bowl commercials, for example, are like this.

It may be ambitious for you to take a simple GDN ad and try to make it a viral success like a Super Bowl ad, but there's no reason why you can't create interesting ads that people genuinely like and appreciate.

Interruption marketing is about gently capturing attention, warming people up with a genuinely enticing and generous offer, and then over-delivering in a way that leaves a pleasant, lingering afterglow. On the other hand, dropping people straight into your order form and asking them to hand over some cash with a GDN campaign probably won't work.

Instead, think of your viewers as being right at the top of your funnel. This means offering them something valuable and intriguing, with few or no strings attached. Give something away, something for free. Maybe it's a coupon, a white paper, a webinar,

Chisel Your Way In with the Display Network

It might "officially" cost $100 to acquire a customer with brute force, but you can still get 'em for $40 if you use finesse.

The Neanderthal way to penetrate a market is to jack up your bid price.

And sure, if you are the guy or gal who can outspend all others, you can become the 800-pound gorilla.

But that is not the only way.

Imagine this:

Getting more of your ideal customers affordably is like penetrating a fortress on a day where a thick fog shrouds everything and you literally cannot see three feet in front of you.

Yes, you can sit there and fire cannon shots into the mist, hoping that one eventually pounds through the mortar.

You hope that if it does get through, you are actually able to somehow know it got through, considering you can't see a single thing.

Or you could shine some other kind of light at some other frequency, like night goggles, clearly seeing that if you stand on a 20-foot scaffolding and fire your gun at the perfect angle, you can take out the castle's entire electrical system in one shot.

Not only that, there are 40 other angles that could work as well. If you just knew where the general was sleeping, a raven could drop a hand grenade down his chimney and it would all be over. There's also a window where you can see the king's chair and a round of bullets would take him out in 12 seconds.

In every market there are MANY angles in.

Understand this: *Every specific way of targeting users and bidding on Google's Display Network is an "angle in."*

Managed placement targeting, topic targeting, keyword and behavioral targeting are the ways of targeting users. Any specific combination of two of these ("target these keywords AND these behaviors") is usually not being used by one of your direct competitors.

Chisel Your Way In with the Display Network, continued

Cost Per Impression, Cost Per Click and Cost Per Action are your bidding angles, ways into the fortress. The point is to choose a specific strategy, then optimize it.

Add to this the fact that specific ad types further specify your strategy.

When you are getting started—or when you are trying to Chisel Your Way In—you need to focus your efforts on a specific combination that *narrows* your focus. So for example you could choose:

- Target keywords related to tuxedos AND user behaviors related to weddings;
- Use Cost Per Action bidding and define your action as people clicking to the tuxedo order page;
- Only use 300x250 pixel image ads.

This targets very finite, clearly defined niche within a niche where the data you generate will be very clear. Again, it is unlikely that any of your direct competitors are using this exact strategy, so there will be pockets in the GDN "space" where your strategy is superior.

The way to Chisel Your Way In to the fortress is to gain a toe-hold—find a tiny spot where your ads are working; then get a foothold, and eventually, a strangle hold.

a mindmap, or a software demo. There's nothing I can think of more effective for a GDN campaign than giving away something for free that contains genuine value. It creates a good impression of your brand and it enables you to entice them to return to your website at a later date. Plus you can use the word "free" in your ads! That's every customer's favorite word.

Try putting your free gift behind an email capture form. Or you can simply direct clicks straight to your download page. That's especially worthwhile if you're doing remarketing. (More on that in a later chapter.) This approach is also a winner because it will attract more clicks. It causes Google to recognize your ad as relevant and show it more frequently. Which will result in even more clicks. Which causes Google to show your ad more frequently, and just like that, you've got yourself a virtuous cycle.

> ### Forget Branding: This Is about Results
>
> Pure branding-only on GDN will get you nowhere. In the early days of Google, a few advertisers would try creating display ads with their brand name, but worded in such a way so as to discourage clicks. The goal was to get free brand exposure without having to pay for those pesky clicks. Don't bother trying to do this now. Google is long since wise to the practice. If your ad receives no clicks, Google will soon stop showing your ad altogether.

YOUR QUICK ACTION SUMMARY

In the next chapter we're going to look at some advanced GDN techniques and discover how to really tap into the power of this network. But first make sure you've carried out all of these steps carefully:

- Think of a simple, free offer that can form the foundation of your GDN campaign.
- Go to Google's Display Planner and research your options on topics, interests, keywords, and websites to target.
- Decide whether you want to proceed! If you're a beginner, you may wish to skip ahead and return to the GDN once you've gained some valuable experience on Search.
- Check that your website is probably configured to record conversions. You cannot carry out effective GDN advertising, or in fact any PPC advertising, without a competent system for measuring conversions.
- Choose your bidding option. CPC is best in most cases.

Google's Display Network
The Greatest Testing Playground in History

Imagine that a company named *Generico Housing Insurance Inc.* wants to build an ad campaign to promote its new insurance coverage for egg damage caused by bored teenagers. Which approach do you think will get the company more new signups?

1. *HiPPO Selection.* The graphic designer develops four ads with very different visual styles and reveals them at the next board meeting. The president of the company takes the role of the HiPPO ("Highest Paid Person's Opinion," a term coined by Google Analytics expert Avinash Kaushik). The image in design #2 makes him laugh and the color scheme reminds him

of the new curtains his wife just picked out, so he chooses that one to run online, in print, and on TV.

2. *Street Selection.* The graphic designer develops four ads with very different visual styles. A market researcher is paid a large sum of money to go out on the street and ask people at random to rate the ads, asking them which one they find most attractive, most likely to create trust, most likely to appeal to older people, and so on.

If you're thinking both approaches seem a little shaky, you're absolutely correct. It should scare you that a large proportion of businesses still develop their ad campaigns using these methods.

Marketing becomes a lottery. If you fail, you blame it on the designer. If you succeed you conclude that HiPPOs or random disinterested strangers know best how to choose a winning campaign.

It should be obvious why HiPPO selection is a bad idea. No single individual, no matter how experienced he or she is, can perfectly predict the performance of an ad campaign. But the street selection approach is also flawed. It's one thing to voice an opinion about how pretty an ad campaign looks; it's another thing entirely to actually be motivated to buy. Most folks on the street don't know the difference.

There's a third way. It's inexpensive, easy to set up, and as impartial as you'll ever find.

We're going to use the Google Display Network (GDN). We'll use live, real-world market research on advertising styles, and then plan our online strategy based on concrete numerical results.

THE POWER OF A BLIND TEST

Let's say the marketing department at *Generico* has decided to go with the GDN method to test its campaign. They create two display ads. The copy in both is identical; only the images are different. Ad #1 shows a house being egged by teenagers. Ad #2 shows a pretty home with a nicely dressed, attractive family standing out front. The call-to-action in both is to click through to the website and request an insurance quote.

At first, *Generico* has no way of knowing which ad will generate more quotes. Doesn't matter; Google will show the ads to a few thousand people, and within a week or two there's a clear winner. *Generico* now knows which image to use as it invests more advertising dollars in its website, GDN, print ads, business cards, and even TV commercials.

This works because we're measuring *actual physical behavior* in real time, not just verbal opinions. People are clicking their mouse and filling out forms . . . or failing to. When they see the *Generico* ad online they have no idea they're participating in a split test. They're simply responding based on whether the ad triggers them to want insurance or not.

GDN is never a branding exercise, and it's never opinion polling. It's observing your target market making live decisions and learning what excites their interest or leaves them cold.

Don't waste thousands of dollars creating huge portfolios of advertising and marketing collateral. Spend just a few hundred dollars up front testing ads and you'll know which images, color schemes, headlines, and calls to action give you the results you want.

"TEST THE FOREST" FIRST

Our colleague David Bullock has given us a great verbal rule of thumb for testing ads and marketing campaigns:

> *First test forests, then test trees,*
> *then test branches, then test leaves.*

Test the big difference-making stuff first. Go after finer points later. How far down you drill will depend on your patience for this kind of work and, of course, your budget.

In this scenario, the "forest" is two things:

1. Your headline, hook, call-to-action, offer, or guarantee.
2. The overall aesthetic design of your ad: color schemes, styles, layout, and tone; bold versus subtle, traditional versus modern, serious versus comic, masculine versus feminine, young versus old, and everything in between.

Let's say you plan to test images of people in your ads. Try different ages as well as both genders. Right off the bat, that gives you four variations: older men, older women, younger women, and younger men. Which one will your target market respond to? After a few thousand impressions you'll know.

The one thing split testing teaches you above all else is that there is *no predicting* what will and will not make a drastic difference.

There are so many different things you can test:

- *Image style:* hi-res color photo, black-and-white classic, hand-drawn picture, or even no image at all.
- *Text formatting:* color, font, size, bold or italic.
- *Dominant color:* Colors have a huge impact on ad performance. Different colors and different levels of light or dark will evoke wildly different moods. If you're carefully targeting sites on GDN to show your ads, think about what color schemes will make your ads stand out on the page rather than blending into the background.

■ *Call-to-Action:* Ideally this should be prominent. Even better if it's in the form of a button. We're trained to click on buttons. Your entire ad may be clickable, but if you feature a boldly colored button people will click there more than any place else on your image.

The Power of the Right Call-to-Action

There are few elements of an ad more important than a call-to-action. The more specific you are, the more likely you'll get clicks. Phrases such as "Download Here" or "Go here to watch the video" may seem obvious, but they work.

Related tip: Create a call-to-action button that's a sharply different color from the rest of your ad. For instance, if your ad features an image of a tent in the middle of a wooded area, don't use a green button; use white, yellow, or even red.

WHICH AD SIZE SHOULD I START WITH?

Google's Display Network gives you a wide variety of ad sizes, but you need to stick to just one size until you've identified your winning ad style.

It's simple math. If you create ten different styles of image ads—a good number to start with—but you attempt to test each of these in eight possible image sizes, you'll end up creating 80 different ads. That's unwieldy, and a waste of time.

The first size to test is 300 x 250 pixels. (This is officially called a "medium rectangle," "med rec," or "inline rectangle"). It's one of the most common sizes supported by sites on

An Ad Size Tweak to Boost Your Mobile Performance

Mobile devices support a variety of different ad sizes. For instance, the medium rectangle will display on most smartphones.

There's one size that will only show on mobiles and which is well worth adding to your campaign for this reason: the mobile leaderboard (320 x 50). Few advertisers bother to create ads specifically for mobiles, so here's an opportunity for you to dominate your market. Assuming you've already tested and selected a winning design, adding a mobile leaderboard version to your campaign can significantly boost your mobile performance.

GDN, so you'll be sure to get plenty of placement. Most importantly, in our experience it's the size that draws the highest CTR, which is the key factor at this stage.

The leaderboard size (728 x 90) also gets good impressions. Clicks and conversions won't be at quite the same level as the medium rectangle, but this is the next best size to go after.

Once you've tested those, try the large rectangle (336 x 280), wide skyscraper (160 x 600), and half page (300 x 600).

Tip: Plan on your best ad outperforming your worst ad by a factor of three.

As of this writing, Google supports 14 different images sizes. However, the 80/20 rule applies here: Most of the available sizes will get very limited exposure on GDN sites. There's little point in creating image ads for every size unless you're attempting to completely max out your impressions. Otherwise it's a law of diminishing returns.

HOW TO CREATE GORGEOUS ADS

Once you've come up with the ideas for ten different ads, you're ready to create the ads. Make them the same size (300 x 250) and use static images. Save animated images until after you've identified your best performing static image and style.

Assuming you're not a hands-on graphic designer, you have three good options:

1. Use Google's Ad Gallery

This used to be called the Display Ad Builder (DAB). Find it by going into an ad group within a Display Network enabled campaign, and clicking the red "+ AD" button:

You can use any one of Google's free preset templates and insert your own images and text, or you can use Google's auto-create feature that automatically generates ads by searching your website and existing Search ads. (The results aren't always the best looking but the tool is free, quick, and easy.)

2. Find a Budget Designer

There's a plethora of online services that will create image ads for you. We like 20dollarbanners.com and minibannerszen.com, where for $20 to 30 a piece, you can have some nice custom designs crafted in a few days or even hours. Both of these websites have portfolio pages, which are worth perusing if you're short on ideas.

3. Hire a Pro Designer

Find the right professional freelance graphic designer, one who takes time with the creative process and isn't grinding out dozens or hundreds of designs per day, and you can end up with some stunning and original images for your campaign.

Important tip: There's a downside to this and, no, it isn't price. (In most cases, hiring pro designers isn't substantially more expensive than finding a budget designer.) Most graphic designers don't understand the testing concepts we cover in this book. They'll expect you to brief them on one style that they can recreate in a variety of formats. The notion of creating ten completely different designs, all the same size, will baffle most designers. You need to either educate them or search until you find a designer amenable to this strategy.

We use the services of Laura Husmann at BannerAdQueen.com. We cannot recommend her highly enough. Her prices are good, her designs are outstanding, and she thoroughly understands AdWords advertisers and the concept of testing. If you want top quality images—particularly if you're an agency handling the campaigns of multiple clients—she should be your first choice.

HOW TO KEEP YOUR ADS IN GOOGLE'S GOOD GRACES

If you're hiring a pro designer who's relatively new to GDN ads, send them to this section of the book and have them read it carefully.

Google has explicit rules on what is and isn't allowed in image ads. Check every one of your ads against Google's requirements before activating your campaign. Here are a few the rules that GDN users most commonly fail to apply.

Technical Specifications

- Static images must be in jpg, png, or gif format, and be of a file size no greater than 150 KB.

■ Animated images must be an animated gif or the correct version of Flash (swf), must run for no longer than 30 seconds (looping images are allowed, but must cease movement after 30 seconds), and be no more than five frames per second (fps) for gifs and 20 fps for swf. In either case, 150 KB is still the maximum file size.

Content Specifications

■ No "trick to click" ads. The ad must look like an ad and clearly differentiate itself from the rest of the page on which it resides. If the ad is designed to look like a system warning or error message, it will be flagged and disabled.

■ The ad image must fill the entire image size and be correctly oriented.

■ The ad image cannot be "tiled" or appear to be more than one image (for example, one image designed to look like three different text ads).

■ As with all AdWords campaigns, the ad must be relevant to the landing page it's sending people to.

■ The image must be of a high quality without any fuzziness or blurred images.

■ All text on the image must be legible.

■ Animated images cannot use strobe or flashing lights.

■ The image *must* be suitable for a family audience. Google takes a hard line on this one. Nothing even remotely borderline will be tolerated.

DISPLAY CAMPAIGN OPTIMIZER: IS THERE BENEFIT IN HANDING OVER THE KEYS?

Let's admit it: PPC takes work if you're going to do it effectively.

Large campaigns in particular can be a considerable time sink. Scary as it may sound, you might want to consider letting Google sit in the driver's seat.

Google offers a tool called the Display Campaign Optimizer (DCO). As of this writing it's only available on limited release to select advertisers. It behaves essentially like Conversion Optimizer for Search. You specify a target cost per acquisition and the tool takes control of all your targeting and bidding decisions.

The biggest barrier to this is the issue of trust. Letting Google take ownership of your bids? Isn't that like letting the Doberman guard the ham sandwiches?

A couple of things may alleviate your concern. The first is that Google will never burn through your budget without providing something in return. They know that to keep you as an advertiser they'll need to improve your CTR, hit or beat your CPA target, and decrease your average CPC if possible.

The second thing to consider is the vast storehouses of data that Google can access when deciding when, where, and how often to show your ads. We might be able to see

some of the basic information about the people that click on our ads, such as device used, location, time of day, etc., but Google has far greater depth of information that it can't practically share with us but that it can use to manage your GDN campaigns.

We've found that DCO improves Display Network performance around 80 percent of the time. When DCO works, it can outperform all but greatest of PPC experts.

Some words of caution, however. Google says that you need to hit 15 conversions in 30 days to be eligible to use the DCO. We advise you to wait until you've recorded at least 50. Even better if you have 100. The more data you build up, the better the DCO will be at delivering results. Don't be surprised to see your CPA *increase* initially with DCO, particularly during the first couple of weeks. For example, if you set a target CPA of $50, DCO may only be able to get you conversions for $60 CPA during that first couple of weeks, before eventually dropping it to $50 or less later on.

Once you've established your initial presence on the Display Network, we're convinced that you'll find DCO to be a valuable tool worth testing.

HOW TO TAKE A RIDE ON THE JET STREAM

Once you start seeing some initial success on GDN, you'll notice a surprising effect that we like to call the Jet Stream.

It's what happens when Google notices that an ad is performing above average.

It may even scare you at first.

GDN is vast, and Google always has an enormous inventory of sites to provide ads for. When Google sees that you've got an ad getting an especially high CTR, they'll use it as often as possible. If they show it on more new sites and your CTR still holds strong, the cycle will continue: Google will show your ad in more and more places and begin to "spider" it out further and further across their network.

Let's say you run a campaign that targets owners of Labradoodles. Google will naturally place your ad on Labradoodle sites to start with. But if it gets an unusually high CTR there, they'll try it on sites about German shepherds and Staffordshire terriers. If the excellent CTR *still* holds, any dog-related site will become fair game. And then any pet-related site. And so on. Google will serve your ad on a broader and broader basis until they find sites where it no longer performs.

When first-time GDN users experience the Jet Stream, they sometimes freak out. They see their impressions going through the roof and their ad showing up on all kinds of unexpected sites.

None of this is anything to worry about. You're taking a ride on the Jet Stream because your ad is performing above the average. Your diligent testing has proven worthwhile.

Google will, of course, keep adjusting where it serves your ads to try to maintain your high CTR. If you're unhappy with any of the sites Google chooses to target, you can opt for "Managed Placement Targeting" instead.

YOUR QUICK ACTION SUMMARY

The Display Network is arguably the most effective way to test new advertising and marketing ideas. Why settle for simple brand ads when you can learn exactly what makes your target audience buy from you, for just a few hundred dollars of testing?

- Brainstorm ten dramatically different ad styles.
- Use Google's Ad Gallery tool or hire a designer to create your ads in the 300 x 250 format.
- Test your ads and, once you have a winner, continue to test minor variations on this theme.
- Once your campaign has generated a minimum of 50 conversions, consider activating Display Campaign Optimizer.

Uncle Claude Sez

Now we let the thousands decide what the millions will do. We make a small venture, and watch cost and result. When we learn what a thousand customers cost, we know almost exactly what a million will cost. When we learn what they buy, we know what a million will buy.

Chisel Your Way In with YouTube
Billions of Eyeballs for Pennies

Thanks to Ryan Masters and Antonio Centeno for help with this chapter.

YouTube advertising may well be the most cost-effective AdWords channel available. This chapter will show you five simple steps to get your first YouTube ad campaign up and running, along with three dynamite tricks for getting more out of YouTube, including a method for getting a some your advertising for free.

Having worked very closely with hundreds of business startups, and at a distance with many thousands more, I can tell you that most entrepreneur success stories include some kind of unfair advantage they were wise enough to

exploit along the way. For marketers, surprisingly often that unfair advantage is an *advertising media* advantage.

For example, in 2002, before I'd ever considered going into the Google AdWords business, my friend Ken McCarthy asked me who he should get to speak on Google AdWords at his seminar. I gave him the name of a guy. The guy turned Ken down.

Ken came back to me and said, "He said no. Perry, I think YOU should speak at my seminar." That's how I got into the AdWords business.

Speaking at that seminar was an "unfair advantage" compared to everyone else who was marketing exclusively online. The reason was, Ken had already assembled a hot rabid community of marketers and all I had to do was show a band of cave men how to make fire and they were off to the races.

Two months later, I had a bevy of hot, exciting testimonials and a collection of great customers and raving fans. That became the cornerstone of my new business. That extra head start was enough to propel me through one of the most brutally competitive land-grabs in internet history.

Similarly, during the next five years, AdWords clicks were bargain priced if you knew what you were doing. Thus, I witnessed thousands of businesses launch and thrive; businesses that would have struggled without that media advantage.

Can you still find pockets of media advantage in AdWords? Yes, you can—in YouTube. You can and should use that advantage as your chisel.

Imagine a TV network with an audience of over one billion pairs of eyes, collectively watching over six billion hours of content every month.

Imagine that this television network allows you to advertise on their network for a few pennies per eyeball—in some cases, for free.

Imagine that this television network allows viewers to directly express interest in your product or service, and only charges you a few cents every time that happens.

Imagine that, once you've created your television ad, you can set it to go live in a matter of minutes.

This is YouTube we're talking about. It's the world's second largest search engine behind Google itself. It gives you the chance to reach its staggeringly large audience.

On YouTube you can place promotional videos. Image ads. Text ads. It's all done via Google Display Network (GDN).

So rich is the opportunity here that it's actually worth digging into your pockets and investing in the creation of a commercial *right now,* even if it's simply a "talking head" video of you discussing your main product or service.

Google highlights four main benefits of YouTube advertising:

1. You can tell your own story while protecting your brand in a safe environment.

2. You can reach a large audience that is highly engaged with the content they are consuming

3. You can create a video campaign in minutes.

4. You can accurately measure and track how it's working.

Chisel Your Way In: The most significant benefit of all? YouTube is one of the *most cost-effective* of all AdWords advertising options. It's poorly understood and under-exploited. You can show a video to a precisely targeted audience for a *fraction* of what you'd pay for a plain old text ad on a Google Search page! If you're just getting started or if you're in a hyper-competitive market, YouTube is a great place to get a toe-hold—so you can then get a foot-hold and eventually a strangle-hold.

I cannot emphasize enough how advantageous it is to have an edge in advertising media when you're launching a new business. When you're just starting out, you need every advantage you can get. It's hard to overstate how much it helps you when you can get new customers for half or a third what they cost everywhere else. That one edge buys you some extra grace for the other mistakes you'll inevitably make.

YouTube can be that cheap traffic source you're looking for, if you know how to do it right.

HOW TO CREATE A YOUTUBE ADVERTISING CAMPAIGN

If you haven't already done so, link your YouTube channel to your AdWords account. Instructions for that are here: https://support.google.com/youtube/answer/3063482.

From the "All online campaigns" page, click the red "+ Campaign" button and choose the last option: "Online Video."

You may notice this screen looks a bit different—that's OK. This is the AdWords for Video Tool which is separate from the AdWords dashboard you're used to seeing. This allows you to see more video and YouTube specific metrics, such as subscribers earned and how much of the video viewers watched.

To access the AdWords for Video tool at any point, just click the "All Video Campaigns" link on the left-hand column under "Labels."

You'll begin by selecting the usual options—your daily budget, your preferred locations, how you want to target, etc. After that you have a number of additional steps that include setting up targeting for your campaign, and finally creating ads especially for this group.

See the previous chapter on Google's Display Network for an introduction to this.

Step One: Choose Your Bid Type

The precise name for the bid type you want is "Maximum Cost Per View." Here's where you set the upper limit on how much you pay each time a person watches a portion of your video.

YouTube has a number of different advertising formats. You can either select one single bid that applies to all of them, or you can go the custom route and set a different bid for each format.

For your first campaign, we suggest starting with in-display ads getting the highest priority at $0.10-0.40 CPV and setting your in-stream bid to half that amount.. You can optimize this later, once you've built up a useful amount of data about your clicks and views.

Step Two: Choose Your Target Audience

Which group of YouTube users do you want to reach? You have three ways to slice up the network and zero in on your preferred audience:

1. *Demographic.* Choose from either gender and a variety of age ranges.
2. *Topics.* This is very similar to the types of topics you can target with GDN. There are main topics, subtopics, and sub subtopics. Google gives you roughly 2,000 options. If, for example, you're a developer of antivirus software, you *could* go after the broadest possible group, folks interested in "computers and electronics." But you'll be better off going for the subtopic "computer security." Even better, drill further down to "antivirus and malware."

 This means your ads will be showing on *videos* related to the topics you've chosen. So if you're targeting the topic "computer security," your ads will only run on videos Google determines are related to computer security (from the video tags, comments, titles, and metadata).

3. *People Interested In*. This is a relatively new option. It's Google's attempt at creating targeted groups more like what television advertisers are used to. These are also referred to as "affinity categories." They target people with fairly specific interests such as do-it-yourselfers, fashionistas, news junkies, savvy parents, foodies, and shutterbugs.

Targeting

By default your ads will show to all viewers. Optionally you can refine your audience.

Demographic [?] **Any gender, Any age** Edit

Interests [?]

Enter a word, phrase, or website

⊟ Affinity categories (reach)
 Art & Theater Aficionados add »
 ⊞ Auto Enthusiasts add »
 Avid Investors add »
 Beauty Mavens add »
 ⊞ Cooking Enthusiasts add »
 Do-It-Yourselfers add »
 Fashionistas add »
 Fast Food Cravers add »
 Foodies add »
 ⊞ Gamers add »
 Green Living Enthusiasts add »
 Health & Fitness Buffs add »

DONE Cancel

Narrow your targeting (optional) ▾

This means your ads might show on any video, but are only targeted to *individuals* whose browsing history matches the interest category you choose. So let's say you're a local baker targeting the interest category "foodies." Even though someone may be watching a music video when your ad appears, that's OK because earlier this viewer was on the Food Network reading recipes, so Google labeled them as a "foodie."

4. *Placements*. Just like we discussed in Chapter 17 on the Google Display Network, you can target individual YouTube videos or YouTube Channels by adding the URL as a placement target.

5. *Keywords*. These work just like contextual targeting on the GDN, but apply only to videos on the entire network.

You can combine multiple targeting methods for a more specific, targeted audience. For example, you could target women ages 35 to 54 (demographics) who are dog lovers

(interests) watching videos about dogs (topics). These targeting options allow you to get really specific and clear on your audience so you can create a more relevant video ad to compel them to take action.

Step Three: Target People Who Are Searching For . . .

In addition to targeting YouTube users based on their interests and demographics, you can also target specific keywords people type into the YouTube search bar. Your ads only appear when those exact words or phrases get searched on. Note: At the time of revising this 4th edition, this keyword bidding feature appears to be unreliable.

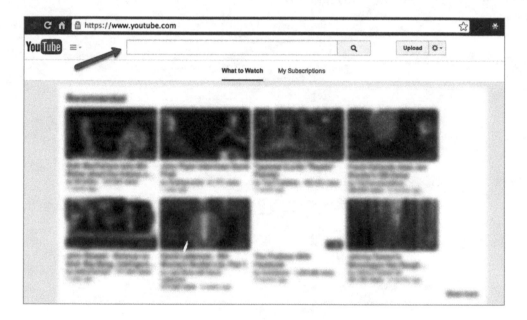

Step Four: Create Your Ad

Creating an ad can be simple. Pick a video from your linked YouTube channel, choose from the targeting groups you selected, and then select your preferred ad format. You have two options:

In-stream videos are the video ads that play immediately before the video the user has chosen to watch. Sometimes after five seconds the user has the option to click and skip.

*This means you want the first five seconds of your video to **grab** the viewer.* These five seconds play a role equivalent to the headline in your Google text ads.

In-display ads are the video ads that you see in the right-hand column on video pages, and at the top of the results of a YouTube Search. When creating these ads, keep in mind the video thumbnail and headline are all a viewer will see in order to entice them to click, so make sure you pick the most compelling combination.

Step Five: Select Ad Attributes

Ad attributes include things like the text of the ad (for in-display ads), the destination URL, the image thumbnail, and the name of the ad. There are some more advanced ones, too:

- *Destination.* Do you want the person who clicks on your in-display ad to be directed to a specific video, or to your YouTube channel? If you haven't taken the time to properly optimize your YouTube channel, go with the first option.
- *Companion banner.* This is a 300 x 60 image that shows to the side of in-stream videos. It doesn't cost you any extra, and it gives you additional branding space. Take advantage of it.

These steps are all you need to start your ads running. But don't forget: *Monitor your results.*

The Reporting feature lets you segment the results in lots of different ways, including formats, network (your video ads can be shown on the GDN as well as on YouTube), targeting groups, and device. Take full advantage of this data so that you can see which ads are working best with the different targeting options you've selected. You can also optimize these campaigns using the peel and stick method and negative placements we've described in previous chapters.

SOME ADDITIONAL YOUTUBE TRICKS

Here are some tricks you can employ with YouTube that you can't use with Google Search or GDN. They let you reap maximum gains from your advertising.

Tracking Viewers

There's a way to track your visitor behavior in Google Analytics more easily. Before you enter a destination URL into your ads, first run it through Google's URL Builder (https://support.google.com/analytics/answer/1033867).

Tell Google your regular URL and then enter your:

- Campaign Source (that's "YouTube" in this case)
- Campaign Medium ("video")
- Campaign Name (anything you like that's relevant)

Ignore the "Campaign Term and Content" for now. Hit "Submit" and Google will provide you with a new URL containing these variables. Insert this new URL as the destination for your ad and this will make it much easier to track your visitor behavior in Analytics.

If you've linked your Google Analytics account to your AdWords account you can see more detailed performance metrics. In your Analytics account click on "Reporting" the top of the page. You'll then see some navigation options on the left. Look for "Acquisition" and click to expand it. Under the "AdWords" option is a link to "Video Campaigns." Here you'll be able to evaluate the engagement and conversion level of viewers who visited your website from your YouTube ads.

Free Ads? Yes!

Google only charges you for in-stream ads if the user watches the first thirty seconds of your video, or all of it if it's shorter than thirty seconds. Consequently, if you can persuade the viewer to click on your ad before that point, you won't pay a cent for the traffic.

The trick to accomplishing this? Give the viewer a strong call-to-action in the first 15 to 20 seconds that invites them to click on your video and visit your landing page. *This is really important.* Our colleagues Ryan Masters and Antonio Centeno get clicks for under ten cents and sales leads for under $2 in very competitive markets, on YouTube, using videos that include a strong call-to-action in the first 20 seconds.

Hint: You can increase your clickthrough rate on this by including at that spot in your video a noticeable graphic that looks like a button. The entire video area is clickable, but the image of a button will entice people to click. This is especially true if you also include a line of text, underlined in blue; that's the universal format for a clickable link.

YOUTUBE CAN DELIVER HUGE TORRENTS OF TRAFFIC

My first "YouTube" epiphany didn't even involve the YouTube-specific ad interface. It was my experiments with Image Ads. I posted a 300 x 250 pixel image ad that happened

to coincide with specific YouTube videos, and *kablamo*! I got buckets of traffic for pennies a click. The conversion rates weren't great; I was getting 4 percent opt-in rates, where other ads in other places got 8 percent. But the traffic was so cheap, and in such volumes, it didn't matter. It was an avalanche.

That was five years ago. YouTube continues to be one of my favorite secret fishing holes. I suspect it may stay that way for a long time!

Simple Branding Using In-Stream Videos

Viewers can't skip in-stream videos for the first five seconds, so pepper the opening frames of your ads with strong branding elements. Even if they skip the video at the first possible opportunity, you will at least have ensured they know who you are and what you were advertising.

Remarketing

Did you know that you can also build remarketing lists based entirely on YouTube users? (See Chapter 24 on remarketing.) Choose from people who:

- Interacted with or viewed your videos
- Subscribed to your channel (or unsubscribed)
- Viewed your in-stream video
- Visited your channel page
- Liked or disliked any of your videos
- Liked or disliked certain videos
- Left a comment (more engaged)

Add these people to one or more of your remarketing lists and you can then remarket to them in the usual way through regular GDN campaigns. You can even remarket exclusively on YouTube.

YOUR QUICK ACTION SUMMARY

YouTube advertising is the jewel in the Display Network crown. It's easy to set up, cost-effective, and gives you virtually unlimited access to the second largest search engine in the world.

- Link your YouTube channel to your AdWords account.
- Choose your maximum bid and target audience.

- Create your ad and select your ad attributes.
- For more advanced tracking, run your YouTube landing page URL through Google's URL Builder and link your AdWords and Analytics accounts
- Get a portion of your advertising for free by adding a call-to-action to your in-stream ads around the 15- to 20-second mark.
- Set up a remarketing list for your YouTube ads to increase your conversions.

The 27-Second Tip That Boosts Your Conversions with YouTube Ads
By Ryan Masters and Antonio Centeno

YouTube is a hidden goldmine gushing with quality, cheap traffic. To date there are millions of customer eyeballs available at pennies on the dollar, and we've gotten them as low $0.02.

And here's the kicker . . .

Your competitors are leaving this traffic by the wayside.

Why?

Because they tried advertising on YouTube and it "didn't work."

Prospects clicked on their ad, watched part of their video, and left.

Dang.

The problem isn't with the ads . . . its the video the ads are sending them to!

This is the critical piece 99 percent of advertisers overlook.

Doesn't matter how good or cheap your ads are: If no one takes action, it's a waste.

People watch videos to be entertained. They will *not* be bored. So if you are not entertaining them, click!, it's on to the next video. You don't need a fancy lighting crew, Hollywood budget, or writers from *Saturday Night Live* to create entertaining videos.

All you need is something we call *the 27 Power Intro*.

It consists of three parts—hook, call-to-action, and credibility.

The 27-Second Tip, continued

1. *Hook*. Think of this as the headline of your video. In the very beginning, tell your audience *why* they should watch the video. What benefit(s) will they gain?

2. *Call-to-action*. What do you want viewers to do? Opt in to an email report? Purchase a physical product? Schedule an appointment? Whatever it is, tell them right in the beginning, while you still have their attention, and be sure to include a link to your website landing page in the first line of the YouTube description. Then, in the video, make sure you point below you, to the ground, when giving the call-to-action. This way viewers will clearly see the link and will be more likely to click through and take the desired action.

3. *Credibility*. Why should they listen to you? Here is the time to mention any certifications, years' experience, or some type of credibility indicator. Keep in mind this can be for any reason—even self-appointed positioning!

You simply need to demonstrate these to your viewers inside the first 27 seconds of your video so they stick around (or go right to your website).

Especially if you're paying for traffic to watch the video.

Let's say John the real estate agent was reading this and decides he wants to capture more leads from a YouTube Video. Here is a *27 Power Intro* he might use:

Hi I'm John, the area's #1 real estate broker [credibility] and in this short video I'm going to show you how to AVOID excess closing costs in your mortgage [hook], BUT before I do that, make sure you assess your preparedness with my free, 60-second online tool, "How much money will you leave on the table when you close? [call-to-action.]

That's all you need, more traffic will go to your website and convert if you simply include a 27 Power Intro.

You can get additional YouTube marketing tips in the online bonuses for book buyers. Go to www.perrymarshall.com/supplement.

Social Media Is the New SEO

Do you have a business that relies on organic, "Search Engine Optimization" traffic? Are you getting sick and tired of all the algorithm changes made by Google seemingly every other week? Why not take control and focus on bringing highly targeted visitors, who already have proven to have a propensity to buy your product or service?

Or, better yet, why not focus on bringing visitors to your site who have similar likes and interests, demographic data, and psychographic data as your current customers?

In the previous edition of this book we discussed how to use "right-angle" targeting to improve your AdWords campaigns. Some of Facebook's newer features are taking "right-angle" marketing to a whole new level.

We also discussed using a Facebook Connect application to collect data from your subscribers. Due to the rapid pace of changes in technology I will tell you that there are many different options for creating a Facebook Connect application, where you can require a potential subscriber to "connect with Facebook" in order to receive something from you. This is essentially an opt-in using Facebook. The great thing about this is that you are getting a good email address—the one he or she uses for Facebook. And, depending on which application you use, you can gather a ton of valuable data on the most common likes and interests of your new subscribers.

You can do a Google search or visit the Perry Marshall blog for the latest reference on Facebook Connect Apps.

THE FACEBOOK SOCIAL GRAPH

As mentioned above you can get very technical and detailed on your target audience and existing audience. However, if you would like to "80/20" this process and get highly relevant data very quickly, just use Facebook's Graph Search.

Note: the Facebook social graph is getting exponentially smarter every month. By the time you are reading this chapter the data they have on users that is available to us will far exceed what it is at the time of this writing. Just go to the Facebook search bar and start discovering what the common likes and interests of your fans and your competitor's fans are.

You can get as granular as you want and as creative as you want with your Facebook searches.

For example, you could specify pages liked by people who "like" Perry Marshall and also "like" the band Rush. See the image on page 193.

HOW WE USED FACEBOOK RIGHT-ANGLE TARGETING TO IMPROVE GOOGLE CAMPAIGNS BY 11 PERCENT, OVERNIGHT

Bryan Todd was driving traffic to the website CosmicFingerPrints.com. This site discusses the intersection between science, astronomy, and religion. Bryan was running ads on Facebook driving traffic to the page and seeking an opt-in to "Learn the Secrets of the Universe."

After a while, Bryan ran a Facebook responder profile report and noticed that his responders had an interest in science fiction, history, and really liked the books *Brave*

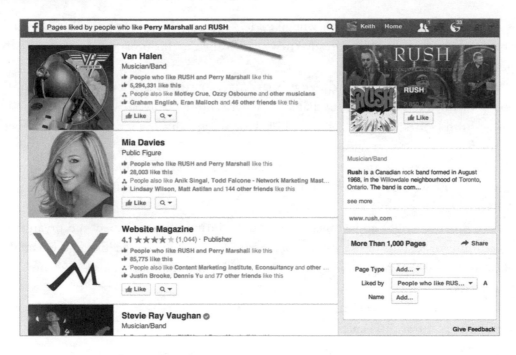

New World and *1984*. So, he split-test two landing pages, which were identical except that one page inserted the following two lines:

> *This ultimate question touches the distant past, and—with the forewarnings in Orwell's 1984 and Huxley's Brave New World—it touches the distant future as well.*

Bryan recognized that people who like science fiction think about the distant future and the distant past, and he already knew specifically that his prospects liked these two books.

In hindsight, like most right-angle marketing connections, they all go together. If you're inclined to click on an ad that says "Where Did the Universe Come From? Did It Come from God?" you probably do all of these things. Bryan added this one sentence to the page.

The conversion rate for the page increased by 11 percent. That 11 percent improvement worked across the board, not just for Facebook traffic, but for Google AdWords traffic as well!

To prove the right-angle concept, at no time during this experiment did Bryan ever specifically target fans of *Brave New World* or *1984*. He didn't change his targeting at all. He only proved that people we targeted for completely different reasons also responded to these book titles.

(Of course we do use right angles to laser in on new target audiences, too! But that wasn't the point of this experiment.)

THE REVOLUTIONARY "ONE SENTENCE" PRINCIPLE

Most people would never expect one sentence to improve conversions by 11 percent the way this did. Especially one that's just innocently added to the third paragraph, with no change to the headline, pictures, or offer! This worked because it pressed invisible buttons in the reader's mind and heart. This technique works in almost any market.

There is a sentence that will increase your conversions 10 to 15 percent. All you have to do is find out what it is and add it to your landing page. But you'll probably never discover it without the assistance of social media.

This is the most powerful thing about Facebook marketing. It's not the ability to post free status messages. It's not the ability to have 10,000 fans for free. This is so non-obvious, it doesn't surprise me that hardly anyone else is talking about it. But it's astonishingly powerful. Because Facebook tracks thousands of bits of information, like peoples' favorite:

■ Books
■ Artists
■ Movies and TV shows
■ Experts people follow
■ Topics people are engaging with right now
■ Sports teams

- Politicians
- Hobbies

Facebook also tracks thousands of bits of valuable offline data (derived from the partner categories), like:

- Personal income
- Net worth
- Type of vehicle
- Value of vehicle
- Job role
- Corporate
- Employment data
- Charitable donation history
- Recent relationship history (Recently married, engaged, divorced, etc.)
- Age of children
- Grocery purchase behavior
- Recently moved
- And much more . . .

SUPERCHARGE YOUR EMAIL MARKETING WITH CUSTOM AUDIENCES

With Facebook advertising, you can export any email or phone list as small as 20 people and upload that list into Facebook as a new target audience. Facebook will go through a mining process of matching up all the emails to their database. After about an hour, you will have a new target audience for your content or banner ads. This is called a "custom audience."

If you upload a list of 10,000 emails (CSV file), you may have 6,500 of those emails match up with the Facebook profile emails. That would be a 65 percent match rate. You can expect about a 30 to 70 percent match rate, depending on the quality of your list. See the image on page 196.

How many different ways can this feature benefit you? Here are just a few examples to get you thinking:

- Not getting 100 percent open rate on your emails? Then run a Custom Audience Newsfeed Page Post Ad that will be sure to get in front of all your subscribers on Facebook.
- Looking for more sales conversions on your leads? Run a Facebook video ad showing a testimonial video from one of your happy customers, with a link in the post taking the user to your sales page or product page.

Create Audience

Information in your file will be matched with people on Facebook to create an audience. Your contacts won't be notified that you've added them to an audience and we'll never contact them without your permission.

Name: Name your audience

Description: Add a description of your audience

Data Type: Select one ▾
- Emails
- User IDs
- Phone Numbers
- Mobile Advertiser IDs

☑ I agree to the Facebook Custom Audiences Terms Cancel Create Audience

- Looking to wake up a dead list? Or run a new promotion to older leads who have unsubscribed? Then run a campaign with a compelling new offer to these Facebook users.
- Looking to get more reviews for your product or book on Amazon and improve your ranking? Then run a custom audience Facebook ad telling people: "If you liked my book please leave a review on Amazon. We'd love your feedback!" Then link directly to your Amazon product review page.

These are just a few examples, but the possibilities are endless, as you can probably imagine.

RIGHT-ANGLE TARGETING WITH LOOKALIKE AUDIENCES

Another new feature that is constantly being improved is Facebook's "Lookalike Audiences" or "Similar Audiences." This is where Facebook will take any existing custom audience you select and create a new, completely unique group of users with similar likes, interests, and shopping habits.

Each time you create a new lookalike audience you are able to optimize for "similarity" or "greater reach." I usually recommend optimizing for "similarity," as the audience Facebook creates will still be fairly large; the more targeted it is, the better.

In fact, because a lookalike audience by itself is usually a large broad audience, we recommend being careful targeting *only* a lookalike audience. In some cases you will

be okay targeting *only* a lookalike audience without any other interests selected, but be careful here. The more hyper-targeted you can get, the better off you will be.

THE HOLY GRAIL OF TARGETING: LAYERING

Do you have a product or service that that would benefit more people, if they *just* knew it existed? If they *knew* the story behind your brand, they would love you.

Keep reading carefully, if this is you or a client of yours. If you are selling crap, then go ahead and stop reading now, because this type of marketing doesn't work very well on crappy products and services that are just ripping people off.

The one thing we know about Facebook ads is that the more precise your targeting is, the better your ads will perform. However, the really sharp marketers with good sales funnels in place, are always looking for ways to be able to scale out. How can they go wider with the targeting and still keep a positive ROI?

One of the best ways to do this is to use a technique we call "audience layering." The basic strategy here is to find a target audience inside Facebook that may be normally too broad to get good results, and overlay that audience with one of your similar audiences.

In the example below, you will see that the interest target of "triathlons" is pretty broad—the "Potential Audience" is 4,800,000 people. This is too big. The advertiser in this case offers training curriculums to triathletes who want to improve their performance. Hardcore athletes. With the general "triathlons" interest you may be getting a lot of regular folks who are not really hardcore athletes. They may just have a friend who runs in triathlons. Or they may have expressed interest in an event like the Boston Marathon, which is a big U.S. annual event.

They typically do much better when targeting small, more precise audiences, like individual races, such as "Ironman Triathlon, Ironman World Championship, Ironman 70.3, etc.

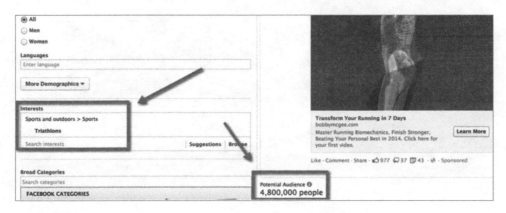

So how do you scale out into that 4,800,000-person audience but leave out the riff raff? You layer that audience over one or several of your lookalike audiences.

You will see in the image below that when you target only the lookalike audience you're *still* targeting a large potential audience of 740,000 people.

Yet when you target someone who likes triathlons *and* is also part of the lookalike audience Facebook created from the "BM Contacts," you will see the potential audience decrease down to 58,000, a much more hyper-targeted audience!

ADVERTORIAL + PRODUCT PLACEMENT = NATIVE ADVERTISING

There is a trend happening right now that leading marketers are tapping into in a big way: It's called "native advertising." Essentially, it's providing useful content to users in the flow and context of the site they're on.

Examples of native advertising include Facebook newsfeed ads, Twitter-sponsored tweets, sponsored YouTube videos, and content advertising networks like Taboola, Outbrain, etc. Note that these content networks are much different than running a display ad in the Google Display Network. You must write a high-quality article that must get manually approved before it is allowed to be promoted. Then if approved, it is promoted on highly trafficked blogs and news sites.

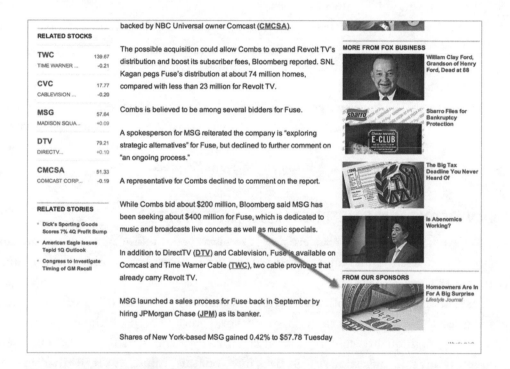

Native advertising really has been around for years. It just had a different name: advertorial. Advertorials have always been (and still are) one of the best performing media channels for direct response marketers.

The great thing about channels like Facebook and these other online channels is that you can create dozens and dozens of different advertorials or product placement ads and test them against each other one click at a time. As you perfect your funnel you can begin to move into other media, or start buying space directly from a proven site or company.

What is an online product placement ad? Just look at any cutting-edge company that is creating content around its products. Video tutorials. Demo videos. Contests. Content created to provide value, not to directly sell a product.

If you want to see an excellent example of this just go take a gander at GoPro's YouTube channel or website.

But the great thing about truly understanding the power of social ad platforms is that you don't have to be a company like GoPro to take advantage of online product placement ads. You don't need a multimillion dollar marketing budget.

All you need to do is follow this five-step process:

1. Create high-quality content that is relevant to your product or service.
2. Host that content on your website. (Even if you are using YouTube, you will embed your video onto a blog post or page on your site.)
3. Amplify that content using highly targeted Facebook advertising, sponsored Tweets, or other native advertising.
4. Make sure you have strong calls-to-action (CTAs) throughout your website to move a percentage of the visitors into taking action with you.
5. Make sure you have retargeting code placed properly throughout your site so you can automatically run retargeting ad campaigns inside Facebook and throughout the rest of the web to bring visitors (who will now be warmed up when they see your retargeting ads) back into your sales funnel process.

HOW DO YOU MONETIZE THESE NATIVE ADS?

The key to monetizing native advertising is to always be thinking about how you can engineer a process to build rapport, trust, and authority, while smoothly transitioning visitors into your sales process.

Instead of spending months or years slowly building up a blog or an authority site, praying for the Google gods to be in your favor, you can speed up the entire process by creating high-quality content, amplifying that content with Facebook ads, then retargeting any nonconverting visitors back into your sales funnel. It's really that simple.

This five-step method is exactly how you clone yourself or your best salesperson and start attending every relevant party, social gathering, or business-networking event possible to grow your business fast. It's how you can provide value, which builds trust and authority, then transition into the phase of customer or client acquisition.

There is one other benefit to this strategy that is sometimes overlooked because it is difficult to measure, but is very powerful nonetheless: The social proof, credibility, and authority you are engineering. When you amplify content with Facebook ads you get shares, comments, and likes on both the post that is promoted inside Facebook *and*

on your blog or website itself, assuming you have social share buttons installed on your posts. This is important, so take advantage! This also creates free, viral traffic.

THE MOST IMPORTANT THING TO CONSIDER BEFORE RUNNING SOCIAL OR CONTENT ADS

What is the *one thing* that you can put in front of your existing sales funnel that will provide value to the end user? Something compelling. Something curiosity driven that motivates people to click to learn more. Something that can give people an "aha moment."

If you can use social advertising to bring highly targeted visitors into your world and quickly give them an "aha moment," the rest is a piece of cake.

Go to www.IsFBforMe.com to find out your Facebook score. In 60 seconds this tool will tell you how seriously you should rank Facebook ads in your marketing mix.

To get a special bonus chapter by Keith Krance called "Social Media and Google" go to www.perrymarshall.com/supplement.

How to Get Customers to Eat Out of Your Hand

Get the Biggest Money from Your Customers When You Give Them Exactly What They Want to Buy

Next time you roll out a new product, you can have a 75 percent or better chance of success by using Google to measure your traffic. You can know exactly how much demand there is for your idea. You can test your headlines and copy, and have your potential customers tell you exactly what kind of product they're looking for.

Google makes this far less expensive and far less risky than ever before.

Here's one such example of powerful, real-time market research on the internet.

How Google Quickly Assessed the Viability of an Event Name . . . for Two Dollars and Seventy-Eight Cents

By Perry Marshall

I was the marketing and publicity director of TruthQuest, a local nonprofit group that hosts speakers and discussions on a variety of hot topics in religion and theology.

After the smash success of the *Lord of the Rings* film, its sequel *The Two Towers* followed suit the next winter. We found ourselves a speaker, Professor Jerry Root of Wheaton College, who could talk about this movie and the philosophical point of view of its author, J.R.R. Tolkien.

No matter how great the speaker may be, it doesn't matter if nobody shows up. So the title of the event was crucial.

Somebody suggested a preliminary title: "Is *Lord of the Rings* Christian?" But I didn't like it. Not intriguing. Too easy to say no or yes and forget about it.

The more marketing I do, the less I trust myself, even, to pick a good title. So our group brainstormed four titles and let the world vote on them. I used Google AdWords and had an answer in just 18 hours.

What Happened When We Ran the Overnight Test

I took our proposed titles and made four ads, all rotating simultaneously. I purchased the keyword "Tolkien," as well as "Tolkein," a common misspelling that people often mistakenly search on.

I started running the ads on Google at about 3:00 P.M. on a weekday and stopped it at 8:00 A.M. the next morning. Here's what the ads looked like, along with their results:

The Two Towers	Lord Of The Rings
Tolkien, The Two Towers, and	and The Spiritual Powers
Spiritual Symbolism	of Hobbits
tolkiensociety.org	tolkiensociety.org
11 Clicks \| 1.0% CTR \| $0.06 CPC	8 Clicks \| 0.7% CTR \| $0.06 CPC

Spirituality of Tolkien

Hidden Messages in
The Two Towers

tolkiensociety.org

20 Clicks | 1.9% CTR | $0.05 CPC

Tolkien Spirituality

Is There Hidden Christianity
In The Two Towers?

tolkiensociety.org

16 Clicks | 1.5% CTR | $0.06 CPC

Keyword	Clicks	Impressions	CTR	Cost
tolkien	48	3,878	1.2%	$2.43
tolkein	7	252	2.7%	$0.35
Overall	55	4,130	1.3%	$2.78

We found out:

1. Clickthrough rates were dramatically different for different titles. The winner was "Spirituality of Tolkien: Hidden Messages in *The Two Towers*."

2. This was *vastly* better than doing a "focus group" or a survey of our friends. Why? Because when people read about this in the newspaper or on a flier, their decision either to continue reading or to ignore it is made *on impulse*. They don't sit and ponder it. The decision to click on a link is equally impulsive.

3. This is a *great* way to come up with titles for magazine articles, white papers, books, and names for new products. And believe me, the votes you get will surprise you. What you *think* sounds cool is probably not what your customers think is relevant.

You can use this exact method to test the marketability of almost *any* idea you have. You can take it a step further than I did, bring visitors to your own website and further test their response to different offers.

HOW TO BE SURE THERE'S A MORE PROFITABLE MARKET FOR YOUR IDEA BY DEVELOPING A PRODUCT *AFTER* YOUR CUSTOMERS TELL YOU WHAT THEY WANT

Let's say you're thinking about writing a software program for doing automotive repairs. It's for do-it-yourself car enthusiasts, and it does engine diagnostics that help increase your fuel efficiency by five miles per gallon.

If a guy bought your software (which you haven't written yet), he could buy a cable at Radio Shack, take his computer into his garage, hook it up to his car, and your software would collect a load of data and display it on the screen. Your program would then tell the guy what to tweak in his engine.

Sounds like a great idea. But how do you know there's a market for this?

You can find out if there's water in the swimming pool before you dive in. You certainly don't want to spend weeks writing software if nobody's going to buy it. So here's what you do:

1. *Write an ebook, white paper, or guide.* Call it "How to Use Engine Diagnostics to Improve Your Car's Fuel Efficiency by Five Miles per Gallon." In it you tell people how to do it the *hard way*. The whole routine that takes you three days, including the spreadsheet and the connector from Radio Shack. (I have a free email course on writing white papers at www.perrymarshall.com/whitepapers).

2. *Head over to Google and bid on starter keywords.* Find all of the major terms related to engine diagnostics.

3. *Post an ad* like this:

DIY Engine Diagnostics
Simple Procedure Improves
Your Car—5 MPG or Better
www.AutoDiag.com

On your landing page, you have a sales letter that tells them about your ebook. You can also follow up with a series of emails that talk more about this.

1. *Get ideas and feedback from your readers.*
2. *Sell the ebook.* Or even give it away for free. But not without a plan. While you're marketing your ebook, you're going to take the next step with your buyers.
3. *Test your customers' response to your actual product idea.* What do they say back to you? Are they interested? Do they pester you to find out when this will be available? Do they offer to pay you for it now, hoping to get first dibs on it when it comes out? If so, you know you've got a winner.
4. *Sell your product,* and the dollars will come rolling in.

You've listened to your customers, you've put together a product in line with what they ask you for, and you've proven to yourself that they're interested. Now when you give them exactly what they want, you'll make the cash register ring.

WHAT YOU LEARN WHEN THIS DOESN'T WORK THE FIRST TIME OUT

Now what happens if it's a flop?

Don't cry in your milk—learn your lesson and get on with something else. You can come up with a new idea and test it for no great sum of money.

And what if the idea is only marginal?

Play with it. Change your ad, change your landing page, fiddle with the title of your report or ebook, adjust the price if you sell it, give visitors incentives in exchange for lots of feedback, and try again. If it won't work, then move on. If you can clear out the bugs, then run like the wind.

Did you know that infomercials also run on this same premise? It costs $50,000–$100,000 to produce an infomercial and run it for a few days. If the producer can get 80 percent return on investment (i.e., only lose 20 percent) the first time out, he won't scrap the project. He'll play with the offer, the upsells, the testimonials, and the other ingredients until he gets it above his break-even point. And he's not afraid to cut his losses if he has to.

When you test ideas that don't work, *fail fast.* Get it over with as quickly as possible. Spend the money, get the results, cut your losses, and move on.

"Wait a minute," you might be thinking, "I don't have hundreds of dollars to blow on pre-testing. I can't afford to do that."

The reality is, you can't afford *not* to. Spending those dollars and going into the red now could save you *thousands* of dollars later in botched advertising and mediocre returns and can prevent you from having to start again from scratch.

The Insights You Get When Customers Vomit All Over You

By Bryan Todd

I spent more than four years in mainland China, during which time I went from not even knowing how to say "hello" to becoming conversationally fluent in the language. It saddened me as I watched many of my Western friends there struggling with the language and getting nowhere.

I learned through trial and error a host of practical, working methods for acquiring the language. Multiple times during my stay there my American and European friends

would tell me, "Wow—you need to share your whole method with me, because whatever it is, it's obviously working."

So I listened. And after returning to the USA, I sat down to write a book that would teach other English speakers to do just what I did.

I then decided to take our marketing advice: I wrote a series of autoresponder emails and bought Google traffic *first,* planning to sell the book to customers later.

I was a newbie at the time. I set up my Google campaign, sent traffic to my new website, and let it go.

And here are two of the responses I got:

> You have shown me absolutely nothing. You have wasted my time and paper printing off your worthless emails. I learned more in five minutes from a Chinese business website than I could ever expect to learn from your time-wasting activities.
>
> —D.M.

> You have not provided me with any practice Mandarin lessons, which is what I wanted. Instead you provided generic information, as a "carrot" to buy your course. This is a scam.
>
> —F.P.

Oh, crap! Here I am in the middle of writing a book about learning the language living in China, while these people are in their home country looking for simple online lessons.

Thank God I hadn't created a whole product yet.

But get this: they *did* tell me exactly what they were looking for. The first guy above left me the URL of the Chinese business site he had mentioned, so I could go and compare. The second guy told me specifically that he wanted "practice Mandarin lessons." Others weighed in, too.

These people wanted online lessons. I didn't have the resources to put something like that together at the time. But I logged it away to pursue in the future.

Now what about my ebook? Should I cancel the project?

No. I *knew* from experience with friends that I had something of tremendous value. But how was I going to find the folks who really needed it?

I finished the book and set my ads to show only in Taiwan and Mainland China—not even in Hong Kong, where Cantonese and English are more common than Mandarin. I turned on the traffic again.

When Your Machine Finally Kicks In

And that's when the positive emails started pouring in. Grateful readers who had moved to China and Taiwan from the U.S., Israel, Germany, Australia, the UK, New Zealand, India, and from all over the globe wrote in to tell me that they were finding my email course to be helpful and relevant.

More importantly, *they were buying the book* and telling me that they were using it. I even found myself doing late-night telephone consultations to Beijing with my customers now, helping them improve their Chinese-learning strategy even further.

In reality, the book is an invaluable resource regardless of what language a person is learning. The principles are universal and apply anywhere in the world. Still, focusing on China and Taiwan paid off.

One buyer sent me this:

> At about midnight last night, I paid for and downloaded your products. I thought I would take a quick glance before going to bed.
>
> It is now five o'clock on Sunday afternoon, and I haven't been to bed yet. I read the entire document twice; your bonus article three times. During this time, I experienced a gamut of emotions; everything from the knowing smile, kissing the computer screen, wildly punching the air, and dancing around the room.
>
> Your product is excellent, Bryan, and worth every cent I paid for it. For the price, I could not have had a better night! Don't even think about returning my money, as I love your work, and I am looking forward to any stuff you do in the future.
>
> —Andrew V.

When you find your market, *boy, do you ever find them!* Giving people exactly what they need and then having them turn around and thank you for it is the true joy of marketing.

The market spoke. The book sold. I made a profit. People like Andrew wrote testimonials, which in turn sold more books.

When Your Market Speaks, and You Respond, It's Money in the Bank

Start small with Google, and when your market talks, listen. You'll knock your head against a few walls in the early going, but there's no better education to be had.

In fact, behind every angry rant you hear is someone who didn't get what they really wanted. Go with what your prospects tell you they want. And don't ever stop asking. Especially when your *existing customers* talk. That's as good as money in the bank.

Since I lived in China for four years, I listened for *four years* as friends and acquaintances complained about their struggles in learning the language. That taught me *what* I need to create for people.

Then I spent two weeks listening to my Google visitors in order to discover *where* I needed to market it.

Then Andrew used the book. It improved his Chinese. He wrote back to tell me about it. His testimonial resulted in more sales. He went on and told friends and coworkers. Word traveled around. More people bought.

That's exactly what people will do for you when you hit their sweet spot.

We still take our own medicine. The title of this book, *The Ultimate Guide to Google AdWords: Access 100 Million People in 10 Minutes* was derived from the following ad, which was our control ad on Google for four years:

Beat The AdWords System
Access 100 Million People in 10 Min
The Definitive Fast-Start Guide
www.perrymarshall.com/adwords

I did similar tests on Google to arrive at the title *80/20 Sales and Marketing: The Definitive Guide to Working Less and Making More.* I tested more than 50 variations. Google ads remain one of the best places to test product names, bestselling book titles, and anything that's got to pass muster with tens of thousands of people.

Uncle Claude Sez

Almost any questions can be answered, cheaply, quickly, and finally, by a test campaign. That is the way to answer them, not by arguments around a table. Go to the court of last resort: the buyers of your product. . . .

We establish averages on a small scale, and those averages always hold. We know our cost, we know our sale, and we know our profit and loss. We know how soon our cost comes back. Before we spread out, we prove our undertaking absolutely safe.

Supercharge Your Clickthrough Rates with Ad Extensions

A d Extensions boost clickthrough rates. It's that simple.

Some folks dismiss ad extensions as unnecessarily complicated and fussy. But these extra links and lines of copy make your ads more visible and more relevant at the same time. And when you improve your visibility and relevance, you increase your CTR.

Ad extensions let you expand your ads and introduce additional specific information. Your ads stand out on the page and entice more clicks. Here's an example of what these look like on the search page:

Did you know that ad extensions even influence your Quality Score? To quote Google: "If two competing ads have the same bid and quality, the ad with greater expected impact from extensions will generally appear in a higher ad position than the other."

This gives you an automatic advantage over other advertisers.

Even if you're a relative beginner to AdWords, this is an opportunity you want to take advantage of.

Before we get into the specific extensions that are available and how to make the best use of them, here are a few things to keep in mind:

1. Google has final say over when they do or don't show your extensions. They base this on the performance of your campaign.
2. Some extensions you have full manual control over, while others Google inserts automatically.
3. A few of the available ad extensions will only show if your ad is displaying among the top three premium positions, immediately above the organic search results.
4. Some extensions will appear differently on different devices.
5. Most extensions can be shown to users in any country, although some are specific to particular regions.
6. The first extensions we're going to review (the "main three") only apply to Google Search campaigns, not to ads on the Display Network.

Access Ad Extensions via the main row of tabs:

AD EXTENSION #1: SITELINKS

If your ad is showing in one of the top three premium spots, you can show sitelink extensions. These appear as additional links underneath your main ad. You'll typically see three to four links that point the user to different pages on your site:

These can work wonders for you. They don't cost you any extra, they offer more specific and relevant options for your prospect to click on, and they let you take visitors directly to the most relevant page.

Best of all, they take up more space on the Google results page, pushing your competitors and the organic search listings further down and out of the way.

Let's say your website sells a particular brand of men's shirts. You bid on the brand name as a keyword and write an ad that specifically offers a deal on long-sleeve crewnecks. With sitelinks you can also add in three or four additional links in your ad that take visitors to offers for turtlenecks, short sleeve shirts, or even hoodies, all from the same brand.

Or you can highlight other information that may be of particular interest to the searcher, such as your About Us page, or your Shipping and Returns Policy page.

These extensions are easy to add and update. You can even create sitelinks that are specific to mobile devices. And you can schedule sitelinks to show at specific times, which is especially valuable if your offers are seasonal or expire after a specific date.

Google has greatly improved the reporting information that they give you for your sitelinks, making it far easier for you to see which ones are getting the most clicks and activity.

Sitelink	Status	↓ Clicks [?]	Impr. [?]	CTR [?]	Avg. CPC [?]	Cost [?]	Avg. Pos. [?]
💬 80/20 Time Management	Approved						
💬 For Consultants	Approved						
💬 The 80/20 Seminar	Approved						
💬 Free Marketer's Report	Approved						
💬 5 Days to Success	Approved						
💬 4-Man Intensives	Approved						
💬 Roundtable	Approved						
💬 Renaissance Club	Approved						
Total - all sitelinks							

A word of caution: Google allows you to set up different sitelinks for different ad groups. That sounds like great a great idea . . . in theory. Problem is, it adds a level of complexity that only the most experienced AdWords users should be grappling with.

If you're just getting started, stick to activating sitelinks at the campaign level.

A Feature That Gives You Higher CTRs

There's a feature called "Enhanced Sitelinks," which allows you to add the equivalent of a headline (up to 25 characters) and two description lines (35 characters each) to each individual sitelink. With this in place, your ad will take up even more space, effectively creating *four miniature ads* that display underneath your main ad.

That can't help but improve your CTR.

Those will only show for high-volume keywords, however. Let your account run for a couple of months before trying out this feature. Start with your highest-traffic campaign.

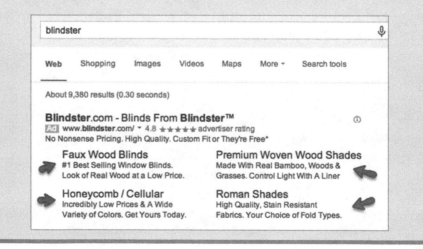

AD EXTENSION #2: CALL EXTENSIONS

Frankly, this is a wonderful feature. Our best students and colleagues use these extensively, especially when doing work for clients.

In late 2013, Google adjusted their editorial guidelines so that you can no longer include a telephone number in the headline or text of your ad. That's actually a good thing, because the phone number option is now available through the call extensions feature instead. Activate this and the telephone number of your choice will appear underneath your ad *as an additional free line.* That buys you extra space for ad copy, and it allows your ad to catch more eyeballs by taking up more space on the results page.

Call extensions are especially powerful when they show on mobile phones: You can set it so that users click on your telephone number and connect to you directly from your ad.

That's particularly handy if you have a site that doesn't display well on mobile devices; better still, if the primary call-to-action on your landing page is to call your phone number. Your contact number will show at the top of your ad in place of your headline, highlighted in blue to indicate that it's clickable.

> ### How Much Does Google Charge You for Calls?
>
> Charges for phone calls and clicks to your ads can get tricky. If someone clicks on your call extension to ring your telephone number directly, you'll be charged the cost of a regular click. If that same user also clicks on your ad's URL to visit your landing page, you'll be charged a second time. You won't, however, be charged a third time for any subsequent clicks on the same ad by the same user.

The cost to have a mobile user click on your telephone number is the same as a regular click. That makes this an extremely cost-effective method of driving calls to your business. This is also a good feature to combine with ad scheduling if, for instance, you only want your call extensions activated during business hours.

AD EXTENSION #3: LOCATION

This is similar to call extensions except that, instead of showing your contact phone number, Google will show your physical location. This is an excellent feature for local brick-and-mortar businesses that want to increase foot traffic to their location.

A drawback to this is Google is firmly pushing AdWords users to use Google+ Local, also known as Google Places for Business. For this extension to work correctly you'll need to have your Google+ Local page claimed and optimized. If you're unsure about where to start with this, I recommend an excellent guide by Guy Kawasaki called *What the Plus!* that covers everything you need to know.

If you're dead-set against using Google Places, there is a way to use location extensions in isolation. Go to the Ad Extensions tab, select "Use Location Extensions," and then look for the dropdown box with the word "Upgraded" in it.

If you change the option to "Not Upgraded" this will downgrade your Location Extension tool to the version before Enhanced Campaigns were introduced. This way you can add addresses manually. If you're struggling to get your head around Google+

Local, doing this can be a lifesaver. (The only limitation is that you have to apply this change to each campaign manually, whereas the "upgraded" version can be applied at the account level.)

AD EXTENSION #4: IMAGES

If you want to increase the visibility of your ads, this is arguably the most effective of Google's ad extensions. Plus, very few AdWords advertisers make use of image ads. That's a huge advantage for you.

When you activate this extension, three images appear above your ads, featuring your product or brand. That's a feature we usually associate with Google's Display Network, but here you can use it with Search.

This is a great opportunity to simultaneously improve your visibility, your branding, and your CTR. But it'll take some work to get this extension up and running. This only activates for ads in top position on the page, and you'll have to talk to your AdWords account representative to organize the setup process. Currently only five of your ad groups can have this feature enabled, so choose wisely.

AD EXTENSION #5: REVIEWS

This is different from "Seller Ratings" that you get on review sites (see "Annotation Extensions" on page 220). It specifically refers to reviews, not by individual buyers, but by reputable media outlets or blogs.

This is another extension that's tricky to set up. As a result it's rarely used. To qualify for this, you'll need the URL of the webpage that contains your review, and then either select a direct quote or write a paraphrased version of no more than 67 characters, including the source name. You then need to provide Google with the URL of the third-party site on which the review can be found. And you'll need to post the same quote on your landing page.

If you're willing to do the dance, once you activate it, this extension will display the review quote as an extra line below your ad.

AD EXTENSION #6: APPS

If you're one of the small subset of AdWords users with an app in the Apple App Store or on Google Play, you'll find this exciting.

Give Google the location of your app, and when this extension activates, viewers will either see a link to your App Store page or a direct link to download your application. (iOS users will see an Apple apps link and Android users will see a Google Play link.)

AD EXTENSION #7: ANNOTATIONS

Annotations are additional snippets of text or information that appear below your ad. They come in three types:

1. *Seller Ratings*. If your product or service is featured on renowned independent review sites (such as Yelp, Bazaarvoice, PriceGrabber, Shopzilla, etc.), Google will compile the results and show your average rating out of five stars. You need to have had at least 30 unique reviews during the previous 12 months and an average score of at least 3.5 out of 5. Be proactive with this and ask your customers to leave reviews of your product.

2. *Social*. If your AdWords account is linked to your Google+ page, this annotation will display your number of followers or fans. This will increase your visibility by making your ad stand out. Plus, if you have a significant number of followers it will add social proof, which can in turn increase your CTR and your conversions. To qualify for this extension you must have a verified URL from your Google+ page, the domain of your Google+ page must match the domain in your ads, and your Google+ page must have what Google calls "high-quality posts and a significant number of followers." "Significant," in this instance, generally means 100 or more.

500 **Hotels** in **New York NY** - Booking.com
Ad www.booking.com/**New-York-Hotels** ▾
Half-Price **Hotels**. Book your **Hotel** in **New York NY**
Booking.com has 2,030,701 followers on Google+ ◀━━

3. *Previous Visits*. This feature is controlled entirely by Google. They'll displays your prospect's previous activity in connection with your website. For example, appearing as an extra line below your ad, it might say: "You visited xyz.com three times. Last visit: today."

YOUR QUICK ACTION SUMMARY

Not only do Ad Extensions increase your visibility and CTR, they expand your ads to considerably greater sizes, giving you a bigger piece of Google real estate. Best part: This comes at no extra cost.

- Add sitelink extensions and use the reporting interface to see how they're helping your results.
- If your primary goal is to generate phone calls to your business, activate call extensions.
- If you're a local brick-and-mortar business, link your AdWords account to your Google+ Local page.
- Review the other four ad extensions and find the one with the biggest potential to help grow your business.
- Once your campaign has been running for a couple of months, consider adding enhanced sitelinks to your highest-traffic campaign.

Uncle Claude Sez

The best advertisers . . . learn their appealing claims by tests—by comparing results from various headlines. Gradually they accumulate a list of claims important enough to use. All those claims appear in every ad thereafter.

Quality Score
Making Google's "Bozo Filter" Work for You

I once did a consultation for an adoption agency. My wife and I adopted a little girl from China. We love her like crazy, so adoption is near and dear to our hearts!

When I looked at the agency's Google account, it broke my heart. It was an absolute mess. All kinds of keywords dumped into this campaign or that, willy-nilly, with no rhyme or reason. The keywords didn't match each other, the ads didn't match the keywords, the landing pages didn't match the ads. The whole thing was like a Picasso painting. That is great if you're doing art, but it's a terrible way to run a business.

Luckily, their AdWords account was still working, and it was bringing them some customers. As I looked closer, I saw the only reason their clock wasn't getting totally cleaned was Google's Quality Score algorithm. Because everything was so mismatched, most of their keywords had Quality Scores of 1 to 3. The keywords were underwater and the ads weren't showing at all. Only a few keywords, which were lucky enough to be OK, were getting traffic at all.

It was at that point that I realized Google's Quality Score algorithm is mostly designed for the lowest common denominator. It saves the average advertiser from paying a hideous stupidity tax and ensures that what little they accidentally do right does generate some results.

As the client repaired the damage, slowly but surely their Quality Scores went up, traffic went up, cost per click went down, and more adoptive parents came in.

GOOGLE PAYS YOU TO BE RELEVANT!

Can you think of any aspect of your business where making more money results in third-party suppliers charging you less?

We're not talking about vendors giving you bulk discounts. We mean—literally—the more profit you make the more your provider slashes your final bill.

It just doesn't happen, right? It's always the opposite:

- When your business earns more, you pay more taxes.
- When you ship more, your shipping invoice is larger.
- When your TV commercial produces sales and you want to increase your airtime, the network ups the bill.

There is one exception. Google's PPC network rewards success. Simply put:

The better your ads perform, the cheaper they get.

How is this possible?

When AdWords first sprang into life circa 2000, it catered to large websites with lots of financial clout. But Google anticipated far more profit if they could attract a healthy percentage of the world's small and medium-sized online businesses as well.

With this in mind, Google did an AdWords reboot in 2002 and successfully signed up scores of new clients.

However, Google had already seen other PPC companies like Overture stumble badly with poor quality ads. If the top spot was sold only to the highest bidder, then the system would always favor the largest companies with the deepest pockets, not unlike large airlines squeezing out independent operators. Big dumb companies could write stupid ads and still show at the top of the page. Most small businesses couldn't compete.

So Google added a layer of sophistication: They made your position on the page a function not only of your bid price but of your clickthrough rate as well. If your CTR was higher than your competitor's, your ad would show higher on the page, even if you bid less.

The concept was simple: Make quality more important than money. If you bid lots of money but wrote terrible ads, you'd disappear from the results page entirely. If you had little money but clear, interesting ads, you could get to the top of the page.

Google believed this would result in:

- Better, more relevant results pages, making Google more attractive to users than other search engines;
- More money for the smartest advertisers, who would in turn be eager to spend more;
- Increased profits for Google.

In other words, a win-win-win.

They made some modest tweaks to this over the subsequent years, and in 2005 they started calling this the "Quality Score."

Then it became time for Google to tackle a second issue: Advertisers fighting over clicks using bait-and-switch tactics.

Let's say you ran a site that provided information on treating gout. You could get scores of clicks to your site by writing ads such as, "Britney Spears Gout Photos." (She was still a big deal then.) It didn't matter squat if your website had no such photos or content; your CTR would be through the roof and your clicks would be cheap.

So Google had to deal with that, too. In 2006 they introduced the landing page Quality Score to the mix. Now the content on your site had to be relevant, too. No trickery, no deceit, no useless content that made visitors hit the back button.

Google's prediction came true: a better experience for everyone searching on Google, more affordable clicks to the smartest advertisers, and more profit for everyone.

Craig Danuloff, CEO of Rewind Me Inc., calls the Quality Score system a "bozo filter." It weeds out the "accidental bozos" who write bad ads because they don't know how to be relevant, and it weeds out the "intentional bozos" who are trying to game the system.

As long as you're not a bozo, the system is heavily weighted in your favor. Think of it as a preferred customer program (what Australians like to call "mates rates").

If there's any downside at all, it's that Google's exact Quality Score algorithm is confidential. Not unlike their main search engine algorithm. To create a level playing field for advertisers they're not above sharing general principles and a few details here and there. But they keep specifics to themselves. And they regularly tweak the system.

WHAT'S YOUR QUALITY SCORE?

To find your Quality Score, log in to your AdWords account, choose a campaign or ad group to view, click the Keywords tab, find the "Columns" dropdown button to customize your columns. Under "Select metrics" click "Attributes" and add Quality Score as a column.

Once that column is displayed, you'll see a score between 1 and 10 for each of your keywords:

Note that you as the AdWords advertiser only get to see one Quality Score number, shown for each keyword. However, behind the curtain there's also a Quality Score for each of your *ads*, calculated in real time, and which varies depending not just on how you construct your campaigns but on what Google knows about the person searching.

For instance, your ad may have one Quality Score for a searcher from the UK on an iPhone, and another for a searcher from Australia using a laptop.

Although it's possible to find a Quality Score number for each of the keywords in your AdWords account, consider it a general guide rather than a mathematical certainty. At best, it will help you to figure out which of your keywords and ad groups could use a little work and which are best left alone.

Again, remember this is a guideline, not a precise set-in-stone number. It's an average score for each keyword, with a much more complicated calculation happening invisibly behind the scenes. The rating you're given in each case is also the most recent calculation. It may have recently increased or decreased, but there won't be any indication in the AdWords interface.

Now that you know your numbers, what should you do about each keyword and its Quality Score? Here are some guidelines:

- *9–10 Excellent*. Don't change anything. You're right on point and are probably paying the lowest possible price for your clicks.

- *5–8 Good*. You're doing fine. You could push your score a bit higher and it might be worth checking that you're not missing anything obvious (such as having this keyword crammed along with too many others into a single ad group). But don't spend huge amounts of time trying to improve it.

- *3–4 Poor*. This is a warning. Your ads for this keyword aren't showing very often and when they do you're probably paying well above average for each click. If the keyword in question has the potential for high volumes of traffic, then fixing the Quality Score here should be your priority.

- *1–2 Terrible*. At this level Google is barely showing your ads for this keyword and charging you a fortune per click. Take action immediately!

SO WHAT FACTORS GO INTO QUALITY SCORE?

You could compare Quality Score to monthly mortgage payments that vary depending on how you look after your house. Mow the lawn, take out the trash, and your payment goes down.

But does Google prefer your house to have a red roof or a black one?

That's where things get tricky. Maybe you paint your house red this month. Maybe next month your mortgage payment goes down even further. But was it because you painted your house or some other cause?

Plenty of PPC experts have experimented and drawn helpful conclusions about how Google rates its advertisers. And at the very least, Google has been up front about the *most important factors* in its Quality Score.

You can visit https://support.google.com/adwords/answer/2454010 for the most current explanation, but below is our summary of the key items, along with our assessment of the ones we feel are the most significant.

Clickthrough Rate (CTR)

This should be a priority for every PPC marketer. Of all the things Google cares about, CTR is always at the top of the list. According to Larry Kim of WordStream, your CTR (compared to your direct competitors) contributes about two-thirds of your Quality Score.

The logic is simple: If users click on Ad 1 more often than Ad 2, then Google assumes that Ad 1 is the more relevant and interesting one. But Google doesn't look at the CTR of each ad in isolation; it also take into account the CTR that other advertisers obtained for the same keywords that you're bidding on, the position on the page on which your ad was shown, as well as the overall CTR you're receiving for *all* your ads across *all* your ad groups.

You're graded on the curve, in other words.

Landing Page

Google measures the quality of your landing page in a number of different ways, but there are two factors that stand out:

1. *How transparent is your landing page?* If the thing promised in your ad is available immediately on your landing page, Google considers this "transparent." If you require the visitor's email address before providing any information, benefits, or freebies, then Google will be less impressed.

 You can always ask for email addresses ("squeeze pages" are *not* forbidden), but you must ensure that your landing page allows visitors to find good, useful information first without any strings attached.
2. *How relevant is your ad to your landing page?* Yes, this is subjective. If there's a match between the words in your ad and the words on your landing page, this is a good start, but that alone doesn't necessarily translate into quality.

Google measures how long each visitor stays on your landing page before clicking the back button. If visitors jump back to Google after only a few seconds, Google concludes that you didn't deliver what you promised. If visitors stay on your landing page for several minutes or don't return to Google at all, this suggests you provided something of genuine value.

Some site owners try to create a unique landing page for every ad. That certainly makes for relevant landing pages. The problem is that it's time-consuming, expensive, and may make tracking your conversions unnecessarily complex. The truth is that the relevance of your landing page is only moderately important compared to the CTR of your ad.

Keyword-to-Ad Relevance

This is about the relationship between the keyword typed in by the person searching, the words in your ad, and the words on your landing page.

See Chapter 5 on organizing your ad groups. Every ad group needs to center tightly around a keyword theme and contain a small number of keywords. You can certainly dump all your keywords into just one or two ad groups, but your CTRs will suffer.

For example, if I type in "chiropractor," I'm not likely to click on your ad unless it has "chiropractor" in the headline. If I type in "sciatica" and your ad says "sciatica relief," I'm far more likely to click on your ad. If it only says "back pain relief," then I'm far *less* likely to click.

The only way to account for all this is to have separate ad groups for each of these types of keywords. In this example, one ad group for variations on "chiropractor," one on the theme of "sciatica," and one about "back pain relief."

Geographic Performance

Google keeps track of *where* people are clicking on your ad. If, for instance, users in New York are clicking on your back pain ad more often than users in Philadelphia, your ad will be given a different Quality Score for each of these two different areas. (Note: You won't see this reflected in any of your AdWords reports; it happens behind the scenes.)

Targeted Devices

It's no longer possible to create different ad groups for specific devices, but Google does keep track of how well your ad performs on each device and they'll assign you a different Quality Score accordingly.

HOW TO IMPROVE YOUR QUALITY SCORE

Here's a quick summary of the fastest and most effective methods for cranking up your score by a few notches:

Aggressively Split-Test Your Ads

CTR is the biggest factor in your Quality Score, and the best way to improve CTR is by testing new ads. The object is to beat the performance of your old ads. The quickest fix for improving the CTR of an ad has always been by "keyword stuffing"—using the keyword in the headline of your ad.

Split Out Your Keywords to 3-4 Per Ad Group, Max

Keyword stuffing—generating as many keywords as possible—does work, but it's difficult if you have too many diverse keywords in each ad group. The fewer keywords you have in each one, the easier it is to make your ads relevant, and the easier it is to push up your CTR.

Important tip: One factor in Quality Score is *your overall CTR across your entire campaign*. Optimizing *all* of the ad groups in each campaign is critical.

Let's say your campaign has ten ad groups. Nine of them have three or four keywords and their CTR is solid, but the tenth ad group has 50 keywords and a very poor CTR. That tenth ad group *alone* is enough to drag down your Quality Score for the other nine. Subdivide that campaign by breaking out its keywords into separate ad groups with closely matched ads. You may save your entire campaign as a result!

Make Your Landing Pages More Relevant

Think of the landing page element of your Quality Score as pass/fail. If your page is good and improving, then spending time on it is only going to make a small difference. If your page is especially bad, go after the obvious issue you can find and fix it. For example, if your landing page contains nothing but an email opt-in form, you'll want to put some additional copy, information, and even navigation on your page so that visitors have the freedom to learn more about you before deciding to share their information with you.

As a general rule, if your Quality Score is 4 or lower it's because your landing page is poorly thought out. If you're already at 5 or higher, your landing page is probably fine and you should make it a priority instead to improve your CTRs.

Negative Keywords

This is a dynamite method for improving your CTR—one tiny change can literally *double* your results—but it's definitely not for beginners. One wrong negative keyword

can flatline your account. If you're going to give negative keywords a try, roll them out carefully into your ad groups, a couple of keywords at a time, and allow several days or even weeks between attempts so you can measure the results of your changes.

What are negative keywords?

Imagine you sell a product that treats hair loss in men. Pretty good chance one of your main keywords will be the phrase match "hair loss." But people search on "hair loss" for their pets, too. How do you deal with those folks?

That's where negative keywords come in. You can prevent your ads from showing for any person who searches on hair loss for their pet. Open the Keywords tab, scroll to the bottom, locate the Negative Keyword section, and enter the words you want to exclude:

		Keyword	Status ?	Max. CPC ?	+ Clicks ?	+ ↓Impr. ?	+ CTR ?	+ Avg. CPC ?	+ Cost ?	+ Avg. Pos. ?	+ Converted clicks ?
☐	•				26	1,148	2.26%	$0.28	$7.36	2.4	2
☐	•				41	1,143	3.59%	$0.33	$13.47	1.2	8
☐	•				121	771	15.69%	$0.08	$10.08	1.1	16
		Total - all keywords ?			188	3,062	6.14%	$0.16	$30.91	1.6	26
		Total - Search ?			188	3,062	6.14%	$0.16	$30.91	1.6	26
		Total - Display Network ?			0	0	0.00%	$0.00	$0.00	0.0	0
		Total - all ad group ?			188	3,062	6.14%	$0.16	$30.91	1.6	26

⊞ Negative keywords ?

Negative keywords are always preceded by the minus sign:

 –dog
 –pet
 –animal
 –cat

You can apply a set of negative keywords to one specific ad group or to an entire campaign. In the case of your hair loss treatment, the latter makes the most

sense. Now, whenever someone searches for the words "hair loss" but also includes the words "dog," "pet," "animal," or "cat," your ad is automatically prevented from showing.

Negative keywords are powerful because they *eliminate irrelevant impressions.* If you have 1,000 impressions and 50 clicks, your CTR is 5 percent. If you use negative keywords to cut out half of those impressions and show to 500 people, but you still get 50 clicks, then your CTR just went from 10 percent to 20 percent.

Fewer irrelevant impressions means better CTR and better Quality Score. That's the power of negative keywords.

The easiest way to find negative keywords is to go back through your keyword research and pick out words that you rejected because they referenced product lines or services that you don't provide.

You can also find negative keywords using Google's Search Query Report. Within any one ad group, click the check box to the left of one of your broad or phrase match keywords, then click the "Details" dropdown button, and under "Search Terms," choose "Selected."

Google will show you all of the related search queries that they chose to show your ads for, along with data on how you're performing for each one. Find an underperforming keyword and turn it into a negative:

Search term	Match type [?]	Added/Excluded [?]
☐ address	Broad match	None
☐ princess dresses	Broad match	None
☐ wedding dress	Broad match	None
☐ prom dress	Broad match	None
☐ salad dressing	Broad match	None
Other search terms [?]		
Total		

This is a great way to efficiently clean up the performance of your keywords and ads and boost your Quality Score.

That said, be sure to apply negative keywords slowly and monitor your numbers carefully. One wrong word in your negative keyword list can seriously damage your results.

YOUR QUICK ACTION SUMMARY

Remember that Quality Score is about having the best possible CTR. Focus on this above all else.

- Add the Quality Score column to your AdWords account report.
- Start by rescuing the keywords with scores of 4 or less.
- If you're convinced that your landing page is relevant and transparent enough, focus on improving your CTR across your entire campaign.
- Regularly review your Search Query Report to find irrelevant impressions and consider adding negative keywords to your individual ad groups or even across your entire campaign.
- Regularly review your Quality Score and be quick to act on scores of 4 or less.

Uncle Claude Sez

People are hurried. The average person worth cultivating has too much to read. They skip three-fourths of the reading matter which they pay to get. They are not going to read your business talk unless you make it worth their while and let the headline show it.

Remarketing
The Single Most Profitable Online Advertising Strategy

Have you ever been reading an article on *The Huffington Post* and suddenly noticed an ad there for the espresso maker you were looking at on Amazon a few days ago?

That's no coincidence. You've been targeted by a remarketing campaign.

Remarketing, sometimes called behavioral retargeting, is a way to advertise to people who have previously visited your website.

One member of my Roundtable, which is my highest level peer advisory group, sold software as a service product. Employers used it to monitor employees'

performance. This was a product that a person would probably not go looking for, but which intrigued visitors when they saw it, which of course made it a great candidate for Google Display Network (GDN). However, one look and a 30-day free trial alone was usually not enough to convince them to buy.

What he discovered was that people would download the free trial, then forget about it and move on. However, he found retargeting ads were effective at coaxing them into installing the software on his employees' computers and actually trying the software out. Then they would experience the value and buy.

Interesting application for retargeting ads, don't you think?

Imagine you ran a hardware store, and *every visitor who came through your door willingly handed you their mailing address, whether they made a purchase or not.* What would you be able to do with that?

That's the power of remarketing.

Set up a remarketing campaign in your Google AdWords account and you have the freedom to reach out again to every person who visits your website, long after they've left.

Consider all the visitors to your website in the last month who showed some interest in your product. They may have added items to their shopping cart, but for some reason left without completing the checkout process. Maybe something distracted them. Maybe they don't get paid until Tuesday. Maybe the price was just beyond their budget.

Whatever the reason, they came very close to adding to your bottom line. Here's where remarketing gives you a second chance—actually, as many chances as you like—to regain the attention of your previous visitors and give them a reason to come back for another look.

In pay-per-click terms you'll never have a group of people to advertise to with more potential for bringing you profit than the folks who have visited your site. They know your brand, they've already demonstrated that they have at least some measure of interest in what you have to offer by, and many will only need the slightest nudge to go from warm lead to new buyer.

Remarketing is most popular among ecommerce site owners, but it's also every bit as effective if you're a content or affiliate marketer whose primary goal is to add subscribers to an email list. Even if your website is so efficient that a full 20 percent of your visitors complete your lead capture form, that still means 80 percent of your audience is leaving without taking action. This large group of people is ripe for targeting with a remarketing campaign.

Much of the setup process is fairly self-explanatory but in this chapter we're going to highlight some of the areas that people sometimes forget to address, and answer some questions that our students ask most frequently.

The New Bicycle: A Remarketing Tale

Our colleague Jeff Martyka of Neckties Inc. tells this remarketing story:

Last summer, my nephew told me he was going to get a new bike for his birthday. I asked him how he planned on convincing his parents to buy it for him. "Easy," he said. "They'll ask me, and I'll tell them what I want."

I realized he had made the same strategic error that many businesses make. He was going to take one shot, and one shot only, at closing the deal with Mom and Dad. No further followup, no method to ensure they bought him the model he wanted—nothing.

Most buying decisions aren't made easily, whether you're a parent deciding what to buy your son for his birthday, or making other, more weighty purchasing choices.

In the case of my nephew, he needed a way to "remarket" to his parents! So let's reframe the situation: We have a nephew (website) that has been asked by his parents (shoppers) what he wants for his birthday. He says he wants a bike (landing page). Does he get the bike with this minimal a marketing plan? Maybe . . . maybe not.

To help my nephew out I developed a "remarketing campaign" to get repeated "impressions" in front of his parents so they would be more likely to buy him the exact bike he wanted. He drew pictures of himself with a giant grin and put them in his parents' cars so they might take and display them at work. He cut out ads from the newspaper showing the bike he wanted and taped them to his parents' bathroom mirrors. He found articles about how children in the United States are obese and need exercise, and he taped those to the refrigerator. And while his dad was out in the driveway washing the car, he pulled his own (old) bike out of the garage and washed it right there in Dad's full view.

Needless to say, my nephew ended up with the bicycle—the very one he wanted!

FIRST, UPDATE YOUR PRIVACY POLICY

You should already have a privacy policy that addresses your use of cookies. In fact, the wording on your small print may already be broad enough to cover you for the use of remarketing campaigns.

Even so, please don't skip this part. Google is very strict about its remarketing campaign users having a properly worded privacy policy. Make those changes before you set up your first campaign.

Visit https://support.google.com/adwords/answer/2549063 and follow the directions carefully. You need to make sure that your privacy policy is updated to include:

- A description of how you're using remarketing.
- Notification that the ads you display will show on third-party websites, including Google itself.
- Notification that these third-party websites will use cookies to select appropriate ads.
- Guidance on how to opt-out of Google cookies (which users can do by clicking through to http://www.google.com/settings/ads).

CREATE CODE

Begin by logging into your Google AdWords account, navigating to the Shared Library under Campaigns, then under "Ads" selecting "Audiences" and clicking the red "+ Remarketing List" button:

Google will respond by generating a small snippet of code that needs to be added to every page on your website. Depending on the size of your site this may be a bit of work, but it's a one-time job.

You can then do one of two things with this:

1. Ask Google to email the code to your web developer, which they'll do along with some helpful instructions.
2. Install the code manually yourself.

In a worst-case scenario, you can always hire someone on Fiverr.com to do the job for you.

Once the code is in place throughout your website, every visitor who comes by will have a cookie installed on their computer that will automatically track which pages they visit during their stay.

HOW TO BUILD AN "AUDIENCE" TO REMARKET TO

Your next and most important job is to create and define your remarketing audiences, sometimes referred to as RM lists. Simply put, an audience is a list of people who meet certain criteria. You can see at any time how many people are on each list you build, but beyond the criteria you select, you won't know who they are or anything specific about them. Google keeps this information confidential, for obvious privacy reasons.

And because these audiences are created using cookies, the whole process is completely invisible to your visitors.

We'll get to crafting ads and fine-tuning the process in a moment, but your first focus is on getting your audiences up and running. Your lists grow automatically, but it takes time to build up a sizeable audience that you can remarket to—days or even weeks, depending on the volume of traffic your site receives. The sooner you complete the audience-building step, the better.

Google will ask you to name your remarketing list, and then specify who to add to it:

There are hundreds of different types of audiences you can create based on hundreds of different kinds of actions and behaviors. We suggest you start by creating **three basic lists,** as follows:

1. *Everyone*. Every individual who visits your site, regardless of what pages they looked at or the actions they took.
2. *Buyers*. Everyone who took the desired action, whether it was making a purchase, completing a lead capture form, or something else. Simply give Google the URL of your thank-you page, and anyone who completes an action and lands on that page will get added to this list. (Note that every visitor on this list will also be on the "Everyone" list.)
3. *Interested*. These people arrived at your site and visited certain specific key pages during their stay. Again, you can provide Google with the required page URLs that a person must visit to qualify for this list.

HOW LONG TO KEEP PEOPLE ON YOUR LIST?

Membership duration is key. This is the length of time that individuals remain on an audience list before Google removes them. For example, if you set this at 60 days, anyone who visits your site will drop out of your audience list after two months.

Note that if they visit your site *again* during that period their membership duration is reset and they'll remain on your audience lists for a new period of 60 days. The default period is 30 days but you can increase this to anything up to 540 days, or 18 months.

It might be tempting to just set this for the maximum duration. But keep in mind that the longer the period of time since the visitor has been to your site, the lower the CTR your remarketing ads will get.

TARGETING YOUR HOTTEST POSSIBLE PROSPECTS USING CUSTOM COMBOS

Once you've created your three basic audiences you can begin to think about developing audience subsets. You do this by combining your audience results with a bit of Boolean logic. For example, you can create a list that includes everyone who *is* on your "Interested" list, but is *not* on your "Buyers" list.

This might give you a list of people who:

- Visited one of your product description pages (e.g., any page in your /products/ directory)
- And visited the Shopping Cart page (indicating that they added something to their basket)

■ But didn't make a purchase (i.e., didn't visit your "thank you" or "download" page).

This is simple to set up, and it could prove incredibly valuable to you. *This one audience of visitors has by far the highest likelihood of bringing you new conversions and sales.*

Go back and click the red "+ Remarketing List" button. On the resulting page, find the "Who to add to your list" dropdown and choose "Custom combination."

A Clever Custom Combo Example

One of our clients has a sophisticated array of custom combos that matches ads with specific membership durations. She creates lists for durations of 3 days, 7 days, 11 days, and 15 days, and then creates combinations that include individuals on:

- The 3-day list
- The 7-day list but not on the 3-day list
- The 11-day list but not on the 7-day list
- The 15-day list but not on the 11-day list

This then allows her to create a progressive series of ads that are delivered in a precise order.

It's a complex example, but it may inspire you to create your own clever combos.

HOW TO CREATE A REMARKETING CAMPAIGN

Now that you've created one or more audiences, you head back to the "Campaigns" screen and click the red "+ Campaign" dropdown button. Choose "Display Network Only."

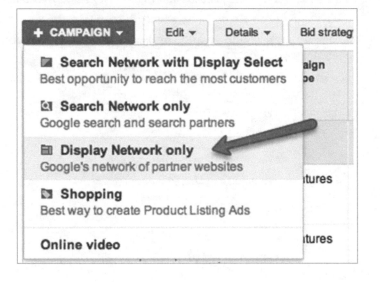

On the resulting page you'll notice under "Type" a radio button for Remarketing. Select it. Now you can choose your bidding strategy and set your daily budget for this campaign.

Your audience lists will start out empty, but over the coming days and weeks you'll watch their numbers grow. While you're waiting for this to happen, make good use of your time by crafting your first campaign with ads aimed specifically at your remarketing audiences.

Don't try to shortcut this process by copying your existing "Search" ads. That is lazy and it's a colossal waste of Google's remarketing system. The audiences you're creating have highly targeted individuals, and need ads that address them clearly and distinctly. Create separate campaigns for image ads and text ads. Within each campaign, create different ad groups for each audience.

A word about these settings. Pay special attention to the following three areas.

Bid Strategy

All the major bidding options are available for remarketing campaigns—cost per click (CPC), cost per thousand impressions (CPM), and cost per action (CPA)—but we suggest starting out with CPC. You can change to CPA later on if you're getting especially good results from your remarketing campaigns.

You should also consider bidding at least double your usual amount. Why? Because these people are warm leads. You can expect a higher conversion rate.

Geography

Look for this further down the page under "Location, language, and device targeting."

Google doesn't recommend adjusting this for remarketing campaigns. If your product is digital you may be fine showing your ads all over the world. But note: If you supply physical products or services and are only able to reach certain geographic areas, then it's essential that you modify this setting to reflect your target locations.

Frequency Capping

Find this option by clicking to expand "Ad scheduling and delivery options." You can set your number of impressions per day, week, or month, and applied per campaign, per ad group, or per ad.

This setting is unique to remarketing and allows you to specify how often any one person sees your ads. If you unintentionally show your ad hundreds of times a day to all the same people it'll kill your CTR, and it won't endear your brand to anyone. We recommend three impressions per day for image ads, and ten per day for text ads.

HOW TO WRITE REMARKETING ADS THAT GET CLICKS AND CONVERSIONS

One of the most attractive elements of remarketing is the way you can write ads specifically to people who have already seen your products and your brand.

However, you never want to forget the Golden Rule of remarketing ads:

Don't Be Creepy!

Remember the first time you became aware that you were being targeted by a remarketing campaign? How did it feel? *"Why does Cracked.com know that I've been thinking about buying a heated toilet seat? Who else knows about this?"*

Remarketing has been around long enough that most people are now accustomed to it. But some people are uncomfortable seeing their web browsing habits follow them around from site to site. How do you respond to that?

Answer: Never draw attention to the fact that you're remarketing to people!

A giant image of your logo with the message, "Hey, we miss you—When are you coming back?" is not smart.

We try to observe two simple methods for getting people's attention without highlighting the fact that they're a recent visitor:

1. Invite them to take the next action step you with you, *without mentioning* any previous steps they've taken.

 Let's say you have a three-step conversion process: A person can watch your video, download your white paper, and then purchase a ticket to your seminar.

 And let's say you want to target visitors who watched your video but haven't taken any of the subsequent steps. You can write an ad that's simply an invitation to download your white paper. For visitors who have already watched the video and downloaded the white paper, your ad can be an invitation to register for your seminar.

2. Follow the "FBI approach." You can spot a real-life stalker fairly quickly once you notice that the same guy is hanging around your street every day. The FBI is smarter than that. They employ a number of different people and rotate them frequently on a calculated basis. If the FBI were following you, odds are you'd have no clue.

 You can accomplish the same level of stealth with your ads. Simply create a wide array of visual ad campaigns and use frequency capping to strictly limit how often each ad is shown on any given day.

SHOULD YOU TRY CUSTOMIZED LANDING PAGES?

In short, yes. But first things first.

Creating a whole new set of landing pages that only your remarketing campaigns direct to could be a substantial amount of work. We'd rather you set up a remarketing

How to Rescue a Failing Remarketing Campaign

Want an example of how to save a bad remarketing campaign?

Let's say you write an ad that mentions a promotional code for use during checkout, but you don't bother referring to it on the landing page. If the customer can't remember the promo code from the ad, they'll give up trying to find it again. And you've lost the sale. Bad remarketing!

But there's a way to fix this.

Have your web developer program the promotional code into the URL so the discount is automatically applied to the shopping cart when your customer clicks on the ad. That's less work than creating new custom landing pages. And it's less "friction" too. The easier you make it for your visitors to get what they came for, the higher your conversion rate will be.

campaign and send people to your existing landing pages than overwhelm yourself with work and give up on the idea.

However, if you you're willing to put in the extra effort of creating customized landing pages with customized offers, your conversion rates will be substantially higher.

The key here is to identify why your visitor wasn't willing to go through with the purchase, and then create an offer that overcomes the objection.

If your most common barrier is price, create an ad that offers a 10 percent discount. Here's where that customized landing page becomes essential. If an ad promises a 10 percent discount, the landing page needs to back it up.

Experiment with different ads and different offers to see which generates the best results. If a 10 percent discount doesn't do the trick, follow up with another campaign that offers a deeper discount, or an exclusive bonus off.

As with all PPC work, watch your metrics carefully to ensure that your campaigns are profitable.

SOME ADVANCED REMARKETING TIPS

If your first remarketing campaigns are a success and you want to dig a little deeper, give these advanced techniques a try.

Analytics Remarketing

This is an incredibly powerful option that pulls data from your Google Analytics to create audiences. Inside Google Analytics are over a hundred metrics, and once your remarketing campaigns have been running for a few weeks you'll have access to a virtually unlimited array of audiences based on any metric or combination of metrics that you can think of.

Want to target people who spent at least five minutes browsing your site? Done. Want to create an ad offer that is only shown to people who read at least six of your blog posts? No problem. Want to reach out to people who arrived on your site via Facebook? Easy.

If you're not currently using Google Analytics, it's worth installing it simply to give you access to this facility. More on this in Chapter 29.

Remarketing Lists for Search Ads (RLSA)

This feature is a way of combining your remarketing lists with your search ads. Although you initially want to keep these separate, once you have some lists created that are working well you can try running them for some of the broad keywords that might not be profitable for general search ads. Another method for taking advantage of RLSA is

to bid on different levels for different campaigns, still showing the ads to everyone, but setting higher budgets for your more reactive remarketing lists.

To set this up, you'll want to go into a specific search-only campaign and ad group. From there, click on the Audiences tab in the middle of the page. You'll see a red "+ Remarketing" button, which you can click. Then click the "Add targeting" dropdown button and select "Remarketing" to add a list to your ad group.

Dynamic Remarketing

This advanced use of remarketing is only available for ecommerce sites that are using the Google Merchant Center. In this scenario, Google already has your product feed and can create ads that feature the products that your visitors have been looking at. If you have a large number of products, this feature can create hundreds or even thousands of precisely targeted ads on the fly. This is incredibly effective and doesn't require any huge investment of time or manual labor.

This option is available when you create a new campaign and designate it as Display Network only and specifically for remarketing. You'll look for "Enable dynamic remarketing" and click the button next to it to connect with your Google Merchant Center account. See the image on page 247.

YOUR QUICK ACTION SUMMARY

Unless your website is achieving unheard-of conversion rates, the vast majority of your visitors are leaving without taking your desired action and, unfortunately, most will

Which Banner Converts Best?

Donovan Kovar, AdWords consultant from Minnesota, offers these tips:

We use both text and banner ads for remarketing, and one will usually work better than the other depending on the niche. Always remember to include the phone number of your business in your banners, with a strong call-to-action so people can call you directly when they see your ad again.

I prefer to use CPM for remarketing ads (starting at $2 to $3 CPM) and I watch the "View Through Conversions" as an indication of which banner or ad is working the best. "View Through Conversions" are people who are returning to your site directly after seeing your remarketing ad, then converting.

Remember to exclude the visitors from your remarketing audience who have already converted so they don't keep getting followed around by your Ads, and you'll have a highly targeted, inexpensive and effective advertising campaign that really makes a difference for your business online.

never return, unless they're prompted to do so. For years, internet marketers have tried to overcome this problem by using pop-unders and exit ads. These had limited success and they were extremely annoying.

Remarketing is the ultimate solution to this problem of "bouncing" visitors. Not only does it allow you to maintain contact with almost 100 percent of the folks who have been to your site, it does so in a way that is completely invisible and carries minimal risk of irritating people.

Yes, remarketing is a bit more involved than most PPC strategies. But if you don't make use of it, your competitors will. For whatever setup effort you put into it, this will return you benefits and profit tenfold.

Here's a quick reminder of the basics and the steps you need to take to get started:

■ Update your privacy policy with four key adjustments. (https://support.google.com/adwords/answer/2549063)
■ Install the code on your website (or send it to your web developer to handle).
■ Build three basic audiences ("Everyone," "Interested," and "Buyers").
■ Create a new remarketing campaign containing at least one new ad group.
■ Set frequency capping for that campaign.
■ Create at least two new ads to go with that campaign (preferably more).
■ Activate your campaigns.

Uncle Claude Sez

Here again comes the advantage of figuring cost per customer. That is the only way to gauge advertising. Samples sometimes seem to double advertising cost. They often cost more than the advertising. Yet, rightly used, they almost invariably form the cheapest way to get customers. And that is what you want.

Google's Search Partner Network

Goldmine or Land Mine?

Did you know that your search ads by default actually show in two very different places?

- Google Search (google.com, google.co.uk, google.com.au, etc.).

- Google's Search Partner Network, or SPN (Amazon.com, eBay.com, Ask.com, other Google properties such as Maps & Finance and many, many others).

Let's be frank: The Search Partner Network is a less effective place to show your ads than Google's regular search page, most of the time. But unless you specifically turn it off, your ads are going to be seen there whether you asked for it or not.

Here's the dilemma:

The name "Search Partner Network" seems to suggest that your ads will show on partner sites that are essentially search engines like Google. For instance, Ask.com (formerly AskJeeves.com) is a key member of the SPN and your ads may be shown when search queries there match the keywords you're bidding on.

This is good business for Ask.com. They can monetize their traffic without having to create their own PPC program. It's also good business for Google, who extends their reach in exchange for shared click revenue.

However, despite the name, not every site on the SPN is a typical search engine. This network also includes sites such as Amazon, eBay, and Gumtree.com. Yes, visitors to these sites can perform searches, but the search results pages look very different from Google's. As a result, the location of your ads there can vary dramatically. On sites like these your ads perform far more like ads on Google Display Network (GDN) than the Google Search pages you're accustomed to.

You may think this is no big deal. Why don't we just create a separate campaign for the Search Partner Network—like we do with the GDN—and use different ads, different maximum bids, and so on?

Because Google doesn't allow it.

In the same way that you can't directly create separate campaigns for mobiles and tablets, you also can't create custom campaigns exclusively for the SPN. Once again, your choice is to either leave your ads running on the SPN, or turn them off altogether.

You're either all-in or you're out.

In our experience, the SPN often performs significantly worse than Google Search pages. Our advice to new AdWords users is to go into your search campaign's Settings tab and next to "Networks" click "edit" and uncheck the "Include search partners" box. See the image on page 251.

However, if you've been running AdWords campaigns for a while, it may be worth your time to dig a bit deeper. There exists a method to create a campaign that is almost 100 percent SPN-only.

HOW TO CHISEL YOUR WAY INTO THE SEARCH PARTNER NETWORK

This is a bit advanced. Are you ready?

Your first job is to look over your stats and decide if an SPN-only campaign is going to be a profitable exercise for you. Go to the Campaign screen of your AdWords account, click on the "Segment" drop-down menu, and select "Network (with search partners)."

This will segment the results for each of your campaigns into three lines: Google Search, SPN, and GDN.

If the SPN results are considerably worse than your Google Search results, there's no shame in simply turning it off and being done with it. But if you sense there's profit to be squeezed out of the SPN, here's what you need to do:

1. *Review your search query report and look for search phrases that suggest SPN.* When your ad is served on an SPN site that isn't a typical search engine, Google doesn't record a search query typed in by the user. Rather, they record text that identifies the content on the page, generally by showing the content of the H1 tag (i.e., the main headline on the page). Phrases like these will jump out at you when you're reviewing your Search Query Report because they're unusually long and contain repeating keywords.

 You can test whether a suspicious-looking phrase is from the SPN. Copy and paste the search query into Google.com and view the first search result. If it's an ecommerce site of some description and the page contains AdWords-style PPC ads, then it's very likely you've found an SPN page that was showing your ads.

 For example, if you see this in your Search Query Report:

 purax pure pads antiperspirant 30pcs adhesive underarm pads

 Copy and paste this into Google's search window and notice the page result that shows up.

 Google never publishes their list of SPN partners but this method is a dead giveaway to finding out which sites are included.

2. *Go into your main campaign, and add an SPN-specific search phrase as a negative exact match.* For example, make this phrase a negative exact match, using square brackets and a minus sign:

 -[purax pure pads antiperspirant 30pcs adhesive underarm pads]

 This will exclude any of your ads from your main campaign from being included any more on this page. It will also exclude your ad if someone manually types this search into Google, but that's unlikely given the obscure nature of the phrase.

3. *Create a new campaign for your SPN ads and start a new Ad Group containing this search phrase—and only this search phrase—as an exact match.* Every time someone visits this page on Amazon, in Google's eyes this particular Ad Group will be a perfect match. Again, unless someone types in this exact phrase into Google, your ad will only ever show on this specific Amazon page. You're now free to tailor your ad to this page, and adjust your maximum bid to better fit the results you're getting.

You may also find it useful to make the name of the ad group the site that you're targeting, along with the search phrase. So, in this example, your ad group would be called "Amazon.com—purax pure pads antiperspirant 30pcs adhesive underarm pads." This makes it easier to keep track of what this ad group is attempting to achieve.

YOUR QUICK ACTION SUMMARY

For most beginners, the best advice is to turn off the SPN in your campaign settings and forget about it. However:

- If you have an established AdWords account, segment your data to find out how your ads are actually performing in the SPN.
- If you're feeling bold, review your Search Query Report to locate sites from within the SPN and set up a campaign that specifically targets them.

Google Shopping Campaigns
A Huge ROI Boost
for Ecommerce

In this chapter we'll show you why Google Shopping Campaigns give ecommerce site owners a far better clickthrough rate and higher ROI. You'll also learn three simple steps to set up your own Google Shopping Campaign (with a little help from your webmaster).

It seems unfair that you can spend days, even weeks, agonizing over and split-testing ad copy, trying to find the perfect combination of words that will attract the maximum possible clicks, when posting a simple thumbnail image of your product and its price can blow those previous best results out of the water.

Unfair, maybe, but it's a boon for you if you run an ecommerce site. Information marketers and service providers don't get this feature. Ecommerce sites alone get to put images of their products directly onto Google's Search pages, via their AdWords account. David Rothwell, a highly skilled AdWords consultant from the UK, tells this story:

In 2008, I was invited to attend a conference at Google's European H.Q. in Dublin Ireland, where they re-launched Google Base/Froogle as the new Merchant Center—a database of your physical products that could show images, plus-box drop downs, and other enticing links in the new and free "Shopping Results."

As long as it remained free, there was not a huge incentive for advertisers to meet Google's strict publishing requirements, and many Shopping Results were initially of poor quality with garbled text and other problems while merchants got to grips with the new medium of data feeds.

This could clearly not continue, and given the emerging commercial value of this service it became obvious that one day Google would have to introduce charges, to "motivate" merchants appropriately to improve the quality of the shopping experience for their users.

Although Merchant Center remains free, in the fall of 2012 Google started to charge for the new Google Shopping service by requiring a link from a Merchant Center account, which has no billing or bidding mechanism, to an AdWords account which has both.

Google Shopping is built entirely around something called Product Listing Ads (PLAs). They're the small, square-ish image ads that appear at the top of the Google Search pages, sometimes under the premium ads on the left, other times just above the

top ad in the upper right-hand corner. Google will stick between four and eight of these onto a single page and feature the image of the product, the price, and the first few word or two of description from the website where the product is found.

These images draw the eye and attract a disproportionate share of clicks. Ecommerce stores that run AdWords PLA campaigns often bring in their highest ROI through these simple ads.

Google used to provide PLAs absolutely free of charge. The gravy train ended in 2013. Then in early 2014 Google introduced Google Shopping Campaign (GSC), and integration of PLAs into AdWords was complete.

If you're an ecommerce site owner using GSC for the first time, you'll be tickled at how easy it is to upload details of your product stock to AdWords.

Depending on the format of your shopping cart, you could have an individual ad for every single product in your inventory up and showing on Google in just a few hours.

HOW TO SET UP A GOOGLE SHOPPING CAMPAIGN

Unfortunately there's no way to just click a button and connect your ecommerce site directly to your AdWords account. You'll have to go through a Google Merchant Center (GMC) account. But there's a step even before you do that. Here's how you set this up.

Step One: Create a Data Feed

How easy is it to plug your product inventory into AdWords? That depends on the technical makeup of your site and shopping cart. Assuming you're not a technical wizard with the ability to code your own site entirely by hand, you'll probably want to speak with your webmaster about exporting your product list as a *data feed,* a specially formatted file containing a list of all your products and all the associated relevant information (price, brand, image, availability, etc.).

The vast majority of modern ecommerce platforms make this easy to do, so you should expect this to be quick and straightforward for any competent webmaster.

Step Two: Open a Google Merchant Center Account

Visit http://google.com/merchants to read about this. It's free. The main purpose is to plug in the data feed from your site. Again, you may prefer to simply arrange for your webmaster to enter your data feed details by providing him or her with the login details of your new GMC account.

This should be a one-time job. If you set up and install the data feed correctly, it will update automatically as your inventory changes.

Step Three: Link Your Google Merchant Center Account to Your AdWords Account

Why isn't there an option to plug your data feed directly into your AdWords account? The answer is that GMC acts as a kind of middleman, assessing your feed, keeping an eye on the data, and making sure the format is correct.

To link these accounts:

1. In your Merchant Center account, click "Settings," then "AdWords."
2. Click "Link another account," enter your AdWords customer ID, and save it.

HOW TO GET A GOOGLE SHOPPING CAMPAIGN UP AND RUNNING

You can now create a new campaign by backing out to your "All online campaigns" view, clicking the red "+ Campaign" button, and choose the "shopping" option. See the image on page 259.

You'll see the usual setup options such as "Default bid," "Daily budget," "Location," and so on. Once the setup process is complete, your products will automatically be placed into one product group called "All products."

You could, if you were so inclined, immediately activate your campaign and set your ads running. For most ecommerce site owners, however, this would be a bad idea. Why?

Because all the items in a group will have the same cost per click. You wouldn't want to bid the same price per click for a 50-inch flat screen television as you would for a cheap pair of wireless headphones.

So start by dividing the "All products" group into a set of subgroups. You can have separate bid prices for each. You can create subgroups of products based on any of a number of attributes those products might share, such as:

- Category
- Brand

- Product type
- Condition
- Item ID

If you choose to divide up the group up by brand, you could create a subgroup for every individual brand and, based on the attributes recorded in your data feed, Google will find and automatically transfer the appropriate product into each of these new subgroups.

Each of these new subgroups can then be divided into a further set of subgroups based on either the same attribute you just used or a completely different one.

And you can continue to subdivide and subdivide and subdivide, literally down to seven levels.

Again, why subdivide them? Answer: So that you can bid separate amounts.

Using our electronics store example, here's how you might subdivide a group:

1. You create the "All products" group, which contains your entire inventory: precisely 500 individual items that are available to purchase from your store.

 All products (500 items)

 You subdivide this group by "category." Your store features five different categories of products, each of which (for this example) contains 100 different items. This gives you one main group called "All products" with five subgroups, each containing 100 products.

 All products (500 items)

 > *Televisions (100 items)*
 > *Blu-ray players (100 items)*
 > *Videogame consoles (100 items)*
 > *Sound systems (100 items)*
 > *Smartphones (100 items)*

2. You subdivide televisions by the "brand" attribute. Your store features televisions by four different manufacturers, each of which has 25 different items in your inventory. So, you now have one main group called "All products," five subgroups containing 100 products each, and one of these subgroups divided into its own set of five subgroups, each containing 20 items:

 All products (500 items)

 > *Televisions (100 items)*
 >> *Samsung (20 items)*
 >> *Philips (20 items)*
 >> *Sony (20 items)*
 >> *Toshiba (20 items)*
 >> *Finlux (20 items)*
 > *Blu-ray players (100 items)*
 > *Videogame consoles (100 items)*
 > *Sound systems (100 items)*
 > *Smartphones (100 items)*

Keep on subdividing as you see fit. Maybe you subdivide your Sony Television subgroup by another category, this time screen size. Next you subdivide sound systems by a different category.

Once you've finished subdividing, you can customize each subgroup, adjusting the maximum CPC for each one, or even excluding particular groups entirely from being advertised.

Warning: Once you've created your full range of subgroups, your product divisions are set in stone. The only way to adjust them is to *delete the campaign* and begin again from scratch.

Power Tips for Success with Google Shopping

AdWords expert David Rothwell shares these insights into how to make Google Shopping work for you:

Track transaction-specific conversion values so you know what you actually earn from sales.

Break campaigns down into as many individual products as possible, so as to optimize your bidding.

Use the Return on Ad Spend feature to understand your profit.

Set high daily budgets with accelerated delivery when your return on ad spend is positive.

Check search query reports regularly for useful negative keywords to avoid wasting your click spend.

Publish your data feed file daily to keep it fresh even if you haven't changed anything. (Feeds expire every 30 days.)

Keep your product titles to 70 characters or less to avoid truncation and poor ad serving.

Use important keywords early and often in titles and descriptions to help Google match your best product to user searches.

Google changes things frequently, so check your campaigns regularly to make sure everything is optimized and running.

Google Shopping Campaigns offer plenty of good reporting options. All the data is available in a single location, namely, your AdWords account. You can segment your data by the groups you created or by individual products and then compare them at as detailed a level as you like.

You can also see information on your competitors, too. This is available when you look at Benchmark CTR, Benchmark Max CPC, and Impression Share. It's averaged and anonymized, so the data won't always be 100 percent accurate, but you're still going to get some good insights from this.

There is no ideal one-size-fits-all system for dividing up your products. For your first campaign, however, we recommend dividing up your "All products" group by "Item ID." Because every product in your inventory has a unique ID, this has the effect of creating a long list of subgroups, each containing a single item. This allows you maximum control when you're setting your CPC for each product.

YOUR QUICK ACTION SUMMARY

If you're an ecommerce site owner, Shopping Campaigns are Google's gift to you. They let you sell your products on Google's regular search pages using images.

- Speak to your webmaster about creating a data feed of your product inventory.
- Open a Google Merchant Center account and add in your data feed.
- Link your GMC account to your AdWords account.
- Create a new AdWords Shopping Campaign, starting with an "All products" group, and then subdivide it into appropriate subgroups.

Impression Share
Get More of the Right Eyeballs to See Your Offer

Once you bid on a keyword, your ad will automatically be shown every time somebody makes a related search, right?

Your ad may sometimes be in a fairly low position on the page, but it'll always be there somewhere, right?

Wrong.

Google almost never shows *any* advertiser's ads 100 percent of the time for a given keyword. There are a number of reasons for this; the most important being that Google wants to test other advertisers' ads to see how they perform.

Plus, Google makes more money showing 22 ads 50 percent of the time than showing 11 ads 100 percent of the time.

Google gets to control whose ads they show and how often. The percentage of the time they choose to show your ads for any given keyword is called *impression share* (IS), also known as *coverage*.

You can increase your impression share and ensure that more people see your ads more often. Google provides reporting data that shows your precise impression share and even provides hints at what you may need to do to improve it.

Imagine you have a profitable ad group, and you discover that your impression share is only 20 to 30 percent. Your ads could be seen *three to five times as often as they are,* and your profit would multiply by a similar factor. There's a huge opportunity to increase your bottom line, simply by improving this number.

HOW TO FIND YOUR IMPRESSION SHARE NUMBERS

To turn on this particular metric inside your AdWords account, go to the "Columns" dropdown menu and click to customize your columns. Then find "Competitive Metrics" and add the following three columns to your stats: "Impression Share," "Impression Share lost due to budget," and "Impression share lost due to rank."

You can view this data at the campaign, ad group, and keyword level. However, "Impression Share lost due to budget" only shows at the campaign level, so we suggest starting there.

> ### GDN Makes Impression Share a Challenge
>
> Impression share can be viewed for Search Network campaigns and Google Display Network campaigns. This chapter focuses on Search Network campaigns—the sheer size of the GDN makes it almost impossible to get anywhere near 100 percent. You would need an unlimited budget, perfect Quality Score, and even then you still wouldn't be able to get the full possible share.

Your impression share number will be a percentage that indicates how close you are to being seen 100 percent of the time. So if your impression share is 50 percent, this means that you're only being seen half of the time you could be. In this case, if you're receiving 1,000 impressions a day on a particular keyword, a 50 percent score means there are up to 1,000 *additional* impressions available to you on any given day—provided you can make the right improvements to your campaign.

"Impression Share lost due to budget" is simple to understand and fix. Let's say your daily budget is $10 but there are actually $100 worth of clicks available out there. Your impression share in this case will never exceed 10 percent, and the reports will probably tell you that your impression share lost due to budget is 90 percent.

"Impression share lost due to rank" is a bit more complex and involves a number of elements we'll look at more closely in a moment. In short, if Google doesn't feel that your campaigns are of a high enough quality, they'll limit your impression share even further.

HOW TO IMPROVE YOUR IMPRESSION SHARE

Impression share is a fantastically simple way of seeing how often your ads are showing, but it's also a quick measure of how Google perceives the quality of your campaign and the potential that exists to increase your profits.

There are two reasons why Google might limit your impressions (apart from the need to test the inventory of other advertisers):

1. *Your Daily Budget is too low.* This is simple to diagnose and fix. It's possible to double or even triple the impressions on a profitable account simply by increasing the daily budget; even raising it significantly above your current spend. With this you naturally need to exercise some caution. How profitable are your campaigns? What can your marketing budget sustain? Answer those questions and you can raise your budget and your impression share accordingly.

2. *Your Ad Rank is too low.* You can improve this by giving attention to three things:

- *Ad Extensions.* If you're not using them, then jump right in and try some sitelinks, location extensions, and call extensions.
- *Quality Score.* Google looks first at whatever campaign is running the highest volume. If the quality of the ads and keywords there is poor, your impression share will suffer. If you're showing a Quality Score of five or below, work on improving it. (See Chapter 23 on Quality Score.)
- *Maximum Bid.* If you need to bump this up to improve your Ad Rank, do so incrementally. Review your max bid every day if need be, and don't raise it more than you can afford or sustain. It's better to have a low impression share in a profitable campaign than to have a high impression share and be losing money!

What Is Exact Match Impression Share?

Google can give you an additional metric, called "Exact Match Impression Share." It's Google's prediction of what your impression share would be if every keyword in your campaign were set to exact match.

When you see this number, don't make the mistake of assuming you can fix a low impression share by switching your entire campaign to exact match keywords.

If impression share is new to you, ignore this number for now. If you're an experienced AdWords user and your exact match impression share is below 50 percent, compare your search query report with your keyword list. See if you have too many broad match keywords or possibly not enough negative keywords.

YOUR CAN SEE YOUR COMPETITORS' IMPRESSION SHARE, TOO

You can spy on your competitors using third-party software applications, but you can also do it within your own AdWords account. You can see your competitors' impression share for individual keywords or even entire groups of keywords.

There's a cool feature called "Auction Insights," which you'll find in the Keywords tab. Pick out a relatively high-volume keyword that you want to research, check the box next to it, and then look for the "Details" dropdown box, just above the "Keywords" list:

Choose "Auction Insights" from this dropdown box. This will load a report that shows your impression share for those keywords, as well as that of a few of your competitors.

You can also run this report at the Ad Group or campaign level, again by choosing your target keywords, and then selecting "Auction Insight" from the Details drop-down box.

YOUR QUICK ACTION SUMMARY

Impression share is one of the fastest ways to reveal untapped profit potential in your AdWords campaigns. Tweak your ad extensions and Quality Score first before attempting to increase your daily budget or maximum bids.

- Click the "Columns" dropdown menu and turn on data for "Impression Share," "Impression Share lost due to budget," and "Impression share lost due to rank."
- Consider whether you need to improve your Quality Score.
- Consider carefully if increasing your daily budget and/or your maximum bids could be a profitable way to improve your impression share.
- Activate ad extensions if you haven't already done so.
- Collect additional useful intelligence on your competitors by generating an Auction Insights Report.

Uncle Claude Sez

Don't get distribution by methods too expensive. Or by slow, old-fashioned methods. The loss of time may cost you enormously in sales. And it may enable energetic rivals to get ahead of you.

AdWords Editor
The Power Tool for Managing Campaigns with Ease

I n this chapter you'll learn six ways that AdWords Editor can be invaluable to you even if you're not running an agency.

AdWords Editor is the popular software application provided by Google that lets you edit AdWords accounts from your desktop and upload changes when you're done.

It not only makes AdWords adjustments easier, but also provides a variety of extra functions you can't perform in the browser interface. It's ideal for offering a birds-eye view of your campaigns and ad groups, and it's invaluable for quickly and easily monitoring the health of your account.

Rumors constantly abound that Google will be taking the Editor away. By the time you read this, it may have already been retired.

But as long as it's around, the Editor remains an irreplaceable part of every good AdWords expert's tool belt. Here's how to make hay while the sun shines, and get the most out of this amazing tool.

How to Get the Latest Version of AdWords Editor

Download the latest version of the Editor for Windows or Mac at http://google.com/adwordseditor.

Once you install it, the software will notify you when new versions are available and it needs updating. Note that it's a small Google development team that manages the Editor. New features from the regular AdWords interface can take months to appear in the Editor, if at all.

WHO IS THE ADWORDS EDITOR FOR?

Folks assume the Editor is only for PPC agencies. Actually, any person with a sizeable AdWords account will benefit from using it. It's good if you want to make swift assessments of your campaigns. It's better still if you have multiple users who are accessing an individual account. And it's invaluable if you want to make any bulk changes.

Google has been gradually adding Editor functions to the regular AdWords browser interface, but there are still some jobs you can't perform without it.

Begin by installing the software. Once it's installed, download your AdWords account data by opening the Editor, clicking on "Open Account," and entering your AdWords login details.

You should also take the time to download stats from at least the last 30 days.

Going forward, every time you use the Editor be sure to click "Get Recent Changes" before carrying out any work.

This is *mission critical* if you're not the only person who accesses the account! When performing this update you'll have a choice between "Basic" and "More Data;" I recommend always going with the latter.

Here are a few examples of the tasks you can perform with the Editor.

Example One: Add Keywords in Bulk

Sometimes, particularly when you're building a new account or campaign, you'll want to add a large number of keywords all at once. Problem is, in the browser interface you can only add keywords to one ad group at a time. If you've got hundreds or even thousands of keywords to add, that could be incredibly laborious.

In the Editor, however, you can add keywords to multiple ad groups across multiple campaigns.

To do this, import your keyword list into Microsoft Excel, format the list of keywords to match the Editor's requirements, and then simply copy and paste the list. Excel formatting instructions are here: https://support.google.com/adwords/editor/answer/56368.

It may take you a couple of tries at first to get Excel into the right format. But once you've got it sorted you can add tens of thousands of keywords across thousands of ad groups, in dozens of campaigns, in a matter of seconds.

Example Two: Edit Multiple Ads

What if you need to change some specific wording in your ad? Maybe you changed a product name. Or maybe you're running a new special offer. Or maybe you've created a new display URL for testing.

The Editor gives you a "search-and-replace" feature that lets you do just that.

For example, if a large number of your ads are advertising a "June Sale," running a simple search-and-replace will let you change every such instance to "July Sale."

Example Three: Change Bids in Bulk

You can change all of your individual keyword bids in one fell swoop using the Editor. Even better, you can adjust your bids based on specific rules. For example, you can instruct the Editor to search all of your campaigns, find every keyword that's

showing in position 8 or lower, and then increase that bid, either by a dollar amount or a percentage.

Example Four: Review Your Campaign Settings

Our friends at Mike Rhodes' company WebSavvy (WebSavvy.com.au) have a powerful but simple practice: Once each week they check the account of every single client to review campaign settings. Sometimes clients try to go into accounts and change things by themselves. One wrong adjustment at the campaign level can temporarily cripple an account. If a client makes an unfortunate mistake like that, it's important to catch it early.

The Editor is a great place to perform this check. It lets you view a huge range of settings and very quickly jump from account to account.

It even lets you copy campaigns from one account to another. The need for that may be rare, but when it comes up, this functionality is a massive timesaver.

Example Five: GDN Targeting Options

Individual ad groups have a huge array of targeting options. If you try to adjust each ad group manually in the traditional online interface you'll find it slow and arduous. But in the Editor you can quickly make bulk changes to large numbers of ad groups.

Not every ad group setting is accessible from the Editor, but this will still save you hours of tedious work.

Example Six: Adding Negative Keywords and Placements

The more experienced you become with AdWords, the more you'll find yourself needing to make ad group, campaign, and account changes on a large scale, as opposed to minor tweaks on individual keywords or ads.

Let's say you're looking over your Display Network campaigns and make the weird discovery that your ads always perform poorly when they show on About.com. (Other advertisers do fine there, but for some reason yours always tank.)

You can exclude the About.com placement so that your ads never show up there again. The Editor makes it simple and fast to add that excluded About.com URL across every campaign:

For more information and training on use of the Editor, visit the AdWords Editor Help Center at https://support.google.com/adwords/editor. For AdWords Editor Troubleshooting, go to https://support.google.com/adwords/editor/trouble shooter/2893845.

AdWords Editor and Microsoft Excel: Working in Harmony

AdWords Editor and Microsoft Excel go together like peas and carrots. Once you reach a point where the majority of your campaigns and ad groups are performing well, your focus will become less on small details and more on your big-picture strategy. It's at this point that you'll really see the value in having these two applications working in harmony. It's actually easier to transfer data between Excel and the Editor than it is to transfer data between Excel and the online interface.

YOUR QUICK ACTION SUMMARY

Get starting using the Editor, even if you still consider yourself a PPC beginner.

- Download AdWords Editor and import your AdWords account data into it.
- Every time you log in, run the "Get Recent Changes" feature.
- Review your campaign settings every week to be sure some mission-critical thing hasn't changed.
- Use the Editor any time you need to make a bulk change involving multiple ads, ad groups, or campaigns.
- Use the Editor any time you need to copy and paste ads, keywords, or ad groups from campaign to campaign or account to account.

Google Analytics
Know Where Your Visitors Come From and Where They're Going

A year after I escaped the *Dilbert* cube and started my consulting firm, I got an ecommerce client who had a large website and sent out a million catalogs a year. When we first began working together, they didn't track much of anything. I slapped my hand on the table and said, "Well, that's going to stop, right now." I was confident and a little cocky, and we rolled up our sleeves and went to work.

MILLION-DOLLAR AD TRACKING DISCOVERY FROM MY FIRST BIG CLIENT

Like I said, this company mailed out a million catalogs a year to a recipient list made up of current and former customers and names rented from 16 different

trade magazines. The impact of the catalog mailings was obvious—sales spiked two weeks after the catalogs went out, like clockwork, as did visits to the website.

But which of those 16 mailing lists actually worked and which lists were a waste of money?

And how much of the website traffic was from the catalog?

How much of the sales on the website came from PPC traffic? How much from organic free listings? And how about blasts to the email list?

At this time, I was solidly grounded in direct-marketing techniques, so I expected this to be easy.

Boy was I ever wrong.

It might be easy to track sales generated by the catalog if we used different part numbers in the catalog than on the website. But that would cause endless confusion. We could track different mailing lists if we printed different versions of the catalog with different part numbers in each version, but that would make things even worse.

Some customers called on the phone, others ordered online. Sometimes the engineer specifying the product ordered it himself and sometimes he sent the order over to purchasing. Sometimes the product got installed in Philadelphia where the customer ordered it; other times the product got shipped to an oil refinery in Houston.

In short, perfectly connecting the dots on every sale was for all practical purposes impossible. I quickly realized that despite my direct marketing dogma about measuring absolutely everything, I had to develop an accurate sense of what *contributing factors* were influential in closing the sale.

The first thing we did was test the 16 mailing lists we were renting from the magazines. We did this by mailing out postcards to portions of each list, offering a white paper. That was easily measurable and we figured that response to a white paper offer would reasonably approximate likelihood to buy from a catalog.

You might not be surprised to find out that 80 percent of the responses came from four of those 16 lists. The other 12 lists were a waste of money. We immediately cut our catalog mailing volume in half with almost no loss of sales.

As we began to measure more and more contributing factors to each sale, we cut out more and more waste. The money they used to spend on stuff that didn't work started going to things that did work. In short, the company quadrupled its sales over the next ten years—despite being in a very slow-moving, declining industry.

Even if you don't mail out a million catalogs a year, even if you don't do a lot of offline marketing, and even if none of your customers hand the order off to a purchasing agent in Houston, you still need to measure those contributing factors. Sure, in theory people should see your Google ad, click on it and buy, and everything should be trackable. But real life is almost always more messy than that. That's why Google Analytics can be a big

help. With Google Analytics, you almost always have at least a decent idea of what things are influencing your customers to buy.

WHAT HAPPENS AFTER THE CLICK?

AdWords is great at telling you which of your ads are getting clicks and even which of those clicks result in conversions. But what about the traffic you get from organic search or through your email campaigns? How do those sources convert? Are their conversions better than what you're getting from PPC?

Also, what about all the people who didn't convert? What did they do on your site? How long did they spend reading your pages? What videos did they watch? What outbound links did they click on?

And which of your pages need improving? Which pages are already working well?

AdWords can't answer those questions, *but Google Analytics can.*

Most people are intimidated by Google Analytics. Even the name sounds daunting, like something über-technical that only geeks would appreciate. But don't freak out. Plug Google Analytics (GA) into your reporting system, learn to watch and respond to it and you *will* become a better marketer. You *will* improve your PPC results.

FIRST STEP: MACRO CONVERSIONS VS. MICRO

Let's say you're an ecommerce site owner and that 1 percent of your visitors make a purchase.

You can study this 1 percent as much as you like in your AdWords reporting—which keywords people searched on, which ads they clicked, where users are located, what time of day they made their purchase, and so on—but none of that will tell you anything worthwhile about the other 99 percent.

You could be converting at 10 percent (a rate most online retailers would kill for) but that would still leave 90 percent of your traffic journeying their way anonymously through your site and leaving you with no clue as to what, if anything, was of interest to them.

This is where GA can help you out. The first step toward learning this is to set up some processes called macro and micro conversions.

What is a *macro conversion*? It's the single prime action that you want your visitor to take. If you run an ecommerce site, you want your visitor to make a purchase. If you run a lead generation site, you want your visitor to give you his or her contact details.

Micro conversions, then, are everything else that represents a positive step *toward* that macro conversion, no matter how small. That could be a whole range of things, such as downloading a brochure, visiting your contact page, going to one of your social media pages, watching a video—anything.

How to Dig Deeper Into Analytics

This chapter is only a very basic introduction to Google Analytics. It's enough to get you started. If you want to fully master this area of marketing, we highly recommend Market Motive's Analytics course (www.marketmotive.com).

The more you know about which micro conversions people are completing—and about the people completing them—the better equipped you are to optimize your AdWords campaigns. With that knowledge you can move more and more of your budget toward profitable keywords and demographics and away from the unprofitable ones.

What are all of the possible actions on your site that you want visitors to do? Browse through your site and jot them down. Seriously—every last one.

Next, set up these macro and micro conversions as "goals" in your GA account. To do that, look under "Conversions" for "Goals" and click "Overview" to start setting them up:

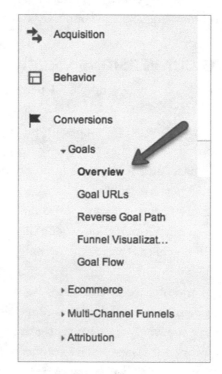

Google will walk you through the process. One of the steps will be to assign a value to each goal.

There's no scientific formula for how many "points" you give to each conversion or goal. The goals that move people closer to converting get more points, and the conversion itself gets the most points. We recommend you start with the smallest micro conversion and assign it one point. Then work your way up.

If, for instance, you're an ecommerce site owner, clicking on one of your social media buttons might be worth one point. Interacting with your store locator could be five points, downloading a brochure could be ten points, and buying a $200 item could be 200 points.

Don't get hung up on trying to assign a dollar value for each action your visitor takes. That isn't the point of this exercise. The idea is simply to set a consistent scoring system so you can directly compare the different metrics on which GA reports.

With a crude points system in place, you can compare traffic sources. If the average visitor to your site via AdWords performs five points' worth of micro conversions but visitors arriving via your email campaigns perform twenty points' worth, you can then dig deeper and figure out what's making the difference.

Maybe visitors from your email campaign are hitting one landing page while your AdWords visitors are going to another, and that's what's making the difference. Comparing your micro conversions in this way tips you off to what is and isn't working.

And you can compare so many other things, too.

Which geographic areas give you visitors with the highest scores? Do visitors from Houston score higher on average than visitors from Chicago? If so, you might want to adjust your AdWords campaign to bid higher and attract more Houston folks.

What about your ads on GDN? Does showing them on site A give you more conversion points than site B? Or are they both flops?

Even Better Analytics Data With Google's URL Builder Tool

If you're running ads on networks other than AdWords, use Google's URL Builder Tool to properly tag your traffic. With that, Analytics can compile data and let you do comparisons.

For example, how does the quality of your AdWords traffic compare to your Bing ads? Or how do either of these traffic sources compare to the direct media ads you bought? You can find the URL Builder Tool with a helpful explanation at http://support.google.com/analytics/answer/1033867.

Are you beginning to see the power that GA gives you to improve your AdWords campaigns?

HOW TO GET ADWORDS AND ANALYTICS TALKING TO EACH OTHER

It's possible to have an AdWords account *and* an Analytics account without the two ever even communicating. That's not helpful. If they're going to work properly, you'll want to link them. Here's how:

1. Make sure you have "admin" rights for both accounts and that both use the same login email address.
2. Go to your GA account, navigate to the Admin tab, find "Account Settings" on the left, and click on "AdWords Linking" below it. Click "New Link" and select "AdWords account" from the list shown.
3. Go to your AdWords account, click on the "cog" icon, and navigate to "Account Settings." On the Preferences screen look for "Tracking," and then something called "Auto Tagging." Make sure this is set to "yes."

4. Finally, also under your AdWords Account Settings, go to "Linked Accounts" and look for the "Google Analytics" section. Click on "View Details" and make sure that your AdWords account is linked to your Google Analytics "view."

Once you've completed this you can start using Google Reports. The two you'll be most interested in are:

■ *AdWords-specific reports.* You'll find these under the "Acquisition" menu. There's lots of valuable data here, so dig in and see what you can find.

Who Gets Credit for the Sale?

"Attribution" is a hot topic. Let's say your prospect hears your radio ad, does a Google search and clicks on your ad, goes back to Google to search on your brand name, clicks on your website link in the organic listings, and finally buys. Which of these marketing "channels" gets credit for the sale?

Officially, Google will "attribute" the sale to your natural search listings. But reality is much more complicated. Every stage in the process played its part, but how significant was the radio ad? How much did the organic listings contribute?

Google has a tool to help answer this, called "Multi-Channel Funnels." Google is currently integrating this into AdWords in the "Search Funnel" section. If you want to unlock the full power of Analytics this is well worth investigating. Read about it here: https://support.google.com/analytics/answer/1191180.

- *All Traffic report.* This is the report you'll need most frequently. At a high level it shows how AdWords (labeled as "Google/CPC") is performing compared to other sources of traffic.

ANALYTICS REMARKETING

We devoted Chapter 24 to remarketing, the single most cost-effective tool in your Google tool belt. The good news is that it works *even better* when you integrate it with Analytics. Another good reason to link your accounts immediately.

Recall that with remarketing you build audience lists based on what actions people do or do not take on your site. Without integrating GA you can only build lists based on pages people visited on your site.

For example, a business owner who specializes in coffee products might create a list just of people who visited pages under her site's /coffeemachines/ directory.

But once you integrate GA, you can create scores of additional lists based on a myriad of other behaviors and actions:

- The device a visitor used to access your site
- The length of each person's visit
- The amount of money a person spent
- The number of pages a person visited

You can even tie your remarketing lists to individual micro conversion goals: everyone who downloaded your brochure, everyone who watched a certain video, etc.

To get access to this, there are a few things you'll want to do first.

Revisit Chapter 24 on remarketing for a fuller discussion but, to access this additional level of functionality, make sure you've carried out these few steps.

1. Update your privacy policy (see the previous remarketing chapter for a reminder of what this requires).
2. Be sure you're using the DoubleClick version of Analytics. As of this writing, the Universal version doesn't currently support remarketing list creation.
3. Go to the Admin section of GA and under the Property column you'll find the "Remarketing" section. Click to expand it, than click on "Lists" to find the option to "Add New Remarketing List."

YOUR QUICK ACTION SUMMARY

Analytics isn't just for geeks. It's a gateway to learning more about all of your visitors and properly comparing your various marketing efforts in real time.

- Make your own exhaustive list of the macro and micro conversions people can take on your site.
- Create goals in Analytics for each macro and micro conversion.
- Assign a value to each goal.
- Link your AdWords and GA accounts together.
- Tweak your GA account to give you a greater range of remarketing options.

Uncle Claude Sez

Advertising is traced down to the fraction of a penny. The cost per reply and cost per dollar of sale show up with utter exactness.

One ad is compared with another, one method with another. Headlines, settings, sizes, arguments. and pictures are compared. To reduce the cost of results even one per cent per ad means muchSo no guesswork is permitted. One must know what is best

In lines where direct returns are impossible we compare one town with another. Scores of methods may be compared in this way, measured by cost of sales.

Keep Your Campaigns
Purring Like a Kitten
The $1,000 Per Hour Job Most People Don't Show Up For

In this chapter we're going to show you three crucial checks you can do regularly that ensure your PPC campaigns remain healthy. Along with that you'll learn seven methods for scaling up your already profitable campaigns, and seven steps for auditing and streamlining an established campaign.

I once had a client who, in three and a half years, had tested a grand total of six ads in his #1 ad group. He'd bought 92,000 clicks, spent over $100,000, and the campaigns were profitable.

"Dude," I said, "You are leaving an astonishing amount of money on the table."

I explained, "For every 100 clicks that comes through, you have the potential to

test one pair of ads and declare a winner. At least for CTR, if not for conversion. During the last three years you could have tested hundreds or even thousands of ads and you'd be getting twice the traffic for one third the money."

He began routinely testing ads, and sure enough, his CTR skyrocketed by 400 percent and his CPC dropped by two thirds.

Months later he was getting eight times the traffic for about half the cost per conversion. *Simply by making a habit of* kaizen *continuous improvement.* This alone can catapult an ordinary player to THE alpha dog in many markets.

One of the great advantages Google AdWords has over most other advertising channels is: *It runs continuously.* Yes, it's a lot of work to set up, but once it's in place it hums along for months and years. I've had ad campaigns run for over two years with an absolute minimum of attention, bringing leads and sales 24/7/365. Which is just fabulous.

But ironically that's where most people go wrong. The typical Google advertiser logs into his or her account only once every month or two. If you have a plan and structure for regularly reviewing and improving your campaigns, your costs will get cut in half, your traffic will double, and your ability to get leads in sales will double or even quadruple. And you'll be much less vulnerable to competition.

Running "real-world" marketing campaigns in television, radio, or print can be torture.

A team of hard-working professionals can slave away for months, sweating over the minutiae of a carefully crafted television commercial or direct mail campaign, only to realize a few weeks after launch that conversions are barely above zero.

An executive can invest tens or even hundreds of thousands of dollars and watch a costly campaign go flat. Then he's faced with a decision: Give it more time in the hopes that it'll turn a corner for the better? Or ditch the project entirely and try to go find more money to restart from scratch?

Thankfully, PPC doesn't have to be *anything* like that.

Sure, compared to the "set it and forget it" nature of Yellow Pages ads and magazine inserts, Google AdWords requires you to be far more hands-on. That's a turnoff for some. But the smartest marketers recognize that this gives you a huge advantage. PPC by its very nature is designed to let you correct mistakes and scale up successful campaigns *quickly*.

A good AdWords account requires ongoing management. That's not a curse and it's not a burden. It's a gift, a golden opportunity to keep testing, measuring, and improving results in real time.

In this chapter we're going to look at the proper way to monitor your Google AdWords campaigns, where to focus your attention, and how to turn failure into success.

Mike Rhodes's company WebSavvy.com.au does campaign management and Google AdWords audits from Down Under, full time. Let's take a look at the checklist that Mike follows with his WebSavvy team when reviewing a client's account.

ONGOING MANAGEMENT: CHECKS

How often do you review your AdWords campaigns and how much time do you spend on each step? That depends on the level of effort you're willing to commit. Ideally you'll want to perform these steps once per month. If your schedule lets you do this more frequently, even better.

WebSavvy breaks down their ongoing management into three phases: Checks, optimizing, and expansion.

Imagine a guy who regularly pays for expensive engine tune-ups but never thinks to check and top off his windshield washer fluid. Too many business owners treat their AdWords accounts the same way. They don't check on the simple, basic stuff often enough.

That's why the "checks" phase comes first. This part of managing accounts is relatively easy to carry out and is *essential* if the rest of your AdWords work is to be effective.

There are three things you want to measure in this step. Each of them is mission critical.

Check Your Conversion Tracking

This is not the first on the list by accident. The first step to any success in any business system is deciding what measurement is going to tell you that your business is, in fact, running like it should.

How to Spot Conversion Tracking Bugs Early

The most common way conversion tracking fails is when a well-meaning web developer tweaks something on your site and unintentionally messes up the process. Sometimes he'll make a change on a page and accidentally delete the tracking code. He might alter the URL of one of the pages, and a seemingly innocuous one-character difference is enough to grind conversion tracking to a halt.

Don't yell at your developers. They have a tough job. But be sure to vet their work and check your tracking processes on a regular basis.

Setting up your conversion tracking is simple, but it's also easy for things to break down. If you're using code on your key pages to measure conversions, check regularly to be sure the code is still present and installed correctly.

Jon Correll of ConversionVoodoo.com, a conversion optimization company, says that he has *never* seen a company that didn't have broken forms, broken conversion tracking, or some kind of other major defect that nobody had caught.

Also, check the conversion process itself to ensure that no glitches have cropped up. Working tracking code on your "thank-you" page is pointless if the lead-capture form itself is broken. Make sure these pieces of your funnel are installed and functioning.

Check Your Campaign Settings

The settings inside your Google AdWords account aren't likely to change without your noticing. But don't take this for granted! Especially if you're not the only person administrating your campaign. Keep a written record of your settings and occasionally check them to be sure nothing has been moved, adjusted, paused, or unintentionally reset.

Check Your Landing Pages

Start by looking for obvious glitches such as broken formatting or dead links. Then take a high-level view and ask whether you're matching the right landing page to the right ad copy. Does what you promise in the ad get delivered in the landing page? Is the connection between the two intuitive and obvious to the visitor? Is there a better landing page you could be using? Is it time to consider building a new one that gives your visitors a better experience?

ONGOING MANAGEMENT: OPTIMIZING

"Outliers" is a term made popular by Malcolm Gladwell's book *Outliers: The Story of Success*. It refers to fringe elements that in some way behave differently to everything else. In Gladwell's case he was referring to exceptional people. You can have "outliers" in AdWords too: campaigns, ad groups, keywords, ads, or placements that perform significantly better—or significantly worse—than everything else.

You could spend your time optimizing every last element of your PPC campaigns, but that's not 80/20. Go for your outliers first.

The goal is simple: Increase the good outliers and decrease or fix the bad ones. If you have a particularly high-performing keyword, for instance, you might want to raise the bid and get more impressions, clicks, and conversions. If you have a poorly performing

keyword, on the other hand, try lowering the bid or even removing it from the campaign altogether.

Before you reach for the "nuke" button, however, ask whether you can improve the bad keyword by writing a better ad or building a better landing page for it. Sometimes your worst player can turn into your star player.

How long do you work on a troublesome keyword or ad group before nixing it? That comes down to your patience, your tolerance for risk, and your budget. If you have a large account with hundreds of ad groups, you can afford to be more aggressive with poor performers.

Either way, don't burn hours of time over a bad keyword, especially if you've got bigger and more profitable ad groups that you could be optimizing for better gains. Pause a questionable keyword and come back to it at a future date if you need to.

ONGOING MANAGEMENT: EXPANSION

Once your AdWords account is well-optimized, think *expansion:* more impressions, more clicks, more conversions. With PPC you can never have too much of a good thing.

There are a number of different ways you can you can expand an account.

Richer, Thicker Search Campaigns

- *Start with new keywords*. The search query report is a goldmine for this information. (To access this, look under the Dimensions tab and in the "View" dropdown box select "Search Terms.") This shows you the actual search terms people typed in that Google chose to show your ad for. Look for common phrases that aren't yet in any of your ad groups. Add them in.
- *One useful thing you'll find in the Opportunities tab is Google's list of additional keyword suggestions*. This section is useful for finding new ideas, but beware: don't be too quickly sucked into Google's insistence that the best thing you can do is increase your maximum bids. There's a time and place to raise bids. *Do not* do it in kneejerk response to Google's pestering.
- *Pay regular visits to Google's Keyword Planner*. We also recommend third-party applications like SpyFu, AdGooroo, WordStream, and Wordtracker. Go digging there on a regular basis to find new keyword ideas.
- *Try aiming for the top positions*. When your ad moves from the ordinary listings down the right side of the page and starts showing up in one of the three premium spots at the top of the page above the organic results, the positive difference in CTR is massive. Use your "Top vs. Other" report to see this spelled out in hard numbers.

> ## Do Higher Positions Boost Your Quality Score?
>
> Getting your ad into the top three positions will virtually always give you a huge bump in CTR. However, that doesn't necessarily translate into a huge bump in Quality Score. Remember, Google is grading you on the curve. Google knows being in prime positions will improve CTR for even poorly written ads, so they apply something called "normalization." They will only kick up your Quality Score if you're performing better on average than other ads do in a given position.

Display Campaigns with Vibrant Ads That Show Everywhere

- Never assume that the performance of your display campaign ads has hit its ceiling. Keep testing new ads with fresh ideas and try to beat your best CTR. This rule holds especially true for image ads. You can often get a really quick win just by testing a vibrant new image.
- If you're using a managed placement campaign, always be looking around for new sites where you can feature ads. If you're using contextual targeting, always be looking for new keywords or topics you can introduce that will expand the range of sites where your ads can show.
- Experiment with different targeting methods. If you're only using managed placements, give contextual targeting a try, and vice versa. And if you're not using remarketing, this should be at the top of your idea list.

HOW TO AUDIT AND DIAGNOSE PROBLEMS QUICKLY

If you've been running AdWords campaigns for any length of time it's a good idea to perform a full audit. WebSavvy audits hundreds of client accounts each year, and here are the main steps they follow. These are an excellent way to quickly identify and address problems and issues that have crept in unnoticed.

1. Structure Your Account Just Right

Start by getting a bird's-eye view of your Google AdWords account. Remember the 80/20 rule? Look for the 20 percent of problems that are causing 80 percent of your slowdown or cash loss, and which will give you 80 percent of your potential improvement once you fix them.

Here are some clues to where some of your biggest problems might be hiding:

- *Not enough ad groups.* The key to PPC success is matching the right ads with the right people. If a campaign only contains one ad group, then every one of your potential prospects is seeing the same generic pair of ads from you regardless of what keyword they searched on. We know with near-100 percent certainty that that's going to earn you some terrible CTRs. In Chapter 23 we shared an example of a doctor bidding on "chiropractor," "back pain," and "sciatica." Each of these themes needs an ad group of its own, with custom ads written to match the keyword. Peel and stick those keywords and give them the exact ads and campaign settings they need for maximum performance.
- *Number of keywords per ad group.* Now dig a little deeper and see how many keywords you have in each group. Ideally you want to see no more than 20 keywords per group. If you've exceeded this amount, create new ad groups and split your keywords into more tightly focused sets.
- *Number of ads per ad group.* If most or all of your ad groups only contain one ad, you're making a big mistake. You're missing valuable opportunities to test and find new, better-performing ads. Just two or three ads per group is plenty for the vast majority of campaigns. Note that it's perfectly acceptable to have two ads targeting desktops along with two ads targeting mobile devices, for a total of four. But that should be your limit when starting out.

2. Find the Right Devices to Show On

Google no longer gives you the option to create ad groups that specifically target mobile users. However, you can see numbers that will help you decide whether or not to show your ads to mobile audiences.

If your impressions, clicks, and conversions are substantially lower for mobile users, odds are the mobile version of your site isn't functioning properly. Updating your site for mobile users could give you a huge boost in conversions. But before you invest time in that, look over your results, and do the math. If you want to prevent your ads from showing to the mobile market, see the previous chapter on bid modifiers. At the campaign level you can set up a bid modifier of -100 percent for mobile devices, and that will keep you from showing there.

3. Know Your Best Networks

As with mobile targeting, you don't have a massive amount of control over which of Google's networks you show on. You can keep your Search Network and Google Display Network campaigns separate, but targeting Google's search partners is limited to "on" or "off." Check your search partner network numbers. If they're good, consider increasing your bids across the board. If they're poor, it may be wise to opt out of the search partners network completely.

4. Show in Positions on the Page That Convert

Hint: Unless you're already a master of ad copy, nothing will boost your CTR faster than improving your ad position, *especially* when you make the jump from the right side of the results page to the premium positions top and center.

This is why the "average position" metric in your campaign reports can be incredibly helpful. The "Top vs. Other" report we showed you earlier will give you this data.

Check to see how often your ads are at the top of the page versus other positions, such as on the right. There's no perfect place for everyone; you'll need to test to see which positions give you the best ROI. But the premium listings at the top will give you a much higher CTR—up to *15 times* that of the other places on the page.

If you're in position one or two, odds are you're getting the maximum potential traffic. If you're ranking lower, somewhere "below the fold" where searchers have to scroll in order to see you, then you've got room for improvement.

How do you push your ad up one or two places? Answer: Bid more. If it means the difference between you being in the top three or not, it's almost always a profitable move.

Note: Your ranking on the page is a function of your bid price *and* your Quality Score. That means that if you improve your CTR by testing new ads, your Quality Score goes up. If you tweak your landing page to make it more relevant, your Quality Score goes up. And when your QS goes up, Google will rank you higher on the page (and give you more impressions) *without* you having to bid more per click.

Regardless, don't expect to bat 1,000. Placing in the top three 100 percent of the time for any keyword is nearly impossible. Aim for a minimum of 50 percent and consider anything around 80 percent to be a job well done.

5. Use Keyword Match Types for Efficiency

With your keywords, there are two common pitfalls to look out for:

1. Too many broad matches, or
2. Too many exact matches.

Rely too heavily on broad match keywords and you'll end up with huge numbers of irrelevant impressions. Fill your ad groups with exact match keywords only, and you'll miss out on huge volumes of traffic.

Take a careful look through your Search Query Report. It will tell you which matching options are being associated with your ads most often, and how successful each one is.

6. Test to Find Winning Ad Copy

Find an ad group that has at least two ads and ask: How different are the ads from each other?

Same headline? Same offer? Same body copy? Same hook? Just a word different here, maybe a comma there?

Remember David Bullock's ad copy maxim from Chapter 18:

First test forests, then test trees, then test branches, then test leaves.

If you've only been running the ads in a particular ad group for a few months or less, you want to be testing "forests," not minor tweaks. You want to see different headlines, different offers, even different display URLs where possible.

For a campaign that's been around for years, small tweaks make sense. Otherwise, make every ad test you run as fresh and creative as possible.

7. Landing Pages That Convert

Compare each ad to the landing page it directs to. Are the two consistent? Is the landing page *obviously* about the keyword? If in the ad you promised information or an opportunity to take action or get a free gift, is that clearly and obviously available on the landing page? Is there a clear call-to-action? If not, your conversions will suffer.

YOUR QUICK ACTION SUMMARY

Thankfully, PPC is not a one-shot deal. Start with a good foundation and then put a solid ongoing campaign management schedule in place so you can continually revise and improve your results and, ultimately, your bottom line.

- Schedule time for routine campaign management, at least once per month. Weekly if at all possible. (That simple, weekly AdWords account checkup, which includes testing a few new ads and improving conversions, can earn you as much as $1,000 per hour. No joke. It is one of the highest-paid 15–30 minute activities you can do.)
- Check your conversion tracking, campaign settings, and landing pages for obvious mistakes and screw-ups.
- Focus more time, money, and effort on keywords and ad groups that are performing well. Find the especially bad ones and fix them, or more likely nix them for good.
- Expand your campaigns through keyword research, bid increases, and new targeting methods.
- Run an audit. Go through established, long-running campaigns and check their structure, the devices and networks they target, and how well each is performing. See what your average ad positions are and how your different match types are performing.
- Test new ad copy and revisit your landing pages to ensure they echo your ads perfectly.

How to Hire the Right AdWords Agency

Did you know that having an agency manage your campaigns may very well trump hiring an in-house employee? It's true. In this chapter we'll walk you through 11 key qualifying questions you should ask before hiring any agency and suggest the best payment model for getting the results you need. We'll also show you how to sidestep the deadly pitfall of handing full ownership of your AdWords account to someone else, while still getting the management help you need.

One of my Mastermind Club members, Bill Crawford, owned a basement waterproofing franchise in Chicago. Bill honed his AdWords chops and found

out (as is often the case) that even in a narrow niche like "basement waterproofing" in a local area like Chicago offers a great deal of traffic if you build your campaigns properly.

His lead flow expanded dramatically in three months. His business went from struggling to prosperous. Inevitably, he started talking about his success at franchisor meetings. Almost without trying, he picked up 16 clients, other franchisors around the country. He was able to easily replicate what he'd so painstakingly set up in other metro areas. Suddenly he had a bunch of raving fans and unwittingly became the world's #1 expert on basement waterproofing for Google AdWords.

Many PPC experts, consultants, and agencies have grown from similar circumstances. Hiring the right agency can be a huge boon for your business, too.

But hiring the right agency is hard. It's a lot harder than finding a good accountant or attorney!

Still, would you rather be doing work that's worth $10 per hour or $10,000 per hour?

If you're managing things right, your AdWords account will grow and your business right along with it. And as your business grows, every minute of your working time will become more valuable.

Eventually you'll reach the point where you make more dollars tackling big projects and opportunities than by managing keywords and ads. Optimizing your AdWords campaigns might be $100 or even $1,000/hour work, but you'll know there's $10,000/hour work to be found elsewhere.

At that point it's time for someone else to take over the reins. Plan on it. Decide you're going to hand this off to capable individuals long before your PPC campaigns start to show signs of neglect.

Before we go on, though, let me make two things clear:

1. AdWords is *not* easy to outsource. Generally it's one of the hardest marketing jobs you can hand off to an outside person or firm.
2. You should not outsource it too soon. It's doubly hard to outsource if you don't thoroughly understand it yourself. Time spent learning AdWords is never wasted. I can't tell you how many customers have said to me, "Perry, I learned AdWords from you in 2005 and I've applied all the stuff I learned from you in all kinds of other situations that had nothing to do with AdWords." AdWords itself is the best direct marketing education I know of.

Onward. You have two options for finding a manager for your AdWords account: 1) hire someone in-house or 2) hire an agency.

With the in-house route you get a person who will have more intimate knowledge of your business, your objectives, your values, your immediate plans, and such.

Most people choose the in-house option to save money. But in our view this is false economy. Any savings you get by hiring someone internally can easily be dwarfed by the increase in profits that a quality agency can provide.

AdWords-focused agencies also give you a number of other benefits that internal employees will struggle to match:

- PPC is all they do. Keeping up with Google's perpetual changes, improvements, and tweaks is a challenge that PPC agencies have both the time and motivation to stay on top of.
- By managing multiple accounts, an agency is able to observe patterns and effective strategies that you may never notice working on a single account.
- Good agencies will have direct access to a Google representative, possibly several.
- Google often provides agencies with early access to various beta features before they're rolled out to the general public.

If you're ready to let a professional take the wheel of your AdWords account, nine times out of ten an agency is the smartest choice.

But knowing that you plan to go the agency route doesn't mean your decision-making is over. No exaggeration: **The difference in class between the best and worst agencies is a gap the size of the Grand Canyon.**

Here are some guidelines to help you make a confident decision.

WHAT PAYMENT MODEL SHOULD YOU FOLLOW?

Most PPC agencies will use one of the following three payment models.

Percentage of Spend

Expect something in the region of 10 to 20 percent of your total AdWords spend. An agency may charge a bit more if your account is small, but anything above this is dangerously close to overcharging.

Frankly, we're not fans of this payment model. Under it, the agency's immediate incentive is to increase your AdWords spend. Yes, you want your business to grow, and you want to be able to spend more to attract the best customers. But a truly good agency should be motivated to decrease your overall costs.

Fixed Fee

This is simple, straightforward, and you never wonder where your agency stands. A good, reliable payment model.

Performance-Based

The agency offers to reduce your cost per action (CPA) to a fixed number, or perhaps to an agreed-upon percentage that's below your historic average. You pay them when they achieve it.

This sounds good in theory, and it can work sometimes. But tread carefully.

Let's say you have three keywords on your account with CPAs of $5, $10, and $20. An agency might offer to reduce your average CPA to below $10. But how do they accomplish this?

An unscrupulous one would just shut down the $20 CPA keyword, even if it's the one that brings in 80 percent of your leads and sales.

A good agency will be motivated to maximize your profits. You need to be absolutely sure that the agency has your best interests at heart if you're going to go with this model.

You can combine incentive models. You can pay a retainer plus a percentage of ad spend plus a percentage of sales, for example.

11 QUESTIONS TO ASK BEFORE HIRING AN AGENCY

Some carry more weight than others, but none of these questions here are trivial. See how many of these you can answer by researching the websites of the agencies you've shortlisted. After that, speak to each agency directly to obtain answers to everything else.

1. Did the Person Who Is Going to be Managing Your AdWords Account Learn AdWords on Their Own Dime?

This is the acid test for account managers. There is something about learning to make your Google campaign profitable *using your own money* that makes you get smart faster than anything else. Your mistakes are directly painful and you never forget the lessons you learn.

This is in stark contrast to the employee who is guaranteed three square meals a day regardless of whether the traffic converts or not. The two are not even remotely comparable.

If you are going to hire an agency (or employee or contractor) to manage your campaigns, *ask them to prove to you that they built a successful, profitable campaign with their own money.* This is the gold standard.

The next best thing after that is the contractor, employer, or agency who learned on someone else's dime, but was incentivized by commissions to make the campaigns successful. Again, they need to prove to you that they made campaigns hit pay dirt.

2. Is the Agency Really an Agency?

You want to find out if the company is really just a one-man band. You want an agency with lots of resources, lots of experience, and personnel. You don't want your AdWords account to be neglected because your lone worker has gone on holiday or come down with the flu.

Now mind you, we do have a small handful of expert colleagues who work solo, without a big staff around them. They know AdWords inside and out, and network closely with other experts in making strategic decisions. We trust them because we know them, and they come with the respect of all the best experts in the business. They're an exception to this rule.

But beware of lone-ranger account managers who come with no credentials, no certification, and no backing of any kind by the big players.

3. What Services Does the Agency Offer?

The best answer? They specialize in PPC, and little else. If they also offer search engine optimization (SEO), social media, web design, print fulfillment, and lots more, this is a red flag. Some multi-service companies will say that they offer PPC when it's really only a sideline.

If you need knee surgery, you don't go to a general practitioner or a heart doctor. You get a specialist. PPC campaigns are no different. You're looking for stone-cold, PPC-obsessed professionals. Your business deserves nothing less.

4. How Did You Hear about the Agency?

The absolute best circumstances under which to hire an agency are:

1. A trusted colleague recommended the firm to you, or
2. You heard one of the agency's senior managers give a brilliant talk at an event.

Always get references or case studies from previous or current customers.

If you hire an agency that contacted *you* out of the blue by email or by cold calling, without you seeking them out first, what does it mean? A firm like that usually has other priorities—they may be more focused on grabbing market share than on doing a high-quality job for you the client.

5. Have They Worked with Anyone Else in Your Specific Market or Vertical Niche?

If not, it isn't a deal-breaker. But it's a good sign if they have prior experience in your sector. Every niche has its own idiosyncrasies.

6. How Do They Report Their Results?

The first answer you're looking for is: They'll connect your AdWords and Analytics accounts and will always report your AdWords results in the context of your other traffic data.

Beyond that, you need to know what kind of reporting cycle they have and the format in which they'll deliver it. They are to provide what you need—weekly, monthly, quarterly, annually, and anything in between!

7. What Key Performance Indicators (KPIs) Do They Use?

Bad agencies talk about number of impressions, number of clicks, CTRs, or even the position of your ads. Good agencies talk about CPAs, volume of conversions, and profit.

How to Manage Campaigns Intelligently for Profit

WebSavvy, a trusted AdWords management firm based in Melbourne, Australia, uses its own proprietary system for measuring its performance as an agency for every client, known as a SavvyNumber™. By making a calculation based on all the main metrics, it provides clients with an assessment of the total profit their AdWords account has achieved each month.

Overall profit should always be the primary measure of any PPC agency's abilities.

8. What Account Management System Do They Use?

Agencies may hold back specifics in the early stages of their discussions with you. That's not unusual. The important thing is to know that they have a system and that they don't just manage accounts on an *ad hoc* basis.

9. Who Exactly Will Be Working on Your Account?

Once the relationship begins, your account isn't managed by a computer or a company; it's managed by one or more highly trained PPC experts. Don't be afraid to ask for specifics about the people that will be physically working on your account. Even better if you can meet them in person.

WebSavvy, for instance, manages each client's account using different people who specialize in different aspects of the work. The technical experts look after things like

Excel pivot tables and AdWords scripts, whereas creative experts handle the writing of ad copy and the design of Display Network ads.

10. Is the Agency Certified?

The agency should be at least AdWords Certified and part of the Google Partners™ program. Don't be fooled into thinking that this automatically gives the agency legitimacy; certification requires passing a couple of fairly easy exams, as well as maintaining a minimum monthly AdWords spend of $10k—which is a fairly low bar in the scheme of things.

However, if an agency doesn't even have Google certification, you're dealing with amateurs.

11. What Does Your Gut Tell You?

Don't be horrified by this question. PPC isn't an exact science. There's always a level of artistry that goes into the equation. Similarly, choosing an agency can't be made solely on cold, hard facts.

Continue to talk to the agency until you feel comfortable with your choice, whether it's to hire them or look elsewhere. The right agency will talk the talk, have good business sense, communicate without using impenetrable jargon, understand the important elements of your business, and have an in-depth knowledge of the AdWords machine.

If you have positive answers to the first of the above nine questions, and you instinctively feel that the agency understands you and your business and what you're trying to achieve, you might just have found your winner.

WHO WILL HAVE OWNERSHIP OF YOUR ACCOUNT?

We've left this to the end in order to give it some extra emphasis.

No matter how professional and successful an agency appears to be, even if they tick all the boxes, you must *always* retain ownership of your AdWords account. It's *your* business asset, and you're granting an agency access to your property.

Completely relinquishing control of your AdWords account to an agency is like giving full control of your bank account to your bookkeeper—utterly unwise, and a recipe for disaster down the line.

How so?

For one thing, if your relationship with the agency breaks down, you want to be free to turn access of your account over to a new firm. You could always start a new account from scratch, but that's a massive headache, especially since your account's history is a factor—albeit a minor one—in your Quality Score.

You may also be considering selling your business at some stage, in which case your AdWords account is a valuable asset to pass on to the new owner.

Even if you're completely new to AdWords and don't yet have an account, you need to open one in your name and grant the agency access. Do not have the agency create their own account on your behalf.

If you're unsure what does and doesn't qualify as account ownership, consider the following:

- Can you access your account from http://google.com/adwords? If you can't, and the agency insists that you log in through its own custom interface, you probably only have partial access.
- Do you have admin-level control of your AdWords account, including the ability to add and remove other people's access to your account? This is essential.
- Do you know your Account Customer ID (usually referred to as your CID)? This is a 10-digit number that looks something like 123-456-7890.
- Do you pay Google for your clicks or do you pay through the agency? You should always pay Google directly, if possible. And not just to get the loads of free air miles. When all is said and done, Google considers the person or business who pays for the clicks to be the owner of the account and the data it contains.

YOUR QUICK ACTION SUMMARY

Hiring an agency is a natural next step in your AdWords management and the growth of your business. The right choice of firm can reduce your costs, cut your time commitment, and greatly improve your results.

- Shortlist one or more agencies based on trusted recommendations or your own direct personal experience.
- Research the websites of your shortlisted agencies to answer as many of the 10 key qualifying questions as you can.

- Speak to the agencies directly to get answers to the remaining qualifying questions.
- Be certain that you maintain admin-level ownership of your AdWords account.
- In the end, listen to your gut!

How Email Transforms Those Expensive Clicks into Long-Term, Profitable Customers

No discussion about Google AdWords would be complete if I didn't show you how to turn that expensive split-second click into a long-term relationship. When someone clicks on your ad, Google charges you 50 cents regardless of what happens next. If the guy leaves after five seconds, he's gone, and you'll probably never get him back without paying *again*.

Fifty cents for five seconds of someone's attention—dang, that's $600 an hour! Kind of depressing if you look at it that way.

On the other hand, if that person gives you his email address, you can communicate with him on a regular basis for little or no cost.

If you're trying to sell a $1,000 product, which is easier to get from your prospects: a $1,000 order or an email address?

The more complex your sales process, the more important it is to break it up into bite-sized steps. That is why the main Google AdWords page at www.perrymarshall. com/google is an email opt-in page:

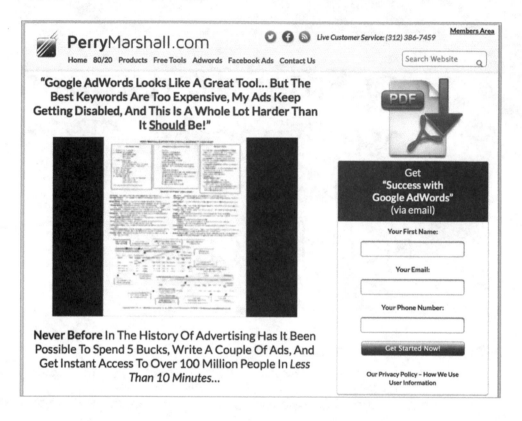

Visitors can either opt-in to take our free cheatsheet and email course or leave. We figure if a person's really interested in Google AdWords she'll at least give her email address first.

This is better than only getting email addresses from people who buy the book on the first visit. And it's better than having only one shot at selling people our services.

HOW TO PUT PERSONALITY AND PIZZAZZ INTO YOUR EMAIL MARKETING

In a day when much of the manufacturing industry is downsizing, cutting management, laying off employees right and left, and moving in a panic to India and China, B&B Electronics in Ottawa, Illinois, has been setting growth records.

It had to hire more staff to handle its growing number of incoming catalog orders and mounting list of willing buyers.

Most people would never think to utter the phrase "infectious personality" and "electronics manufacturing company" in the same breath, but B&B is both.

It refuses to surrender to the dull, corporate geek stereotype. Instead it has loads of fun with the stereotype. B&B regularly courts its growing customer list's inboxes with witty, lively messages that celebrate the stale, geek image of the Dilbert-cubicle engineer. Marketing director Mike Fahrion graces customers with his regular "Mike's Politically Incorrect Newsletter" rant column.

A techie's girlfriend recently wrote B&B to thank it for turning the engineer stereotype on its head:

Hey Mike,

This is the hapless girlfriend who shares an email account with a techie who subscribes to your newsletter.

The amount of dry, poopey emails that we get in our inbox is criminal, and it's pathetic that the other electronic types are perpetrating the geek image that's out there by sending those incredibly boring messages.

I mean, come on! "All you've ever wanted to learn about C++, Extensive Layer Management Plug-In for mental ray Pipeline"? BRUTAL!

Thank you for the sense of humor in your newsletters.

Mike, I think you need to start a "How to Write a Cheese-Free Newsletter" course. I can think of many companies that need your help!

Signed,

Disgruntled Dish

Does B&B owe its stellar growth in a stagnant industry all to its email? No, but it's a vital ingredient of its carefully thought-out marketing strategy.

Build a Business Around Your Uniqueness

Use email correctly, and your customers will stick around three times longer. It's the most personal online medium there is. With it you can sell to your customers again and again by building trust and creating an entire business around your own unique personality.

Mike understands this, which is why he originally hired Perry Marshall to ghostwrite his "Politically Incorrect Newsletter."

Whether you're B&B Electronics or Martha Stewart, capturing a person's email address turns a one-time click into an opportunity to build a relationship that can work for you again and again and again.

Buying Google traffic is only the first of many important steps in our marketing process. If we had to credit our own success to just one thing, it would be the use of email and autoresponders.

POWER IN THE PERSONAL: SIX KEYS TO EMAIL MARKETING SUCCESS

Run-of-the-mill advertisers have little respect for the personal nature of email. They don't realize how easy it is to turn off otherwise receptive prospects to their message, just by violating that.

You need to write to the person as one person. Unless the person you're writing to is part of a group where he or she personally knows each of the other members, then the last thing you want to do is write as though you're talking to a crowd.

This is you, an individual, talking to your customer, an individual.

1. A "From" Field That Shows You're a Real Person

So if that's the case for the actual text of your email messages, chances are that same principle will apply to other details in your email. Such as your "from" field, for example. Consider the different impressions these "from" lines create:

- Bill Kastl
- William Kastl
- William D. Kastl
- Nakatomi Corporation
- William D. Kastl, Nakatomi Corporation
- Nakatomi Sales Department
- Bill Kastl, Nakatomi Sales

You want to be warm and personal without looking like spam. This is a challenge because spammers are themselves always trying to make their messages look like they're from some forgotten friend. The key is to say something that is so specific to readers' particular interests they know no spammer would ever come up with it.

Pick a "from" field that your customers will understand, and stick with it.

2. A Provocative Subject Line

The most important thing about email is that its success or failure is all about *context*. Email subject lines work *not because they follow standard copywriting formulas* but because *they tap into what specific people are interested in at a particular time.*

If I showed you generic examples of email subject lines, it would be almost impossible for them to not sound like spam.

So let's take examples from a specific context that *you* understand: Google AdWords. Here are the subject lines of some of the emails I've sent out to my Google AdWords customer list:

- When Google is NOT the Best Way to Get a Customer
- Are Google Employees Spying on You?
- Google's "Don't Be Evil" and all that
- 5 Insidious Lies About Selling on the Web
- Fistfight at the Board of Directors Meeting

These headlines do not assault the reader with cheesy-sounding promos, but they do hint very strongly at a story. They provoke curiosity rather than scaring people off.

3. Everybody Loves a Good Story

B&B Electronics sells industrial communication hardware via catalog and the web. A "boring" geek business if there ever were one. But when Perry Marshall writes its monthly newsletter, he turns that dull, geek image on its head and interrupts a dreary day of engineering with wry humor.

The method? Storytelling.

Subject: **ZIGBEE AND THE GEEKS' REVENGE**

Leslye was the girl who made my heart go pitter-patter in junior high school.

I was always sure to take the long way to Social Studies, down the stairs to first floor, past her locker, then back up to 2nd. Just checkin' up.

I was not the boy who made her heart go pitter-patter. She liked Sam, and maybe Rodney, too.

She wasn't interested in me. And she never discovered that I liked her. It was my little secret.

Now maybe you didn't run the sound system in Junior High like I did. Maybe you ran the film projector instead. Maybe you programmed Apple II computers in BASIC and belonged to Chess Club.

Still, you and I were geeks, and the pretty girls took no notice of us.

But it's 2009 now, and we geeks rule the world. We're the people who really know what's going on. All the pretty boys and their material girls have viruses on their computers and they can't function without us. They're at our mercy.

And the latest Geek Revenge these days is . . .

ZigBee.

ZigBee is sort of like wireless instant messaging for sensors and smart devices. You drop ZigBee nodes wherever you want, no cables necessary, and the more nodes you have, the more communication paths there are and the more reliable your system is . . .

It's a little wonky. It doesn't surrender to the stereotype that engineers are dull, lifeless geeks who only understand ones and zeros. No. It *celebrates* it. It turns it into the central message. It plays with the concept and has no end of fun with it.

More importantly, though, while it celebrates the engineer stereotype, at the same time it smashes it to pieces.

Engineers make buying decisions on emotion no differently than the rest of us do.

Storytelling *does* work when marketing to them, no differently than people in any other profession. Plus, every geek out there has suffered the heartache of unrequited love.

Every time B&B sends out an email blast, it gets emails from customers saying, "Your newsletter is the only one I read every time it comes" and "I always look forward to getting emails from you guys."

WHY WE CHOSE ENGINEERS AS AN EXAMPLE FOR EMAIL MARKETING

Most people stubbornly insist you can't use storytelling and humor to sell to "logical" people like engineers and scientists. Most people also think that business-to-business marketing has to be dreadfully serious.

This campaign shoots holes in both beliefs because we're doing both at the same time here—using emotional, human-touch email marketing to sell business-to-business products to engineers and scientists.

Does this work in other markets? You bet it does. Bryan Todd sold more books on learning Chinese and ignited more feedback and fan mail through this one message than anything else he sent out:

Subject: **WOMEN WHO HOLD HANDS; MEN WHO HUG**

William kept brushing against me as we walked down the street.

Now I'm a guy like he is—and I'm straight, too—and I found this a little unnerving. This was back during my first month living in mainland China, William was my new friend, and he had some habits that were awfully strange.

And when we'd go out walking somewhere, he always rubbed his shoulders up against me. I kept thinking I was crowding him, so I'd move to the right. Then he'd move right too, get closer and rub up against me again.

Sooner or later I figured out that this was just his way of being friendly. No, not "friendly," just friendly—you know, normal, nice-guy friendly.

It's that classic issue of personal space.

Every culture has different rules. My Chinese guy friends rubbed shoulders with each other, and with me, as they walked down the street.

Americans don't do that, unless they're in a relationship.

Younger women in China hold hands. Sometimes regardless of age. Arm in arm, hand in hand, they saunter together down the street.

Ah, but do they HUG you?

None of my friends ever did.

At least, not until I was with a couple of guys being visited by a lady pal of theirs from Shanghai . . .

This email was part of Bryan's regular, timed email autoresponder series and didn't even explicitly promote his book. But it got a *reaction* from people. Still does. It turns the spotlight in a sensitive yet eminently funny subject.

It paints Bryan as completely and totally human. Not a peddler, not a salesman, not a pushy marketer, but as a regular guy whose experiences his mainland or Taiwan-based readers all share.

Most importantly, this approach *trains* people to read your emails by convincing them that you've always got something interesting to say.

4. People Can't Forget You When They Hear from You Often

Get an autoresponder series going and you can win the hearts of customers for life:

- We like five-day sequences. Five is a good number. Prime numbers like 3, 5, and 7 are good.
- After that five-day sequence is done, keep in touch at a slower rate. In our "The Nine Great Lies of Sales & Marketing" e-course (www.PerryMarshall.com/9), messages continue every few days and taper out for more than two years afterward. (You read it right: two years.)
- Your unsubscribe rate should be 3 to 10 percent. If it's more than that, your message isn't matching your market. (If it's less, you may not be edgy enough.)
- Want to squash refunds and returns? After people buy from you, send them a series of messages that show them how to use your product more effectively and shares features they might have missed.
- When people complain that they've missed a day or two from you, it's a sign that your content is good *and* that the spam filters are doing their job.

5. If You Violate the Expectation of Relevance, You Damage Your List

Let's say you're a chiropractor and you've just launched a new herbal remedy. It's a fantastic product, and you want to tell your customers. What should you do? Should you blast your entire list with it?

Odds are, you could maximize your sales total for that day by doing so.

But you're going to pay a price. All the people on your list who aren't interested in herbal stuff are now going to be *less responsive* to everything else you do—even if they don't unsubscribe. You've just taught them that you like to send out emails about stuff they're not interested in.

Which means they're that much less likely to read your next email.

It's a nasty mistake to treat everyone on your list the same unless they really are. If you've got a back pain newsletter, it's likely only a few people on that list would ever be interested in a knee pain newsletter.

The typical marketer will treat everyone the same and when he gets a back pain subscriber, he'll also send knee pain stuff, neck pain stuff, herbal stuff, environmental stuff, whatever.

The smart marketer will not. The smart marketer will have different lists for each topic—different sublists.

So if you're the chiropractor, you build an herbal sub-list, and then sell the herbal remedies just to those folks. That way you maximize the value of every single list you have.

In email—and by extension, direct mail and other forms of communication—that means that some of your prospects and customers don't ever want to hear from you (the bottom 5–10 percent). They, of course, do not matter. They can unsubscribe. But for the people who do:

- Some of them (maybe 50 percent) would like to hear from you no more than a few times a year.
- Some of them (20 percent) would like to get your three-, five-, or seven-day autoresponder sequence for a few days, then only hear from you if something really important happens.
- Some (5–10 percent) would like to get all your newsletters, and if you have email lists for six different problems or products, they'll want to be on every single one.
- Some (1–2 percent) would like to hear from you every day.
- A tiny handful (less than 1 percent) would literally read 10 emails from you every day, if you were willing to send them.

6. The Human Touch Sells

Don't hide behind your email. Use it to express more of yourself. You're not a faceless corporation; you're a person. Show that side of you, and people will remember you. And buy. And tell others about you.

Express a personality that people can instantly recognize. This is free branding. When you introduce new products or make changes in your marketing program or message, now you can attach those to a name—your name or another person that your business is known for—and now your name itself has even more meaning and credibility.

A MEDIUM THAT WILL NEVER GO AWAY

When you communicate with your customers in multiple media rather than just one, it greatly solidifies your power in the marketplace.

There's power for you in adding offline marketing to your arsenal. Communicating with your customers via direct mail (or even fax) takes you out of the ephemeral, fly-by-night online world and plugs them into you by an entirely new medium—a medium that is harder to break into but potentially more rewarding and enduring.

You can bank on the fact that the guy in the blue-gray uniform who comes to your house every day is going to *continue* coming to your house every day pretty much as long as the earth keeps rotating on its axis (or as long as politicians depend on him to deliver their campaign mailings).

A customer who finds you offline and goes to you online is usually more valuable to you than a customer who knows you only online. In the same way, a customer who

knows you offline through physical mailings and physical products as well as online is going to be a much more valuable customer than one who only knows you online.

OPT-INS: MORE THAN JUST AN EMAIL ADDRESS?

Most opt-in pages only ask for a name and email address, but is that all the information you want? Many, if not most, businesses should also collect physical addresses and fax numbers. Asking for this information, even requiring it, makes your database much more valuable.

It also gives you a valuable communication medium besides just email. What if you accidentally get on a spam blacklist, if your email service goes belly up, or email suddenly gets a lot more expensive? It's a mistake to rely solely on email.

THEY CAN KNOCK OFF YOUR PRODUCT, BUT THEY CAN'T KNOCK OFF *YOU*

Anybody can have a TV talk show, but there's only one Oprah. Anybody can rant about the Democrats, but there's only one Rush Limbaugh. Products can be replicated and ideas can be stolen, but personalities cannot be duplicated.

Use email to express your own personality and you'll have a unique bond with your customers that nobody can take from you.

Uncle Claude Sez

A person who desires to make an impression must stand out in some way. Being eccentric, being abnormal is not a distinction to covet. But doing admirable things in a different way gives one a great advantage.

That's why we have signed ads sometimes—to give them a personal authority. A man is talking—a man who takes pride in his accomplishments—not a "soulless corporation." Whenever possible we introduce a personality into our ads. By making a man famous we make his product famous. When we claim an improvement, naming the man who made it adds effect.

Persuasive Ad Copy—The Ultimate Silver Bullet
How to Mint Money with the Printed Word

When I left the *Dilbert* cube in 2001 and hung out my shingle, my copywriting skills were more than adequate for corporate client work—writing press releases, product descriptions, and magazine articles. However I wanted to sell information: toolkits, books, ebooks, and the like. I wanted a sales-on-autopilot business, not a consulting project business.

That kind of business required far greater copywriting and persuasion skills. My skills were not up to the task. I needed a mentor.

I hooked up with the legendary copywriter John Carlton. He would rip my pages apart and bust my chops. Then he'd bandage my damaged body parts

with some words of encouragement and instruct me on how to re-assemble my message for killer persuasion power.

Then . . . the first letter he made me rewrite went from 1 percent response (not quite breaking even) to 2 percent (solidly profitable). I was elated!

John's guidance got me over the hump. I can attribute my business "escape velocity" to his tutelage. His help was essential to moving my rocket ship from launch pad to orbit.

So I asked John to contribute a chapter to this book. He's taught more people to successfully sell in print than almost anyone alive, so pay close attention.

The dirty little secrets behind effortless selling . . .

Your First Rookie Lesson in Classic Salesmanship

Here's your launching pad to finally transform your ability to persuade, close deals, and earn the Big Bucks . . . with the time-tested fundamentals of getting your sales message across that nobody told you about.

By John Carlton

(The most respected, ripped-off, rabble-rousing marketing expert alive)

Is it OK if I teach you three super-simple secrets—right now, today, right here—that will systematically transform your ability to:

- Get the undivided attention of your best prospects . . .
- Convince them to listen to what you have to say . . .
- Earn their sincere respect . . .
- And turn them into buying customers.

And to do all this whether you're speaking directly to a prospect . . . or reaching him through an ad or website or email or TV commercial or any other media?

Is this something you feel could affect your bottom line?

It is? Okay then. Let's get going.

First, let's do a little "spot check" on your current Sales IQ, with a sneaky question: What is the *single most important thing* you need in your personal "tool kit" to become independent . . . wealthy . . . respected . . . and happy?

Go on, think about your answer for a few moments. The single most important thing. Most folks get it wildly wrong, including many entrepreneurs who should know better.

All right. What did you come up with?

If your answer included anything about brain power, or investors, or an MBA, or any kind of "advantage" you feel should give you a head-start on attaining independence, wealth, respect and happiness . . .

. . . please reconsider how you think about success.

Because the answer to this question is much simpler: **You need to learn how to *sell*.**

Oh, the shame of it all. The *horror* of resigning yourself to being "that guy" who has ulterior motives whenever he talks to you, because he wants to "sell" you something. That just can't be the answer. It's too . . . creepy.

So let's get straight on this basic secret of lasting, empowering success, right off the bat.

Consider this: Do you have a *great* product? Something that people can really use to improve their lives, save more time, save money, get better results? Do you run an ethical business that fulfills on all promises and delivers exactly what you say you can deliver?

You do?

Then guess what.

If you have a product that your prospect needs . . . and can put to good use . . . especially if it's something that addresses a critical, life-changing situation he's in . . .

. . . and you can't *explain* this to him in a way that makes him realize that he needs to become a customer right now . . .

. . . then *shame on you*.

Because you are HIDING your product from people whose lives would be better if they knew you existed. And that you can deliver exactly what they need.

Salesmanship is nothing more than the ability to move past the natural (and very solid) resistance that people have to "being sold" . . . and help them get their hands on your product (which can change their lives in amazing ways).

It's what separates the failures in the business world from the folks who become successful. What kind of entrepreneur *are* you if you can't sell? The "Marketing Graveyard" is crammed to bursting with great products, really superior stuff . . . that *died* because no one figured out how to sell them.

Yes, you need all the other things that business experts and technology wizards insist you use in your marketing. All the software and equipment, the order taking processes, the SEO, the traffic-capturing tactics, the auto-responders, all of it.

But you need to know how to sell, FIRST.

All else is just a detail to getting your sales message out to the world.

Have you ever watched a YouTube video that made you laugh? That you wanted to show your friends? That you told others about?

After watching that video, did you then send a dollar to the person who posted it?

No, you didn't. Because no salesmanship took place.

Yet, this is how too many business owners run their operation—they believe that getting page hits, clicks, or opt-ins is important. And it's good to have those things . . .

. . . but they will do nothing for your bottom line if you *can't close the deal*. And make a sale happen.

Selling isn't magic. It's a very simple process most anyone can master. It's the essential element of all great marketing. However, it's also misunderstood and avoided.

So, first breakthrough: Stop pretending sales will happen because you have a great product, or you're a nice person, or you pump a lot of money into your business.

The fact is, a nearly broke entrepreneur at his kitchen table who knows how to sell can bring home a fortune . . . while even the biggest companies on the planet can crumble into dust if they ignore salesmanship.

It happens all the time. Many of the most famous success stories start with a lone person, lacking funds and connections and experience . . . but knowing how to sell . . . conquering the world.

This knowledge will be your secret weapon no matter what you do with your life. You will know how to close a deal, which is the prime talent of anyone who strives to be successful.

It's the Missing Link between having a dream . . .

. . . and making it a reality.

I am not a "natural born" salesman. I was clueless about business and selling until I was in my 30s . . . and only began my now-legendary career because I admitted that nothing good was going to happen to me "accidentally." And I needed to get busy learning how the world worked.

I made every mistake possible in my climb to success as a renowned copywriter and creator of ridiculously effective marketing campaigns. I blithely wandered down every blind alley, made every dumb decision, suffered all the consequences possible for a clueless dude out in the wilderness of advertising seeking clues.

However, I also hunted down the best mentors I could find, read voraciously and critically, and *applied* everything I learned to the harsh test of the real world.

And, I took notes. This is how I became a decent teacher. I made the blunders, fixed the damage, and forced my way into the party. I spent *decades* in the front trenches of the business world, watching businesses rise and fall and new businesses spring up from the ruins.

If something worked, I continued to use it.

If it didn't work—out there where you get zero credit for a "nice try"—I ditched it.

The advice I'm able to give, at this point in my long, battle-scarred career, has been proven over and over and over again.

You want theory, go somewhere else.

You want hard-core tactics and specific steps to take . . . keep reading.

Now, I am NOT going to teach you to write ads today. I'm also not going to teach you to be "creative".

Instead, I'm going to teach you the three simple fundamentals *behind* every great ad, and every great "creative" idea that actually produced sales.

These three tactics are lifted directly from my notorious "**Simple Writing System**" course, which Perry can get you a special deal on, just as soon as you're ready to rock and roll.

Relax. Even if you're terrified at the thought of having to write an ad, certain that you cannot possibly get up the nerve to actually ask another human being to buy what you offer . . .

. . . just get over your bad self.

With these same simple tactics I'm about to share with you, I've taught the most stubborn, self-sabotaging scaredy-cats you've ever met to get past their fears . . .

. . . and start selling stuff like crazy. Using every type of advertising media out there.

This stuff works in spite of your effort to ignore it. It's only one tenth of one percent of everything I have to offer you . . . but it's easily enough to help you transform your ability to persuade and close the deal. Just play along.

Here Is Simple Selling Tactic #1:
What Are You Really Selling In Your Business?

Think about this for a moment. Write down your answer here. I'll even help you get started:

"I sell _____

_____."

Just fill in the blank.

When I do this exercise at seminars, the most common answers I hear are "I sell a book on making more money," or "We sell the finest equipment in the industry," or "We sell a proven way to do xyz."

I also hear a number of people insist they sell "hope." Or "the opportunity to succeed."

All are wrong.

Most entrepreneurs and business owners are NOT selling what they THINK they're selling. You're not selling a book, or a service, or a consultation, or widget, or a new life.

No.

Rather, what you are selling . . .

. . . is what your book, service, widget, or claims of spiritual rejuvenation . . .

. . . *DOES for your prospect.*

It's not the "thing." **It's the RESULT.**

I don't want your book. I want, instead, what *happens* to me as a result of reading your book.

If there was a magic way to get that result *without* reading your book . . . I'd do that.

This is what trips up so many marketers. You get caught up in the weight, heft, bulk, the "thingness" of what you offer.

But it's just a thing. A DELIVERY SYSTEM for what I really want. And I want results.

So get clear on this: If you, or your competition, come up with an even simpler, easier, faster, tidier, and cheaper way to get what I want . . .

. . . like freedom, wealth, happiness, fun, revenge, health, beauty, another chance at life . . .

. . . then I'll go do that instead.

Don't get trapped in admiring the "thingness" of what you offer. What really matters is what your prospect believes he can GET from it.

As Perry likes to say, "Nobody who bought a drill wanted a drill. They wanted a hole."

See? That's wasn't so hard to understand, was it? And yet, it's one of the fundamentals of persuading people to buy that is commonly ignored (or never realized) by biz owners frustrated at their lack of sales.

Let's Go to Simple Selling Tactic #2: "The Elevator Chat"

This tactic can change your life, right now.

Consider this scene: You step into an elevator with another person . . .

. . . who just happens to be your perfect prospect. They're in dire need of what you offer, but you don't know this yet.

They politely ask you what you do for a living.

And what do you say?

If you cannot explain to a total stranger who you are and what you offer . . . in the time it takes an elevator to go from the 9th floor to the lobby . . .

. . . in a way that instantly alerts your perfect prospect to your value in their lives . . .

. . . then you do not have a sales message at all.

This is where many biz owners stumble. Standing right next to someone who should go goggle-eyed at meeting you . . . because they desperately need exactly what you're offering . . . you cannot clearly and succinctly tell your story.

It doesn't matter how "hot" this prospect is. Most of your prospects out there don't know who you are. They don't know what you offer, or what you do.

No matter how they got to your website, or your ad, or in front of you . . .

. . . you're just a cipher to them. They're distracted, uninterested in hearing a stranger mumble about his business, and SKEPTICAL of anything you say that smacks of ego, or confusing detail, or (worst of all) a long story that you can't seem to spit out.

Your perfect prospect has a problem or situation that requires a *solution*. And if you cannot deliver your credibility at providing this solution simply and concisely . . . they will move on. And you've lost any chance at a sale.

It's the same face-to-face as it is online, or in a magazine, or on television. You get one brief moment to capture her attention, and get her interested in what you offer.

Here's how the Elevator Chat formula works: You must be able to fill out this template (or something similar):

> **"We help [this group of people] . . . do or get [this benefit] . . . [better, cheaper, faster, easier] . . . even if [worst-case believable scenario]."**

That's it. That's the "starter kit" for an elevator chat that will get the attention of a perfect prospect.

Want some examples? Here is my own elevator chat:

> "I help small biz owners and entrepreneurs . . . create their first killer sales messages that bring in the Big Bucks . . . even if you flunked English or are scared to death of writing."

Another one, from a former client:

> "We help golfers with huge handicaps . . . to immediately start hitting long, straight, gorgeous tee shots, and score so low they win all the money from their buddies . . . even if you've been slicing, hooking, skulling, hacking, and putting like a baboon your entire life."

For an accountant:

> "We help understaffed biz owners grossing one-to-ten-million a year . . . to pay the least amount of taxes legally owed each year . . . without adding a minute of extra work to your day . . . even if your bookkeeping is a total disaster zone right now."

For a financial advisor specializing in debt restructuring:

> "We help broke people buried in debt . . . to get *out* of debt within a short time . . . and have more money in your pocket without taking on another job, or borrowing. Works best if you have no understanding of finances or economics whatsoever."

For a weight-loss product:

> "We help overweight people . . . to lose 15 to 30 pounds of body fat within one month . . . without ever feeling hungry or deprived or sweaty from exercise. Works even if every diet you've ever tried before has failed for you."

Can you see how quickly telling the story of what you do for people, in ways that directly address the needs of your prospect, can help you position your business in their eyes as a positive solution to their situation?

This process is, more or less, the lazy man's way to find your "unique selling position" . . . that particular story about who you are and what you offer . . . which is the foundation of persuasion.

This Is Simple Selling Tactic #3: "Why You, Why This Product, Why Now?"

Your prospect needs information before she can make a satisfying decision to buy anything. She lacks knowledge about the quality of competing products out there . . . she is not on the "inside" of your market and so doesn't know if your price is high, low or outright theft . . . and she has no clear criteria to help her make a good decision, most of the time. Even if she's familiar with the products available and has experience with the market.

Even worse, she sometimes has to answer to the skeptical people in her life *after* making a buying decision. The nosy neighbor next door who loves to make her feel like she got ripped off, her spouse who is aghast that she's bought this particular product; her friends who are highly critical of everything.

So it's your job to help her make a good decision. To answer the fundamental questions: "Why should she deal with you and your company . . . why should she buy this particular product . . . and why should she buy it now?"

The way to do this is to position your product against all the competing products out there . . .

. . . uniquely . . .

. . . in order to sell.

All long-time salesmen know that it's often easy to get someone to agree with you that, yes, that is a mighty fine product you have there. It certainly seems to address the solution she's looking for. And it's priced attractively.

And, yes, at some point down the road, she thinks she may indeed decide to maybe buy it.

This is called "not closing the sale." A recipe for a starving salesman with skinny kids.

Instead, give her all the "ammo" she needs, in simple sound bites, to help her feel secure she is making the right decision to buy now . . . and has answers to the skeptics in her life, should they start harping.

You help her see how your product is—for example—a better overall value (if you're priced higher than the competition) . . . or a genuine bargain (if you're priced similarly).

It is unique, because it's easier to use . . . works faster . . . is bigger or smaller or more substantial . . . or whatever it is that sets your product apart.

Most of all, you help her overcome her natural tendency to *put off* making a final decision . . . by pointing out the urgency of the deal, the temporary opportunity presented right now, the extra goodies available in this version, or whatever helps you to seal the deal NOW.

The basic formula for this (no matter what you're selling) is:

- Here's who I am.
- Here's what I've got for you.
- Here's what it will do for you.
- And here's what to do now.

This is the essence of good advertising and selling. It's the building blocks of a sales message that addresses your credibility (who you are) . . . the nature of what you're offering (what you've got) . . . the results that make this product a solution (what it does) . . .

. . . and, most important for your bottom line . . .

. . . how to OWN this product right now. Tell her precisely what to do next in order to have this product start doing it's thang in her life.

This is why entrepreneurs and biz owners who know how to sell succeed, where others fail. Your sales message must be clear, concise, and targeted at the "sweet spot" of need in your prospect . . .

. . . while educating her on all the reasons this purchase is a great idea . . . and should be completed right now.

Face-to-face, it's easy to see why this process can work. Poor salesmen wait for prospects to ask questions, and leave it up to her to figure out whether to buy or not.

But the world-class salesman becomes an *advocate* for the prospect—explaining precisely why this product is the best choice (or even a good choice), among all the other choices available . . .

. . . and why making a decision now is the right move to make.

There's more to all this, of course. You cannot argue your way to a sale—you must *persuade*. And you must know your competition as well as a spy would . . . so you can speak knowledgeably about the uniqueness of your product, and why it's a bargain (even if it's priced higher . . . Not all prospects are looking for the cheapest option, especially when their ideal solution is critical to their survival and happiness).

However, this is a good overview of how a solid, built-for-success sales message is constructed.

And here's the main thing for entrepreneurs: Once you understand how a good sales message is created . . .

. . . you can use the exact same process to create ALL of your advertising and marketing needs.

Spoken, this sales message will persuade prospects face-to-face. Written out, it will be the best ad you ever create (either for printed ads, or for websites). It will be the fuel for your video sales letters, your radio spots, your television segments, your email campaigns, your product launches . . .

. . . everything you do to get your message out there.

A great sales message can be used with any media you choose, to reach your best prospects, and to persuade them to buy from you.

If this little primer on sales messages has helped you . . . and you would like to learn even more proven, time-tested ways to make your selling abilities sizzle . . .

. . . then listen to my interview with Perry here: http://www.perrymarshall.com/copywriting/

This is the very simple, do-it-yourself-quickly track that has helped transform thousands of entrepreneurs, business owners, professionals, and even rookie marketers into sales-generating monsters. And it doesn't matter whether you've ever sold anything before or not, or where you're at with your career, or even if you previously failed at biz.

There, you'll also get access to a special deal on my Simple Writing System.

The process of acquiring, and using, the best salesmanship tactics in the world is not brain surgery. It's actually very simple and straightforward . . .

. . . and once you learn it, the skills are yours forever.

Having a great product is one part of the equation. Having all the gizmos and technical wizardry is another part.

However, the KEY to making any business work . . . will forever be your ability to persuade someone to buy what you offer. It's the foundation for true independence, legitimate access to wealth streams, and the chance to fulfill your dreams.

I hope this has helped. Now go get 'em.

Uncle Claude Sez

Many of the best accounts in agencies are the accounts developed from small beginnings. Often much is at stake on these advertising possibilities. A mistake may ruin a fine prospect. Mediocre service may result in a small account where a big one might have been. That is why competent ad-writers are paid such large incomes.

So You Have a Killer Sales Machine. Now What?
The New Army of Next-Generation Marketers

A new breed of direct marketer is emerging: the one who's learned from the first-hand experience of split testing rather than the second-hand tutelage of gurus. And these marketers learn fast, too, because with Google and the internet the answers are all but instantaneous.

When you first join this new and elite crowd, you'll find paybacks on a level you'd never have imagined.

This can create unexpected problems, sometimes. Conrad Feagin, one of our coaching students, grew his business from $7,000 a month to over

$100,000 a month in 12 months. A couple of months after that I got this email from him:

> Hey Perry,
>
> I have been dealing with my merchant account provider for the last two days. The Bad News: They are tying up some of our funds. The Good News: We apparently "broke the bank," so to speak. We went from $103,000 in February to $175,000 and counting in March. Should end up around $190,000 or so. This is all a little scary. Hopefully I will not have any problems but, needless to say, I am applying for another account at another provider. Thanks for all the help!

I love getting emails from people who have problems like this! It proves that the commies haven't killed the entrepreneurial spirit in America yet.

And this guy is no old-school copywriter. I doubt he even knew what copywriting was a few years ago. He got these enormous results by steadily testing and improving his website.

Most niche marketers don't have big enough numbers to easily test lots of stuff, and they certainly don't have a whole staff of bean counters to help them do it. So they rely heavily on gurus, "best practices," and copywriting courses and seminars.

And many of the best niche copywriters I know, people like John Carlton, the late Gary Halbert, and Scott Haines, haven't had tons of their stuff split tested the way we're talking about today.

Their craft is really the result of lots of experience and intuition. These guys are good enough that most of the time they can crank out a winner the first time out.

Internet marketers who split test are mastering their trade faster than ever, and the best marketers discover what works by a combination of old-school tutelage and constant testing. The ultimate answer to every marketing question is *test it*. Answers have never been so easily within your grasp.

Now hang on, because the power of this is even greater than it appears. It's *exponential*.

THE IMPROVEMENTS DON'T JUST ADD UP, THEY MULTIPLY!
How to Get Massive Compound Interest on Sales and Profits

If internet marketing is some kind of magic show, I'm about to reveal the secret trick of the whole thing. This is what's truly important! Let's say your sales process looks like this:

1. Your AdWords ad

2. A landing page that offers a free video or white paper, a software trial, or access to video materials in exchange for name and email address

3. A sales letter

4. Your order entry page, or "action form"

We want to split test each of these four steps. We not only test the AdWords ads, we split test two different landing pages, two different sales letters, and two different order forms. What happens when we do this?

2 AdWords ads > 2 Opt-in Pages > 2 Sales Letters > 2 Order Forms

A challenging goal would be to double the effectiveness of each step. This is *not* impossible. And you don't have to be a genius—you just need to try some sensible things.

So if we double the CTR of the AdWords ad, and the landing page, and the sales letter, and the order form, our improvement is:

$$2 \times 2 \times 2 \times 2 = 16X$$

A 16-fold improvement! Notice that the improvements multiply, cascading from beginning to end. Every improvement is magnified in the end result.

If you go into a competitive market on Google—such as anything computer related, weight loss, martial arts, web hosting—these are hyper-competitive categories that are very hard to win in.

It's not unusual to start out losing money at a 4:1 ratio—i.e., for every $4 you give Google, you only make $1 in gross revenue. Not fun.

But now you double each of these four steps—and you improve your numbers by 16X—now you're making $4 for every $1 you give Google. That's pretty amazing. Continuous split testing unlocks the whole thing like the key to a safe.

And like I said, let's take a common scenario—a threefold improvement on AdWords, a threefold improvement in your opt-in page, a twofold improvement in your sales letter, and a mere 50 percent improvement in your order page (order pages are extremely sensitive to small changes—that sale hangs by a thin thread!)—now you've got as much as a 27-time improvement in conversion over what you started with.

What you've done so far would have been very hard to do in the offline world— and ten years ago not a whole lot easier in the online world—because there was never a consistent, controllable source of traffic. Pay-per-click traffic, however, is fairly consistent, and it's always 100 percent controllable. Within two to three months (as opposed to two to three years), you've tested several dozen variables and eliminated all but the best. You've polished a sales process to the point where it delivers killer results.

You're making a killer ROI on your sales process. And because you're so effective at turning visitors into dollars, you can afford to pay more for your traffic than all your competitors. You're getting unstoppable.

What now?

Now we go out with our growing war chest and buy all the traffic we can get, using the Expanding Universe Theory of internet marketing.

You've started out with Google AdWords and refined your marketing machine. Now you take the same messages and sales process, and roll out your product in this order:

1. Google AdWords
2. Search engine optimization
3. Other PPCs such as Yahoo, Bing, and Facebook ads
4. Email promotions
5. Affiliates
6. Banner ads, advertising networks such as Advertising.com
7. Social media (Facebook status updates, Twitter)
8. Press releases
9. Direct mail
10. Print advertising

Items 2 through 10 are more expensive and less controllable than Google. Get it right with Google first, where you have total control, then do email.

Then get help from affiliates. Don't let any of these other things or people be your guinea pig. If it works on Google AdWords first, then you can invest in these other things and be fairly certain it will work.

I can't overemphasize how powerful this is. Usually search engine traffic represents only a tiny percentage of the people who are potential customers for you.

When you roll out items 2 through 9, you may make 5 to 50 times as much money as you were making with AdWords. And remember, no longer is it necessary to risk more than a few hundred dollars on a marketing campaign!

EXPANDING INTO OTHER MEDIA: PROFITING FROM THE WINNER-TAKE-ALL PHENOMENON

The top dog has a disproportionate advantage over the others. The top three players in any market get more business than all the rest combined. This is true on Google as well, and there's a snowball effect.

You enter a market, you start split testing right away, and you use sound marketing techniques, copywriting, and all of the tools at your disposal.

How fast can you go from zero to dominating a market? Answer: As fast as you can split test.

AFFILIATES: THE MOMENTUM KICKS IN

Affiliates want to make money, and the Holy Grail for an affiliate is a program that consistently sends it very good dollars in exchange for its traffic. You never want your affiliates to be blind test subjects for your experiments.

Friends come and go, but enemies accumulate!

Do your experiments with PPC traffic first. Then verify it with email promotions and inclusions in e-zines. Now that you have rock-solid numbers, take it to your affiliates.

Everybody's trying to turn traffic into dollars. Affiliate marketing is what MLM was in the early 1990's—a craze. (It also works better.)

You'll never read about this in *The Wall Street Journal,* but anywhere from 10 to 30 percent of all internet traffic is driven by affiliates. It's an invisible empire.

If you're the guy with the content and the efficient sales process that spins off dollar bills, the world's your oyster.

Good affiliate relationships are extremely profitable. And more affiliates breed more affiliates. The snowball effect multiplies, and you eventually hit the point where you're getting so much traffic you can't make it stop.

HOW TO GRIND DOWN YOUR COMPETITION: A GOOGLE LESSON FROM HAN SOLO

Harrison Ford, aka "Han Solo" and "Indiana Jones," was working odd jobs back in the mid-1970s when he was asked by George Lucas to fill in doing readings for the part of Han Solo for *Star Wars.*

Ford wasn't even being considered for the part. Lucas actually had his eye on Nick Nolte. Kurt Russell and Christopher Walken were prime candidates for the role as well.

But during these test readings Lucas realized that the man perfect for the role was right under his nose. Harrison Ford was in the right place at the right time. George Lucas decided he wanted him for the part, and the rest is *Star Wars* history.

Did he just get lucky? Ford told *Us* Magazine back in 1981:

Right from the beginning, I believed that staying on course was what counted. The sheer process of attrition would wear others down. Them that stuck it out was them that won. That was my belief then. It still is.

According to Ford it was *attrition* that was the key to landing the big roles. Celebrity status and million-dollar title roles came his way because he hung in there

long after other actors had given up and gone back home. Movie history vindicated his decision.

> Sometimes the secret to success is grinding your competitors down, making incremental improvements over time until you're ahead of them.

The secret to staying power, the secret to long-term sales numbers that your competitors will never beat, starts with always testing two ads against each other, two opt-in pages, two sales letters, deleting the losers, and beating the winners.

Bryan Todd
Split-Testing + Attrition = Success:
Brian K. Wins by Attrition and Surprises Even Himself

Some time back a gentleman named Brian, who had a website that sold custom gift products for children, joined our Bobsled Run personal AdWords coaching program (www.BobsledRun.com). He and I had several productive one-on-one sessions together where we examined every element of his whole sales process and suggested changes and new approaches and small tweaks here and there.

A few weeks into the process, Brian was on the verge of giving up the ghost simply because of the amount of work involved in keeping his whole operation running, along with his perception that there were no significant changes that he could ever make that would push this site over the top into serious profitability.

Perry and I managed to talk him out of quitting.

Several months later we had Brian on a group call again. He raised an innocent question about conversion rates on websites, not realizing how far out of everyone's league he had actually progressed: "I'm averaging maybe a 5 percent clicks-to-sales ratio on my whole website. I feel like I could do a lot better and wonder if anyone else on the call struggles with this too."

There was silence on the line.

"Uh, did you say *5 percent?*" one of the callers asked.

"Yes, that's right. Why? Is that kind of low?"

More silence. Perry piped up: "Five percent is really, *really* good!"

One in every 20 of Brian's visitors was saying yes and buying his physical product from him. Just a few months before, Brian had been averaging less than 2 percent—one in 50. What made the difference? There was no point where Perry or Bryan or Howie gave some single Eureka-moment piece of insight that allowed Brian to make the leap from two up to five of every hundred visitors buying.

No, rather it was Brian's very calculated, systematic, methodical approach of simply split-testing our new ideas against his existing old ones and keeping the one that worked better. He did this tirelessly over the course of six months and *more than doubled* the response on his website.

To Brian, this seemed totally commonplace, simply because the process had been so gradual. So unremarkable.

And it really is not rocket science. Of all the secrets that Brian and others in our Mastermind Club learn, this is the least glamorous, and yet the single most profitable. You can do this with any sales process, and every piece of it, and see gradual, unmistakable improvements over time. The answer lies in *split testing*.

GOOGLE MAKES IT SO EASY

What makes Google so elegant is your ability to do such painlessly easy, real-time split testing of different ads. Take an ad that's getting a CTR of 1.1 percent, write a second one with smarter copy, run it live against the first one, and discover after a few days or weeks that you've now got a CTR of 1.4 percent. Then delete the old ad and try another copy idea to run against the new winner. That one gets you a CTR of 1.6 percent.

You repeat this process over and over again, and find that you're eventually, after several weeks or months, pushing CTRs as high as 2.5 percent or better. Maybe even close to 3 percent.

Are you patient enough to do this? I'd virtually guarantee that most—not all—of your competitors are not. They're eventually going to tire of split testing, if they haven't already, and conclude that what they've got going is adequate.

If you are patient enough, you can do what Brian did. He was ready to throw in the towel in March but by September had doubled his traffic, simply through his patient, methodical, can-do mindset of never giving up while making just the slightest incremental steps forward.

When you combine the power of split-testing with the force of attrition, you'll come out the winner.

NOUVEAUX SKIN CARE COMPANY GETS AN UNEXPECTED TURN IN ADVERTISING

Julie Brumlik, who sold an exotic skin care product using Google, happened to have a huge advantage coming into the game: Her product had already proven itself and she had been able to get celebrity endorsements, even winding up on Oprah's show.

When she joined our Bobsled Run program, we advised her to use her keywords in her ads—especially the headlines. This was based on good experience; she tried it and did fine. But split-testing new ideas all the time will sometimes bring you new insights that even beat otherwise sound advice.

Julie followed her hunches and tried a different approach:

Wrinkles Instantly Vanish
www.celebritybeautysecret.com
Oprah, Melanie, Goldie, Demi, Nora,
Beyonce, Marisa and Dr. Weil Agree
2.0% CTR

As Seen on Oprah
www.celebritybeautysecret.com
Age-Defying natural product line
for skin care. Erases wrinkles!
2.2% CTR

10 percent improvement. Not bad.

Don't miss this though: Julie tried this new "As Seen on Oprah" headline and it worked for *some* of her keywords. But not for all of them. The only way to know was to split test in each ad group and see where it worked and where it didn't.

It's no exaggeration to say that *every keyword literally represents a different market.* Julie's approach appealed to women who respect Oprah. In a number of cases it worked but not in all. And eventually the Oprah empire stepped in and demanded that she no longer use Oprah's name in her ads. Julie had no choice but to comply.

Some keywords represented markets where the headline appeal to Oprah turned the trick. In other cases it was a flop. That's the real world for you.

AMERICA'S SECOND HARVEST WINS BY ATTRITION AND WE DONATE TO HURRICANE KATRINA VICTIMS

Our business supports micro-enterprises and AIDS orphans in impoverished countries from Haiti to Africa. Need knows no political boundaries.

One U.S. organization stood out from the crowd, however, and I parted with a donation based solely on its brilliant marketing approach. America's Second Harvest has an ingeniously simple message: It purchases unbought groceries from supermarkets before the products reach expiration and distributes them to the needy.

Its costs of doing this are ridiculously low, and it hits you with a clear and simple claim:

Every $1 you give provides four bags of groceries!

How could you not give to a cause like this, when you know your dollar is stretching that far?

I gave once and continued to receive mailings. It doesn't just send plain, dreary letters begging for money every time. Actually, no two mailings ever look alike.

Each one comes in a different shape and size. One is a large, lumpy, clear package. Another is a postmarked lunch sack. Still another is a full-color brochure on how to volunteer with the needy in your local community.

Always full of pictures, always interesting, always fresh. At Thanksgiving in November it wowed me with a matching promotion offer to buy 300 Thanksgiving meals for just $20.00.

How could I not give?

When Hurricane Katrina devastated the Louisiana Gulf Coast in late 2005, we were bombarded left and right with requests from all across the United States to donate.

Even though I had prioritized giving to third-world causes, sure enough, a letter came—from America's Second Harvest, saying that it was in the thick of feeding hurricane victims through its program, and would I please contribute.

It was a no-brainer. By this time the ASH letters were a welcome and regular part of every week, and I trusted them. My first gift to Second Harvest had been small, but it kept at me. So when disaster struck and it was there again like a familiar visitor, I gave big this time.

The people behind the ASH effort are no slackers. They understand that you win by attrition. Others drop off the radar, but you stand strong—and you win. You always win. This is true with Google; this is true with any marketing effort you put forth.

Harrison Ford landed the part of Han Solo through attrition and a fair share of luck. For you it doesn't need to be luck at all. You've got Google's outstanding system for split testing and the flow of traffic from all over the world to vet your sales funnel.

Uncle Claude Sez

Advertising and merchandising become exact sciences. Every course is charted. The compass of accurate knowledge directs the shortest, safest, cheapest course to any destination. We learn the principles and prove them by repeated tests. . . . We compare one way with many others, backward and forward, and record the results.

When one method invariably proves best, that method becomes a fixed principle. . . . One ad compared to another, one method with another. Headlines, settings, sizes, arguments, and pictures are compared. . . . So no guesswork is permitted.

. . . We test everything pertaining to advertising. We answer nearly every possible question by multitudinous traced returns. Some things we learn in this way apply only to particular lines. . . . Others apply to all lines. They become fundamentals for advertising in general. They are universally applied. No wise advertiser will ever depart from those unvarying laws.

17 Things Yo Momma Never Told You About Google

1: TEN THOUSAND HOURS

Malcolm Gladwell's book *Outliers* is all about his observation that the most talented boy wonders of the world (people like Bill Gates, Steve Jobs, and the Beatles) were successful not because of innate talent but because they got a chance to invest 10,000 hours in their chosen profession and got their 10,000 hours in early.

I like the 10,000-hour theory and I talk about it myself from time to time.

Just the other day I was doing a phone consultation with a customer and he said, "If I were going to invest my 10,000 hours in pay-per-click, where would you suggest I focus my energy?"

I replied, "I'm not sure there's 10,000 hours worth of stuff to even *know* about pay-per-click. There's a keyword, there's an ad, there's a bid price. If you spent 10,000 hours studying that I'm not sure what all you would study."

"However," I added, "You can *most definitely* invest 10,000 in understanding what came before that click and what comes after that click. The story, the psychology, the progression of keywords from first inquiry to sale, the art of gently leading your customer where you want him to go."

Even as complex as AdWords can be, the AdWords machine is not 10,000 hours of complexity. Now I admit that on huge, multimillion dollar campaigns, it can approach 10,000 hours of complexity. But it's the *psychology* of it that's tricky.

If you invest 10,000 hours (five years' worth of career time) aggressively honing your chops, you *will* be a master marketer, and you'll be in the driver's seat of one of the most lucrative careers in the world today.

2: THE "BEFORE" CIRCLE AND THE "AFTER" CIRCLE

Like I said, that click is just one event. The click is a bridge between two circles: The story the person is in before—and the story the person *wants* to be in after.

Before and After. That's the game.

Before the click she had a migraine headache. Not only that, she would experiencing mind-splitting, crushing headaches one to two times per week. Totally debilitating. She's short-tempered with her husband. She yells at her kids. When those headaches come, everyone knows to get out of harm's way.

She's so ashamed, and . . . on some days, so lonely.

She clicked on your ad and for the first time got a coherent explanation why she gets these headaches and why they refuse to go away. It wasn't just a doctor handing out pills; it was something she could sink her teeth into.

She purchased your program (she thought to herself: This had better work 'cuz if I don't find something that works I'm going to go out of my mind . . .) and began following it religiously, day by day.

By week three she was down to one mild headache per week and by the fourth week she was completely free . . .

She's in a story. She wants her story to have a different ending. Your job is to enter into her story and change it. That's what she wants. She's dying for it.

The way you do your job is: You find out what conversation is going on inside her head; you step into it; then you change it.

3: THE PIE CHART OF DESIRES

Name a keyword. Name a market. What I'm about to describe applies to ALL keywords and markets. Let's say the keyword is "splitting headache." Now 100 people search "splitting headache," and you ask them this question: "What is the number-one thing you are looking for today?"

You ask 100 questions, and you get 100 answers. You lump similar answers together. The answers look like this:

- 36 percent have a headache right now and are looking for some action they can take to make their headache go away (i.e., what they're really looking for is a good tip—some kind of information);
- 27 percent have a headache right now and are looking for a medication they can buy online that will make their headache go away (i.e., they're OK waiting a day or two for a shipment).
- 19 percent suffer from migraines more than once a week.
- 12 percent have a friend, relative, or child who has a headache right now and they're looking for a solution.
- 4 percent suffer from migraines more than once a month.
- 2 percent took a medication that made their headache worse, not better and are looking for something different.
- Total: 100 percent.

The pie chart looks like this:

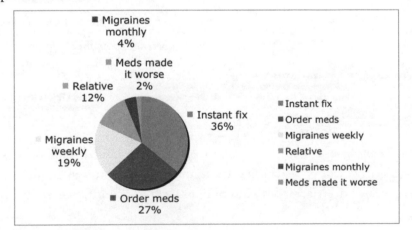

Now the obvious thing to do is write an ad that targets the biggest piece of the pie. But you may not want to do that. Why?

Because the slice of pie you can make the most money with is the question that they're having the hardest time answering.

That means if you're taking a survey, you need to add another question: "How hard has it been to find a solution to this problem?"

The problems where the answer is "very hard" are the ones you can most easily sell a solution to. These are also, by definition, the problems your competitors aren't addressing.

4: TELL-TALE SIGNS OF MARKETS

Search on a keyword. Google returns a result. *FREEZE.* Don't touch that keyboard.

What do you see? What comes up and why? There are many, many clues, and these clues tell you many things about the market that you are trying to compete in:

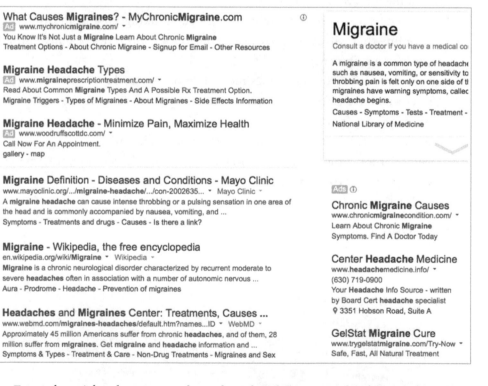

■ *Fewer than eight ads appear, only on the right.* This means this keyword is not very competitive *and/or* its market does not generate enough money to support very many advertisers. It's kind of like the arctic tundra where few plants can grow.

- *There are more than eight ads (there's a second page of results), but only eight ads appear on the first page of results.* Here, no advertiser is getting a high enough CTR/Quality Score to appear on the premium results. This usually means people who search this keyword have a huge range of desires and the market is very fragmented.

- *There are nine to eleven ads on page one, including one to three ads across the top, and no second page of results.* This means a few advertisers are getting high CTRs and good Quality Scores, but most of the other advertisers are doing poorly. There is often a marked difference between the two kinds of advertisers. If you study the difference, you can tell what the market responds to.

- *There are nine to eleven ads on page one, including one that threads across the top, and many pages of results, i.e., dozens of ads total.* This means the market is healthy and competitive, there is money in this market and some advertisers are successfully "nailing" their customers' sweet spot.

- *There are many pages of advertisers but the advertisers change from one month to the next.* This means this market has a high churn rate with many advertisers entering and leaving the market all the time. This is a **bad** sign because it means nobody is making money. This is a very common occurrence in MLM and business opportunity keywords. Those businesses are a revolving door, and you should stay away unless you are a *very* experienced marketer with deep pockets and a better sales process than everyone else.

- *All the ads say fairly similar things.* This means most people searching this keyword want pretty much the same thing.

- *The ads are all over the place in terms of message.* This means that there is no one desire that this keyword represents. There is a whole pie chart of desires and there may be six to eight distinct desires in the market.

- *The lowest-ranking ads advertise sites like eBay, SuperPages, and ReachLocal.* This means you are in a market that is not very competitive and probably easy to win in. Often such markets don't have a great deal of traffic.

5: IMPRESSION SHARE

Most people don't realize this, but Google shows most peoples' ads only part of the time. When you're brand new, they're probably only showing your ads 10–20 percent of the time. Your reports might tell you your ad got 2,236 impressions today, but you don't know that your keyword got searched more than 10,000 times.

Let's say you're bidding $1 per click and Google tells you, "First page minimum bid is $1.50." That doesn't really mean your ad is *never* seen on the first page. Rather, it means that your ad is probably only seen on the first page 5–10 percent of the time.

If you increase your bid, your impression share may grow to 25 percent, 50 percent, maybe even 100 percent. Google is serving up its inventory for maximum clicks. Google knows that people might search 5, 10, 15 times, and it knows if it keeps showing different advertisers, it can get more ads to get clicked on. This strategy is good because it is optimizing your CTR automatically.

But if you have a killer ad that gets a *great* CTR and if you have good Quality Scores, your impression share can approach 100 percent.

Something to be aware of: If you have a competitor who has excellent CTR and Quality Scores, Google may be showing its ad 100 percent of the time. If your CTR and QS are lower than your competitor's, then increasing your bids to get 100 percent impression share may accomplish nothing more than spending lots of money.

Bottom line is, high CTR and Quality Score get your ads shown more often.

6. DOING ADWORDS FOR CLIENTS

All of the best AdWords practitioners I know developed most of their skills by managing campaigns for both themselves *and* clients—as well as masterminding with other AdWords experts. If you want to be an AdWords genius, these are my suggestions:

- *You should always have some project that is exclusively your own.* There is nothing like learning on your own dime. It teaches you more than anyone else. When there's money attached to it, the lessons are imprinted deep inside your mind.
- *You should always have some project that is not your own.* Other peoples' money. Other peoples' marketing results. I'll talk about how to get clients in a minute, but the reason this is so valuable is that it extends your knowledge into markets you would otherwise have no experience with. If one of your markets is CRM software and another market is natural health supplements and another client sells management consulting, you develop a wide perspective that you would otherwise never get. You will also find yourself transferring ideas directly from one market to another. Not just AdWords ideas, but ideas for website design, landing pages, offers, email messages, and guarantees.
- *Join our Mastermind Club. Yes, this is a shameless plug*—but the world's largest private AdWords discussion group online is my own group of paying members. Many of these sharp men and women have been using AdWords for literally years, and know the system inside and out. When you get stuck on something you can post a question to the forum and often get a qualified answer in less than an hour. We hold a monthly coaching call for our Mastermind members and do live Q&A. New members get a huge package of cool educational material. Details are at www.perrymarshall.com/mastermind/.

How to Get Clients

Principle Numero Uno is to understand what you are selling when you are an AdWords consultant: You are selling *dollars at a discount*. What you are saying to your prospective client is:

> Right now you are buying new 1,000 new customers per month for $10 each and this is costing you $10,000 per month. If you pay me $2,500 per month I'll get you 1,200 new customers for $6 each. Your AdWords spend will go from $10,000 per month to $7,200 per month; you'll get 200 more customers than you were getting before, and after you've paid me my fee you'll still be spending $300 per month less than you're paying now.

> So you can leave things the way they are now, or you can hire me and save $300 per month and get 200 new customers every month that you're not getting now.

> Is that a good deal, or what?

Now in order to say this you have to do some research. You need to know how much it's costing them to get a new customer. You need to know what a customer is worth to them. You need to know what they're happy with, and unhappy with. Bottom line is, you need to earn your keep.

You can access a presentation on how to build an AdWords consulting practice at http://www.perrymarshall.com/supplement/.

7: HYPER-RESPONSIVE CUSTOMERS

There are three kinds of customers:

1. Customers who buy once and never come back again
2. Customers who buy from time to time, maybe for years
3. Customers who buy everything they possibly can from you

This last category is only about 5 percent of your customers, but these customers may bring you as much as 50 percent of your profit.

These are the people that you design your business for: The raving fans.

Let me restate that: You want to design your business such that "raving fans" are not only possible, but probable.

Some businesses could not possibly have raving fans even if someone was looking for a business to be a fan of, because everything is so mediocre. You need to be outstanding at *something*. Which is to say you need a powerful USP.

But once you have that USP, you want mechanisms (such as email/snail mail/ autoresponder follow-up and customer appreciation events) that stimulate customers

to come back, and come back, and come back for more. You brainstorm things that will re-ignite your old customers' interest.

If you do the math for a typical website, about one Google click in 2,000 represents a hyper-responsive buyer. That's right, about one person in 2,000 has a propensity to have this kind of buying behavior. These customers buy compulsively from other companies, and they'll buy compulsively from you if you have an appealing offering.

We all know people like this. You know people who are Apple fanatics and own five Apple computers and eight iPods and three iPads. You know people who have 80 pairs of shoes in their closets. You know people who constantly go to motivational seminars. You know people who buy and read every single Stephen King book.

Notice that this kind of buying behavior is personality driven. People love buying from personalities and companies who have a lot of personality. Don't be afraid to have personality.

8: INNOVATION AND THE HYPER-RESPONSIVE BUYER

Pinpoint a major keyword. It gets, say, 50,000 searches a month. Picture all the people who are searching for those keywords. Imagine, even, a person who searches for this not just for a few hours or a few days, but from time to time for months or even years.

That person is a true, hyper-responsive buyer.

I have a question for you: What will get *his* attention?

I propose to you that this person is very jaded, has seen everything before, and is hard to impress.

But if you impress him, if you deliver something that is truly a breakthrough, he will tell all his friends; he'll give you a killer testimonial; and all his friends are hyper-responsive customers, too.

You can "flip" an entire market just by winning the affections of that rabid 5 percent.

9: GOOGLE LACKEYS VS. REAL GOOGLE REPS

There are two kinds of Google reps:

1. *The rank-and-file AdWords person who answers the phone or replies to email inquiries.* This person typically knows very little about AdWords, and unless there is a simple, obvious issue with your account (i.e., a basic problem like when your ad gets disapproved), he often won't know what the problem is.
2. *The professional Google account rep.* If you are a medium- or large-size business that spends upwards of $100,000 per year, you'll likely be assigned a professional

Google account rep. Sometimes these reps know the inside scoop about how Google's system works and the vagaries of Quality Scores, etc.

There *are* people at Google who know how the system works, but you generally have to be spending money to talk to them. Fortunately Google doesn't give big companies a special discount—the clicks themselves are a level playing field—but Google does give them more information.

If you want to be on the leading edge of that kind of information I have two suggestions for you: 1) Our Mastermind Club (www.perrymarshall.com/mastermind) members pool their experience and solve problems together; 2) AdGooroo (www. AdGooroo.com) collects data on hundreds of thousands of Google advertisers—as well as you—and provides competitive data on your ad positions, impression share, and budgets.

10: "WOULD I SEND GRANDMA TO THIS SITE?"

One of my colleagues was asked to help with a site that was severely "slapped" with Quality Scores of 1. Because of his close relationship with Google, he was able to get a "real" Google rep to give him a "real" answer to why the site was slapped.

The answer: "I would not send my grandma to this site."

Yeah, I know, some people will retort, "What does *your grandma* have to do with anything?"

I looked at the site, and I would not send my grandma there, either.

The person at Google didn't elaborate, so please permit me.

This particular site was selling a specific business opportunity. The hype factor was through the roof. It was a pure "squeeze page" with nowhere else you could go to learn about the vendor. All the bullets were tease, and the claims were extraordinary.

It had a smarmy feel.

Google didn't like the site. So somewhere in the account, a Google reviewer punched in a low quality score, and all the keyword and SEO tweaks in the world won't change that.

I realize this is all totally subjective on Google's part. But it tells you a few interesting things:

- Google is *not* just run by robots. It's got more than enough money to put real people on the assignment, and it does.
- In my opinion grandma is a **great** criteria. Grandma knows nothing about the internet, so she trusts you to tell her who's OK to listen to. Should she sink her retirement money into that bizop? Well, in Google's opinion, if there's more than

a 10 percent chance of her getting screwed, then . . . absolutely not. Remember: If grandma doesn't have a tech-savvy grandson, then she has to rely on Google.

- The site failed to prove what it was saying. Let's say this bizop was totally legit. If so, then it should be able to prove it. Names, cities, states, numbers. Qualifications, cautions, requirements.
- The site should have contact information, preferably including street address and phone number, and not appear to be some guy hiding behind his computer.

Might I suggest: Add "Would a Google rep send her grandmother to this site?" to your bag of tricks, and let's all do our best to make the internet a more trustworthy place.

11. EVERY MARKET HAS A HOLE

There is no such thing as a market where you cannot find a way to "chisel your way in." Even if it has 100 or 200 or 500 bidders, I can guarantee that at least a few of the top ten advertisers in that market still have a vulnerability.

That vulnerability can come in many forms, all of them boiling down to inability to convert visitors to sales. And the number-one factor in that is a need in the market (in the pie chart of desires) they are not meeting.

If you want to crack into a new market, the number-one question you need to ask is, "What unmet need in this market are people willing to pay money for?"

There is always some need that few if any of the competitors are addressing. That's your "in."

Tiny little Google ads aren't so tiny. They're a vast universe. The ultimate ad might be a needle in a haystack, but that needle is worth finding. Fortunes lie inside that ad.

12: BOOTSTRAPPING VS. VENTURE CAPITAL

One time I was on the board of directors of an online startup company.

The president of this company had started four other companies. Two had failed, and two had gone public. That is a pretty impressive track record for startups.

His approach was: "If you build it, they will come." Raise venture capital or angel money from private investors faster than you "burn" the money, and eventually you get the attention of some big company who buys you out. Everyone breaks out the champagne and makes millions of dollars.

My approach was far less glamorous than that. My approach was: **"Make ONE dollar."**

In other words, do whatever you have to do, build whatever you have to build, to get to a point where you can predictably spend $1 on Google clicks and get $2 from paying customers.

Which is to say, it's OK if you have overhead and investment and everything else far in excess of that $1. Maybe you've invested thousands, tens of thousands, hundreds of thousands of dollars. But in the marketing department, you're making money at least on a small scale. Once you're doing that, you just scale up.

That's my approach. I have personally coached more than 500 businesses through this process in over 200 industries. It's basic, it's humble, most of the time it's done from a spare bedroom or basement office. But it works. It's made me and countless others literally millions of dollars.

When I joined this company, I was told that we were going to use a hybrid approach. That we were going to "make $1," but we were not in any way going to limit ourselves to the meager growth limits of a self-funded startup. We were going to raise money and scale this thing big and fast.

Gentlemen, start your engines.

So off we went. We built a Google campaign that acquired new members at an excellent low cost-per–acquisition, and we had tons of traffic to the site.

But for whatever confounded reason, I could not get the president of the company to make a dollar. I could not get him to sell something to these people.

At least not anything you could realistically make money on.

Yet every quarter at board of directors meetings, he would chide us for not bringing enough investors.

I finally resigned and sent them all a nasty email telling them that they were defrauding their shareholders because two years into it they still had no business plan that had any hope of making money.

This *could* have been a tremendous success. There was nothing wrong with growing a company fast on the shoulders of investors. But the investors were so distracted by the dog-and-pony show about how big this market was and how much money was in this market and all the grandiose promises that they never bothered to look into the core marketing DNA and sales story.

The DNA of any sales machine is really simple:

What does it cost you to get a customer and how much money do you make on that customer in [one day/one month/one year/one lifetime]?

If you do not have at least a partial answer to that question, you don't have a business. You have a pipedream. Doesn't matter if you've got a $10 million building and a Startup of the Year award from *Inc.* magazine.

On the other hand, if you've got a Google account, a teeny, tiny little ecommerce store built on a free Blogspot site, and a Paypal account, and you're putting $1 in and getting $2 out, *you have a real business.*

13: JUST BUY THE STUFF AND SHIP IT

Notice that the DNA of a real sales machine is not having a manufacturing facility, ownership of the product, a flawless system for customer service, or anything else.

With that in mind, consider a contrarian, renegade approach to building that business.

If the DNA of a real sales machine is the ability to put $1 in and get $2 out, then you're off to a good start if you can put $1 in and get 80 cents out.

So if you're starting out, the FIRST thing you must do is simply prove that you can sell something.

That's it.

Just prove that you can sell something. Doesn't matter where you get it or how much it costs to obtain it.

So let's say that you want to sell some kind of high-end $1,500 bicycle, and it's going to cost you $250,000 to put them into production. You know that after you put them into production, it will cost $600 each to make them and you'll have a $900 gross margin.

Most people will put the bikes into production first, then try to sell them.

Big mistake.

Let's say it costs you $5,000 to build them by hand.

Then what you should do is advertise your bikes for $1,500, take some orders, and THEN bite the bullet and build the first 10 bikes for five grand each.

Yes, I know you're sending out $3,500 with each shipment. Doesn't matter. It's still the lowest risk way to enter the market. It'll cost you $35,000 to sell the first 10 but it's better than spending $250,000 to sell zero!

Make sure there's water in the swimming pool before you jump off the diving board.

The same advice applies even if you're doing something as simple as selling hand soap. Get the orders first. Then if you have to, drive to Walmart, buy a case of hand soap, and sell it at a loss. But get the marketing and sales machine right before you hammer out the fulfillment issues.

14: ARTIFICIALLY HIGH BIDS IN A FEROCIOUSLY COMPETITIVE MARKET

I have a student who's in a particular segment of the printing industry, which is a fiercely competitive niche. Typically he's battling against 90 plus bidders in a price-sensitive commodity market.

He soundly established a presence on one keyword, and after several months of fine-tuning, he got his cost down to $2 per click.

He asked me what he should do next, and I said, "Knock yourself off. Create another brand with a different USP in the same market." So he did.

For the first week, his cost per click was $11.

OUCH.

He was real doubtful at first, but I told him to stay the course.

Sure enough, after some time went by, he "earned" Google's trust, and the cost per click dropped to $2.

What he had just encountered was Google's artificial barrier-to-entry for new advertisers.

It's daunting when you're new, but once you're established, it protects your territory from poachers.

Carefully follow the instructions in this book—and especially this chapter—and you'll be able to enter any market at will.

15: PERSONALITY VS. TRANSACTIONAL MARKETING

There are two kinds of approaches that are most often used in selling products, even physical ones: 1) institutional "brand" advertising and 2) personality-driven advertising.

Examples of the former are Tide laundry detergent, Crest toothpaste, Chevy trucks, and Harvard University.

Examples of the latter are George Foreman grills, Donald Trump's real estate properties, Wendy's Dave Thomas, and Video Professor training courses.

I submit to you that personality-driven advertising is easier to "pull off," happens faster, and costs less money than traditional brand advertising.

Here's a way to think about it:

Think of authors and radio/TV personalities such as Oprah, Dr. Phil, Rush Limbaugh, and Dr. Laura. Think of the late Roger Ebert and the radio personality Paul Harvey. Or coach Vince Lombardi. Consider how these folks deliver news, entertainment, and opinions to people who are, literally, "fans." Their job is to communicate their version of reality to a clearly identified audience.

The way you do personality marketing is, you add a bit of Oprah or Rush Limbaugh to your product. You take a very specific position, you have strong opinions, and you talk about a far wider range of topics than merely what you sell.

People like that.

Thus your website is a platform for you being you, not just a person who sells your product.

I've included a bonus chapter about personality marketing at www.perrymarshall.com/supplement/.

16: WHAT I LEARNED FROM INFOMERCIALS

Some people watch infomercials. Some who watch buy from them. Some don't.

I, for one, have never bought a single thing from an infomercial. I'm not "an infomercial buyer."

In general, I don't even care to watch them all that much, even though they are extremely educational for salespeople. (*Tip*: If you want to see a sales pitch that has been scientifically proven to work, just watch an infomercial that's been on the air for three months. I can guarantee you, it's making money. Take notes and look for ideas you can borrow.)

But anyway, in 2002 when I first began using Google AdWords, I almost instantly knew how the entire AdWords market was going to develop. Even though it was virgin territory, it was undeveloped and nobody understood it.

I foresaw that in 2010 and beyond, it would become a fiercely competitive, dog-eat-dog marketplace and there would be certain things you HAD to do in order to win. I knew that because I had **studied** infomercials.

What does Google AdWords have to do with infomercials?

Back in the '80s, broadcasting laws changed, and it suddenly became possible for TV stations to sell extended slots to advertisers. You may recall that 30 years ago, most TV stations went off the air at 1 A.M. or 2 A.M., and they said, "We'll be back at 6 A.M. . . . "

So people started making 30-minute commercials.

I remember when I was a kid, turning on the TV one night and seeing an infomercial shot at a Holiday Inn meeting room. It was a single camera pointed at an overhead projector, and some guy was pitching information on how to get rich in real estate.

When infomercials were new, the airtime was incredibly cheap. You could actually shoot a cheap video at a seminar, air it, and make money.

Then companies started discovering that this worked. And the bid prices went up.

Today if you want to *test* an infomercial, you're going to spend a minimum of $75,000 to $100,000 to put a show in the can and test it in a few markets. It's going to have to be professionally produced and superbly scripted. Otherwise it doesn't even stand a chance.

Most of the players in the infomercial biz are companies that specialize in this area and do hundreds of millions of dollars of business. The largest such company is Guthy-Renker, whose sales are about $2 billion.

The barrier to entry is now very, very high.

I knew that AdWords would be a niche-market version of the same thing, just on the internet. And as the AdWords market matured, I always knew what was next. Because I knew history repeats itself, I studied history.

Here are some factoids about the similarities between infomercials and AdWords I would like you to think about:

- *It used to be said that infomercials were the most competitive place you could possibly sell anything* because the customer's hand is always on the remote control and she can change channels if she gets bored for two seconds. The same is true online: People have 12 windows open, and the entire internet is only a click away. Smart phones are even worse.

- *Back end is everything.* Real success is seldom achieved from a one-time sale. It has more to do with your ability to win a loyal customer who buys and buys again.

- *Testing is essential.* You have to test ads, landing pages, and offers in order to maximize your sales. The most successful advertisers will be those who test more than everyone else. Fortunately it's not hard to be that person.

17. "PICK THE CHICKEN CLEAN"

Economical cooks find ways to use ALL the parts of the chicken, not just parts of it. Similarly, you want to find ways to satisfy ALL your customers' needs, not just one. Ask yourself these questions:

- If you sell a $50 product, what could you possibly offer that would cost $500? What could you offer for $5,000? There is hardly a market where there is not an answer to this kind of question. There is always a small percentage of people who will spend lots of money to scratch an itch, and those people will contribute a large percentage of your profit.

- What related things do they buy?

- Can you get them to buy on a repeat basis, for example, a membership or monthly shipment?

- Do your competitors offer something that you can sell to your customers, so you can earn an affiliate commission? Your customers will probably buy from the competition anyway (it's not like you "own" them, after all), so you might as well get in on the action. Especially on the internet, you can't keep your customers from finding the other guy. Just decide to profit from the transaction instead.

A FINAL THOUGHT

Joe Polish is a legend in the marketing world. He's a former carpet cleaner turned marketing guru. He's pals with the likes of British billionaire Richard Branson and Paula Abdul. The running joke about Joe is: he always says "Let me introduce you to my good friend ____" because EVERYBODY is Joe's good friend.

A long time ago—one year out of the Dilbert cube, struggling to get my biz off the ground—I cornered Joe in a restaurant at a seminar one night, bought him a hamburger, and picked his brain.

His number-one piece of advice was:

GO D-E-E-P INTO YOUR MARKET.

"Here's what I mean, Perry. Do not just skim the cream off the top of the market, shake off the low hanging fruit and be content with that. If you do that, you'll only get the most fickle customers."

He continued: "If that's all you do, you're super vulnerable to competition knocking you off. Eventually someone will. What you should do instead is be the guy who's willing and able to spend more than everyone else to get a customer. It makes you one stiff competitor and gets you access to customers that nobody else can reach."

He went on to regale me with stories of how he would intentionally drive his competitors out of business by luring them into markets and magazines where they could never even hope to break even—he knew it but they didn't.

Probably five to six years later when I was compulsively, tirelessly banging the AdWords drum and driving my stake deep into the ground—I suddenly remembered where I'd gotten that. I'd gotten it from Joe.

This approach has always served me well. Build a "Star Business" (Chapters 7 and 8), be #1 and go deep. It will serve you too.

My late friend Tom Hoobyar was touring Stanford University one day and he saw a bunch of shiny cages in a dumpster. "Why are you throwing those away?" His professor friend pointed out that lab rats had gnawed the panels of those 20-gauge stainless steel cage walls until they were thin as tin foil. He poked his finger right through the remaining steel and said:

"Feral Rats."

Tame rats gone wild. The mere fact that you are where you are today, that you have gotten as far as you've gotten, is proof positive that you are a true entrepreneurial Feral Human. A Feral Man, or Feral Woman with she-balls.

Today you're going to need every feral skill you've got. If you do, you will make gains you would not have dared imagine just two years ago.

fe·ral 🔊 *adjective* \ˈfir-əl, ˈfer-; ˈfe-rəl\

: of, relating to, or resembling a wild beast

—used to describe an animal (such as a cat or dog) that has escaped and become wild

When Joe Sugarman, founder of BluBlockers and direct marketing pioneer spoke at my Maui seminar, I asked him: "Joe, what was it like to try to grow a startup during the Jimmy Carter administration?"

Joe answered, "Every time the President would do something that showed a lack of leadership, sales would go down. Every time he would do something decisive and authoritative, sales would go up."

Needless to say, sales were flaccid much of the time. A daily uphill battle. Plus Sugarman got slammed by the FTC because a blizzard in Chicago delayed shipments. Then he got sucked into a congressional hearing where Al Gore, uh, shall we say, broke a promise or two. Uncle Sam squeezed the juice out of his nascent company, JS&A and left it dead on the sidewalk.

But the good news is—only a few months later, a crazy opportunity presented itself and evolved into BluBlockers, a blockbuster success. Today Sugarman owns a couple of incredible homes on Maui and his friends include the likes of Bill Gates and Steve Jobs.

Seasons of crisis are times of maximum opportunity.

<div align="center">IF.</div>

IF you're agile enough, discerning enough, if you see the forest for the trees.

If there's anything I hope you get from this book, it's that online success is not merely about clickthrough rates or conversion rates or any one single metric, but it's about you seeing the big picture of what your customers really want from you and delivering it at least a little bit better and with greater satisfaction than everyone else.

If you can be 10X better, great. But even if you're just 10 percent better . . . if you're better than everyone else, you're number one.

Commit to dominating your market.

Uncle Claude Sez

I started with Lord & Thomas at $1,000 per week. But soon we agreed that the right plan was a commission basis. Then the agency paid me only for service which proved profitable to them. On the other hand, I received what I earned. Under that plan I earned in commissions as high as $185,000 in a year. All earned at a typewriter which I operated myself, without a clerk or secretary, and much of it earned in the woods.

Signature Victories

The measure of the moment
In a difference of degree
Just one little victory
A spirit breaking free
One little victory
The greatest act can be
One little victory

—One Little Victory by Neil Peart

The best daily ritual I've picked up in recent years has been writing one little victory, no matter how tiny, in my little black moleskin notebook. Every day. Even if you only have enough energy in the morning to write one sentence,

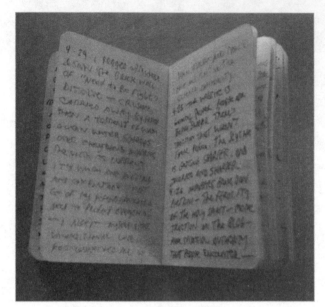

remember something *positive* and write it. It's the 60-second habit that can change your life. A tiny hinge that swings big doors.

If I've learned anything from writing copy, it's that every single person lives in some kind of story. Stories are actually *the* thing that defines any community or culture. Even more so than the language those stories are told in.

You might be surprised to find out how different people's stories can be. In Chapter 20, I told you about using Facebook and social media to profile customer stories.

We ran some ads for a coffee product. Here are the favorite movies for the people who clicked on the coffee ads:

1. *Notebook*
2. *Dirty Dancing*
3. *Juno*
4. *Fight Club*
5. *Princess Bride*

We also ran ads for an astronomy website. Here are the favorite movies for people who clicked on the astronomy ads:

1. *Star Wars*
2. *Fight Club*
3. *Lord of the Rings*
4. *Dark Knight*
5. *Gladiator*

You'll notice that the only movie in common is *Fight Club*. (I'm not sure why.) Except for that one, all the coffee lovers' movies are chick flicks and all the astronomy lovers' movies are combat films.

This shows you that coffee fans and astronomy fans live in *entirely different stories*. Up-and-coming ninja marketers will give this some more thought. There's an insight in what I just told you that's worth about 50 times what you paid for this book.

Hint: If you know what story your customers live in, you can sell to them with ease.

I don't know exactly what story you live in, though I know for most of my customers, *Lord of the Rings* is probably closer to the sweet spot than *Princess Bride*. But there is one thing I know for certain: *You want to make your story **better**.*

Stories run deep. If you want to change the story you've been in to the story you want to be in, it's best to just assume it's going to take everything you've got. If there's a resource that is capable of improving your story, you should avail yourself of it.

Examples of stories that people live in:

It's a good thing I showed up and fixed everything because otherwise those people would've screwed everything up.

Every time we're about to sit down to a romantic dinner, he gets an emergency call on his cell phone and has to go to the ER.

I'm always on the outside looking in.

Politicians are constantly taking advantage of us, and it just gets worse all the time.

The world is going to hell in a hand basket.

Every time I look for a parking space, someone pulls out and the space opens up for me.

Whenever things are looking completely impossible, some opportunity opens up and things work out in the end.

Whenever I'm on the cusp of a huge victory, something bad happens and snatches my Big Win away, and I go home terribly disappointed.

I never allow myself to be in a position where I can be vulnerable. I am 100-percent self-reliant.

I never allow myself to be in a position where I have to depend on myself. I rely on [him] [her] to keep me on track.

Even in the darkest journey, I fear no evil.

I always learn the hard way.

I'm teachable, and I always learn from other people's experience.

When I'm pressing against hard challenges, things might seem hopeless for months, sometimes years. But eventually I achieve a breakthrough, and things suddenly, dramatically improve.

All this stuff is self-talk. It's über-powerful. The difference between losers and champions is, losers believe they have no control over their lives. They've acquired *learned helplessness.* Winners have acquired the belief that they have some ability to affect outcomes, no matter how indirect their actions.

Self-talk is reinforcing, and people stay stuck in whatever self-talk they've been embracing. Telling yourself your own sad story may be comforting, but it keeps you in prison.

Sixty seconds of positive reflection every day changes your self-talk one sentence at a time, one day at a time. If you eat one bowl of ice cream, it makes no difference in your life. If you eat a bowl of ice cream every single night before you go to bed, you gain 25 pounds in 10 years. If you jump on a trampoline for 5 minutes every single day, you're still in good shape at age 70.

And if you focus on what's good about your story every single day, you build a reservoir of positive pattern recognition. That's the micro-pattern, 60 seconds to change your life. Let's talk about the macro.

MEGA-VICTORIES

I did something the other day that I'd like you to do, too. I made a list of about a dozen **signature victories** in my own life, events that were tremendously positive. Allow me to share just one.

Signature Victory: Spent four years in the trenches at a startup company, worked my buns off, company got sold for $18 million. Cashed in my stock options, left the company, started a business.

This one move wiped out our debt in one fell swoop with money to spare. Gave us our first Christmas where we could buy whatever we wanted to buy for each other. Didn't make us "rich" by any means, but it was the first giant gulp of financial oxygen. Felt *r-e-a-l* good.

I still think about that a lot. I've had much bigger victories since then, but that was a *signature victory*—one of those defining moments in life that has so much flavor and impact that it shapes the way you think about everything after.

The time leading up to it was extremely turbulent, and there was always a feeling of *careening* nearly out of control. Yet deep down I had this quiet sense of inner calm, that it would turn out OK in the end.

When all the pieces came together, I had an overwhelming sensation of being set free. Now I can finally do what I really want to do in my life. I can pursue my own purposes instead of somebody else's. *Perry you've been waiting for this chance. Ball and chain just cut off your leg. On your mark . . . get set . . . THE PISTOL FIRES and a new race has begun. Go man, go, go, go.*

No matter what happens to me, I have that signature victory under my belt. Nothing that happens tomorrow can take it away from me. Nothing that happens to you tomorrow can take your signature victories away from you.

Focus on them. Relish them. Savor them. Even the small ones.

I don't know where you are in your journey. Maybe you're like me and you started your business ten years ago. You're reading this book to add some advertising mojo to

an already-running business. Maybe you work at a job, and this book is your reading assignment.

Maybe your entire brand-new business hinges on how well your Google campaigns work.

Wherever you are in your story, I believe what you do is important because without marketers, nobody knows about all the great products and services that smart people are constantly developing. I believe you can make your story bigger and better.

Carpe Diem—Seize the Day!

—Perry Marshall

About the Authors

Perry Marshall

Perry Marshall is an author, speaker, and consultant in Chicago. He is the world's bestselling author on Google's advertising system. Google advertisers who use his methods generate well over a billion clicks per month (conservative estimate).

His company, Perry S. Marshall & Associates, consults with both online and brick-and-mortar companies on generating sales leads, web traffic, and maximizing advertising results.

Prior to his consulting career, he helped grow a tech company in Chicago from $200,000 to $4 million sales in four years. Subsequently, the firm was sold to a public company for $18 million.

Like direct marketing pioneer Claude Hopkins, Perry has both an engineering degree and a love for persuasive copywriting. He's published hundreds of articles on sales, marketing, and technology, and his works include *80/20 Sales and Marketing* (Entrepreneur Press, 2013), *The Ultimate Guide to Google AdWords* (Entrepreneur Press,

2006, 2010, 2012), The *Ultimate Guide to Facebook Advertising* (Entrepreneur Press, 2011), *Guerrilla Marketing for Hi-Tech Sales People*, and a technical book, *Industrial Ethernet* (ISA, 2nd Edition).

He's spoken at conferences around the world and consulted in over 200 industries, from computer hardware and software to high-end consulting, from health and fitness to corporate finance.

Bryan Todd

Bryan Todd is a writer and web traffic specialist in Lincoln, Nebraska. He's worked in both Europe and Asia and has spent most of his career teaching—from foreign language and world history to advanced testing methods for the internet. He has worked with clients in dozens of industries from health care and book publishing to manufacturing and computer software.

Mike Rhodes

Mike Rhodes is an AdWords evangelist. As a popular speaker, consultant and CEO of WebSavvy he loves nothing more than to dive into the machine, pull it apart, deeply understand it and share that knowledge with the world.

He's been asked by Google to consult on how to improve AdWords, worked directly on 1,000+ accounts, and has taught thousands of business owners and marketing managers how to use the power of this tool to grow their business.

Mike founded WebSavvy in 2006 to offer a "done for you" service to those businesses that didn't want to learn, but just wanted to grow their businesses and their profits. His team manages tens of millions of dollars in ad spending and guarantees their results.

A devoted dad and husband, he lives in Melbourne, Australia, with his wife and two daughters.

Quick-Reference AdWords Glossary

Confused by a word or phrase or acronym you've come across? Find it defined and explained here.

Above the fold: The part of a webpage in the browser window readily visible when it first loads, before the user scrolls further down.

Ad group: A collection of one or more ads triggered by a specific set of keyword searches.

Ad rank: The position of an ad on the results page compared to other advertisers. Equals your bid for that keyword multiplied by the matched keyword's Quality Score.

AdSense: The program where a website owner displays Google ads on his or her site and receives a commission when visitors click on the ads. See *Google Display Network*.

Audience: A compiled list of users who have visited your site or taken some specified action with you, which you can target again with advertising. See *remarketing*.

Automatic placement: A domain or webpage in the Display Network where Google has chosen to show your ad.

Average CPC: The average amount that Google has actually charged you for your clicks.

Average position: A number representing the average of where your ads displayed compared to other advertisers for the date range you've selected. The lower the number, the higher on the page your ads displayed.

Ban: The permanent suspension of an entire account due to policy or terms of service violations.

Broad match: A keyword or phrase submitted without quotes or brackets. Triggers ads to show any time users type in close variations, related words, or synonyms.

Campaign: A collection of ad groups that all share the same daily budget, network and geographic settings.

Click to Call: A mobile device feature where clicking on an ad or on a phone number will result in a call to the business at the number listed.

Clickthrough rate (CTR): A percentage representing the number of clicks you got on an ad or keyword (or group of ads or keywords), divided by the total number of impressions received.

Contextual targeting: This allows you to target your ads to people based on the websites and pages they're reading. The assumption being that if they're reading content directly related to the products and services you sell, then they ought to be more likely to click your ad.

Conversion: Any measured desired action (opt-in, purchase, signup, phone call) a customer or prospect takes with you after the initial click.

Conversion rate: A percentage representing the number of actions (opt-ins, purchases, signups, phone calls) your visitors or prospects have taken, divided by your number of clicks.

Coverage: See *impression share*.

CPA: Cost per action, also called cost per conversion. The average amount you pay each time a user takes a desired action (opt-in, purchase, signup, phone call).

CPC: Cost per click. The average amount you pay each time a user clicks on your ad.

CPM: Cost per thousand impressions. The average amount you pay each time Google displays your ad to users 1,000 times.

CTR: See *clickthrough rate*.

Daily budget: A user campaign setting that dictates the maximum amount of money that Google will charge you for clicks to that campaign on a single calendar day. Once this has been spent for the day, Google will stop displaying your ads.

Destination URL: The web address users are routed to first when clicking on your ad. Can be a tracking link or a final landing page destination.

Disapproval: Google's official rejection of a single ad from showing due to ad content, URL, or landing page policy violations.

Display URL: The web address users see displayed in your ad.

Exact match: A keyword or phrase submitted with straight [] brackets. Triggers ads to show any time users type in only this word or phrase verbatim.

GCO: Google Conversion Optimizer. The system where you indicate a target cost per conversion you want to pay, and Google optimizes your placement and CPCs to bring you conversions at or below that amount.

GDN: Google Display Network, formerly called the Content Network. The vast network of sites on the internet that display Google ads.

Impressions: The exact number of times your ad was displayed when someone searched on your targeted keyword (or visited a page on the Display Network that you targeted).

IS: Impression share. A percentage representing the number of times your ad was displayed, divided by the total number of times someone searched on your targeted keyword (or visited a page on the Display Network that you targeted).

Jet stream: A state ads reach when they get high CTRs and Google shows them all over the internet, including pages unrelated to the subject of the ad or to keywords or themes you originally targeted.

Landing page: The first page on your website a user sees after clicking your ad.

Managed placement: A domain or a webpage in the Display Network that you've specifically chosen to have your ad shown on.

Max CPC: Maximum cost per click. A user setting where you dictate to Google the maximum amount you're willing to pay for any single click.

Modified broad match: A keyword or phrase submitted with a plus sign + directly before one or more of the words in the phrase. Triggers ads to show any time a user's search query includes each of the words marked by the plus sign.

Navigation: Links to other areas of content on your site.

Negative keyword: A custom keyword that tells Google not to display an ad whenever a particular word or phrase is typed in or used.

Organic: Free, unpaid listings on search engines such as Google or Bing. See *SEO*.

Pay per click: The form of advertising where advertisers pay only when a user clicks on an ad or link, rather than paying per impression or per action.

Peel and stick: A method for increasing CTR or conversion rate by pausing or deleting an underperforming keyword (or group of keywords) in its current ad group and creating a new ad group for it with one or more ads better matched to it.

Phrase match: A keyword or phrase submitted with straight quotes (" "). Triggers ads to show any time users type in a search query that includes this exact word or phrase verbatim.

PLA: Product listing ad. An ad on Google Search, usually with an image, displaying a product for sale on an ecommerce site.

PPC: See *pay per click*.

Proof: Testimonials, images, screenshots, endorsements, or any other placed features on your page that give you credibility in your market (and promote sales).

QS: Quality Score. Google's 1–10 measurement of how good an "experience" users will have if they see your ad on a page.

Remarketing: Also called "retargeting." The strategy of showing ads on sites around the Display Network to users who have already visited your site or taken some action with you.

SEO: Search engine optimization. The strategy of optimizing websites and pages to rank higher in Google's organic or "free" listings. See *organic*.

Slap: A temporary suspension, either 1) of an ad group, campaign or account due to terms of service violations, or 2) of specific keywords from triggering ads to show, due to low Quality Score.

Split test: A setup where two or more different ads (or landing pages, email messages, etc.) are rotated to show over the same general time period to people searching on a specific keyword or group of keywords.

SPN: Search Partner Network. The network of other search engine, information, and ecommerce sites (e.g., Amazon, Ask.com) where Google displays ads in response to a search query.

Statistical significance: The state of having enough data over time to trust the patterns you're seeing.

Topic targeting: The system where Google shows your ads based on topics or categories you've chosen rather than specific keywords or websites.

USP: Unique selling proposition, also called *value proposition*. The features of your product, service, sales process, customer experience, or guarantee that make you unlike any other seller in your market.

Index

Thank You for Purchasing the *Ultimate Guide to Google AdWords, 4th Edition*!

Get a stream of updates and valuable resources (conservatively valued at $85.00) that will help you get more clicks from Google for less money, convert more visitors to buyers, and make your online business more effective than ever before.

Here's what you get:

- Updates on Google's ever-changing system

- Special reports, audios and videos, including videos for all five "Chisel Your Way In" strategies: YouTube advertising, advanced Display Network strategies, Building Killer USPs, the Swiss Army Knife Formula for Bionic Google Ads, and Savvy Market Selection.

- Links to dozens of resources and tutorials for getting all your online bases covered: registering a domain name, setting up a website, selecting an email service, choosing a shopping cart service, finding products to sell, and starting up your Google Adwords account.

- Scientific Advertising by Claude Hopkins.

- Special report on "Personality in Marketing"—how to make you and your unique approach to everything a key element of your business Unique Selling Proposition.

Go to www.perrymarshall.com/supplement